Verse, Voice, and Vision

Poetry and the Cinema

Edited by Marlisa Santos

THE SCARECROW PRESS, INC.
Lanham • Toronto • Plymouth, UK
2013

Published by Scarecrow Press, Inc.
A wholly owned subsidiary of The Rowman & Littlefield Publishing Group, Inc.
4501 Forbes Boulevard, Suite 200, Lanham, Maryland 20706
www.rowman.com

10 Thornbury Road, Plymouth PL6 7PP, United Kingdom

Copyright © 2013 by Scarecrow Press, Inc.

British Library Cataloguing in Publication Information Available

Library of Congress Cataloging-in-Publication Data

Verse, voice, and vision : poetry and the cinema / edited by Marlisa Santos.
p. cm.
Includes bibliographical references and index.
ISBN 978-0-8108-9209-5 (cloth : alk. paper) — ISBN 978-0-8108-9210-1 (ebook) 1. Motion pictures and literature. 2. Poets in motion pictures. 3. Poetry in motion pictures. I. Santos, Marlisa, 1970– editor of compilation.
PN1995.3.V48 2013
791.43'657—dc23
2013018679

™ The paper used in this publication meets the minimum requirements of American National Standard for Information Sciences Permanence of Paper for Printed Library Materials, ANSI/NISO Z39.48-1992.

Printed in the United States of America

To Slowpoke,
who taught me how to read.

Contents

Acknowledgments

This volume began with a panel at the South Atlantic Modern Language Association conference in 2011; its theme that year was "The Power of Poetry in the Modern World." I won't say that I had no idea that such a project as this anthology was possible, since from the moment I learned of the theme, I knew that it had potential for something much larger than our small group of presenters in Atlanta that year. So I would like to begin by thanking SAMLA's conference coordinator, Lara Smith-Sitton, for providing inspiring leadership in the organization and for her professionalism and kindness. I would also like to thank all my contributors, particularly Carolyn Kelley and Carrie Messenger, whose papers were the starting point of this project. And most special appreciation goes to my colleagues Susan Redington Bobby and Suzanne Ferriss, both of whom have been very supportive to me in my professional and personal endeavors and have given me their love and friendship in countless ways over the years; it makes me so happy that we have been able to work together on this project.

Thanks as well to Cynthia Miller, who pointed me in the direction of Scarecrow, and to Stephen Ryan, who has been most responsive and collegial along the way.

I must also thank my colleague and friend Ben Mulvey, whose love for *Splendor in the Grass* was an inspiration. And I give special thanks to Dean Don Rosenblum, who has been most encouraging and supportive.

Finally, and most importantly, I am unspeakably grateful for the love and support of my brother, Radleigh Santos, and my mother, Myrna Santos. My mother is the epitome of grace under pressure and is a continual source of inspiration to me. And to my husband, Randy Burling, who gives the gifts of silence and sound, whenever they are required, in addition to his constancy and love, I am eternally thankful.

Introduction

The ancient Romans and Greeks called the poet "seer" and "maker," respectively. Sometimes these terms can be placed in opposition to one another, to highlight the differences between art and craft, between the prophetic or stylistic expressions of creativity. In their most original senses, however, they are inseparable: What is the value of "seeing" if one cannot "make"? And indeed, the creation of the poetic product fueled by elevated inspiration can be viewed as the highest form of human artistic pursuit. In his *Poetics*, Aristotle argues that poetry has value precisely for the reason that Plato argues it does not: for its "imitation" of the human experience. Aristotle would not likely have imagined the mimetic qualities of the motion picture when making these arguments, but his principles hold to both verse and film alike—that the representational art of humanity holds great instructional, moral, and aesthetic value.

"Poetry" may have a wide variety of connotations, from the dusty volumes of the past, calling to mind Chaucer, Donne, or Dickinson, to the revival of contemporary poetry in our age, that of Billy Collins or Richard Blanco. But as "hip" or as "relevant" as poetry tries to be in contemporary life, it may always be a bit more divorced from everyday life than other art forms. That is, until it makes its way to the screen. Take, for example, Robert Aldrich's *Kiss Me Deadly* from 1955. The frame of that lovely and twisted film noir is the unlikely Christina Rossetti sonnet, "Remember." The combination of the poetic text and the filmic text provides the kind of delicious parallels and absurdities that arrest the viewer's attention and breathe unimagined life into Rossetti's nineteenth-century verse. Elizabeth Willis, in her definitive study on the use of Rossetti in *Kiss Me Deadly*, comments, "One can hardly think of a more devastating slur than to have [Mike Hammer] brought to his knees before the federal government by the quintessentially dead Victorian spinster poet."[1] *Kiss Me Deadly* spins a cinematic narrative wherein the violent and sexist Mike Hammer is strung along and even emasculated by a mythological thread that originates in a Rossetti sonnet. This is one of the more tantalizing ways that the intersection of poetry and cinema can both arrest the viewer's attention and inspire newfound—or new—interest in the poems of the past. Willis argues that "Rossetti is the perfect counter to Spillane's Hammer not so much because she represents an old-world innocent in the city of sin but because she makes sense within it."[2] This apparent incongruity creates a unique edge that reinforces Hammer's drive and vulnerability within the film. His interactions with cops, killers, and femmes fatales all inevitably focus back to the haunting refrain of Rossetti positioned within the film's narrative, her invocation to "remember me; you understand / It will be late to counsel then or pray."[3]

Unlike the other uses of literature in film, poetry seldom functions in a purely adaptive nature. Fiction and drama are often adapted into film, with varying levels of fidelity, but aside from epic poems, such as *The Odyssey*, that may be converted into a poorly made blockbuster or television miniseries, when poetry appears in film, it has a specific, and usually serious, function. Stacey Harwood points out that filmmakers "appreciate how verse creates a change of register, a complicating of character and plot . . . the quoted poem acts the way a metaphor does within a poem, concentrating or crystallizing the emotion by extending, virtually doubling, the means of its expression."[4] Think, for instance, of the function of e. e. cummings in Woody Allen's *Hannah and Her Sisters* (1986). The intense yearning felt by Michael Caine's Elliott for Barbara Hershey's Lee can be shown in many ways on-screen, but perhaps the most memorable sign of his affection is his recommendation of "the poem on page 112" in a volume of cummings's work, "Somewhere i have never travelled, gladly beyond": "(i do not know what it is about you that closes / and opens; only something in me understands / the voice of your eyes is deeper than all roses) / nobody, not even the rain, has such small hands."[5] The love that Elliot believes he feels for Lee is founded on his belief in, and his desire to protect, her fragility, her remoteness, her potentiality. Poetry acts almost as a kind of shorthand, to distill and capture the complexity of such emotion in a minute of screen time, with Hershey's voice-over reciting the lines and then a cut to her tear-stained face.

Often poetry is remembered for its use within a film for the brief and sudden, but intense, impact it has on the film's narrative. Harwood argues that "just as minor-key strings alert movie-viewers to imminent danger, poetry tells them that something important is about to happen, or that some profound truth has been revealed. The poem provides a pause to allow for an investigation of emotion, like a briefer and less self-conscious version of the song-and-dance number in a musical."[6] As an example, when watching Orson Welles's *Citizen Kane* (1941), the viewer's attention is arrested by the title card preceding the newsreel account of Kane's life that reads, "In Xana-du did Kubla Khan a stately pleasure dome decree—." Even if one cannot identify the lines as belonging to Samuel Taylor Coleridge, most viewers would recognize the concept of Xanadu and the legend of Kubla Khan as a fanciful, but futile, expression of grandeur. References to "Xanadu," Kane's palatial estate filled with valuable art objects and created as an expression of love and ownership of his young wife, continually surface in the film, like rising thought bubbles. One of the most memorable references, expressed by Kane's former friend and colleague Jedediah Leland (Joseph Cotten), sar-donically pokes fun at Kane's aspirations: "Five years ago, he wrote from that place down there in the South, uh, what's it called? Uh? Shangri-La? El Dorado? Sloppy Joe's? . . . Xanadu, yeah." The real character and estate was modeled after William Randolph Hearst's San Simeon, but Welles's choice to invoke the Coleridgean idea of Xanadu from the 1816 "Kubla Khan" adds a dimension of lost regality and an ironic stab at hubris that would have been difficult to achieve without such a reference.

This volume approaches the intersections of poetry and film in various ways that overlap, yet remain distinct. The first section of the anthology addresses personifications of the poet on film, whether historic poets or imagined poet figures. Susan Redington Bobby argues about the fragility and tenacity of love and poetry in the modern world through the exploration of two fictional poets, who seem eerily historical, and the academics who pur-sue their mysteries, in Neil LaBute's adaption of A. S. Byatt's *Possession* (2002). Carolyn Kelley tackles the complicated personality of Dorothy Park-er from Alan Rudolph's *Mrs. Parker and the Vicious Circle* (1994) and the way that Parker's poetic talent was undercut on-screen as it often was in life. Ellen Moll's essay, in its exploration of the commodification of poetic pro-duction, draws on the real figure of the poet John Keats in Jane Campion's *Bright Star* (2009), as well as on the symbolic influence of Walt Whitman in Richard Kwietniowski's *Love and Death on Long Island* (1997). When turn-ing to depictions of fictional poets in film, it is refreshing to consider the only true comedy in the collection, Thomas Schlamme's *So I Married an Axe Murderer* (1993), in which Liz Faber examines the connections between poetry and cinema as popular narrative and "vital, cultural media." Finally, Carrie Messenger, in her investigation of the shifting identities of a celebrity Indian poet in Guru Dutt's *Pyaasa* (1957), and Qi Wang, as she probes the meanings behind the poet figure in various contemporary Chinese films, expand the cultural implications of the poetic author beyond the English-speaking world.

Other films in the anthology, comprising its second section, focus on the way that individual poems are superimposed upon a filmic canvas to create an interwoven narrative of voice and vision. Jim Jarmusch's *Dead Man* (1995) is illuminated by Hugh Davis, who explains how the allegories of

William Blake are brought to life in a postmodern Western setting. Nichole DeWall's essay on Peter Weir's *Dead Poets Society* (1989) examines how the poetry of Shakespeare's *A Midsummer Night's Dream* creates a haunting subtext within the film. Finally, my own contribution to the volume considers metaphors of consumption, desire, and deprivation within the application of Wordsworth's Intimations Ode to Elia Kazan's *Splendor in the Grass* (1961).

The final section of the collection concentrates on the medium of film as a kind of poetry in and of itself, the way that films become a self-reflexive poetic expression, largely through the use of encapsulated visual images, and not relying as heavily on verbal narrative to advance meaning. Avant-garde films that subscribe to this philosophy seek to separate the medium of film from language—indeed, as Dziga Vertov asserts in his introduction to *Man with a Movie Camera* (1929), to separate it from all other art forms. This conception of film, to many, is the purest—the truest and most unique expression of a completely new medium to the modern world. But the closest anchor for understanding finds a resting place with poetry, hence the appellation of "film poems" or "poetry films" to such creative endeavors, as the deepest expression of metaphor is grounded in poetic pursuits. Not surprisingly, many of the filmmakers included in this section can be considered as "Renaissance" in the diversity of their talents, especially poet, critic, and filmmaker Pier Paolo Pasolini, whose forays into "mimetic fiction" through film are explored by Roberto Cavallini. The work of another filmmaker considered to be among the most "poetic," Terrence Malick, is examined by Suzanne Ferriss in her study of *The Tree of Life* (2011) and its function as a cinematic poem paralleling Wordsworth's Intimations Ode. Walter Metz's essay stretches itself beyond the innate expressions of poetry on film to consider how the sensibilities of poet Frank O'Hara and filmmaker Otto Preminger intersect in compelling ways to illuminate the ephemeral nature of everyday human interaction. The final two essays in the collection address the function and translation of language on the screen to poetic ends: Jennifer O'Meara draws insightful connections between the films of Hal Hartley and Jim Jarmusch and their unconventional use of the spoken word to convey poetic energy, and Juan G. Ramos investigates the space between word and image that lends meaning to Eliseo Subiela's creations of magical realism.

Many incongruities may come to mind when considering the intersections between poetry and film. The obvious one is their relative ages: poetry can be counted among the world's oldest art forms, while film can be counted among its youngest. Another is their mode of genesis: poetry is a solitary art, while film is a collaborative one. But here is where I think this volume beautifully merges those two sensibilities: in the diversity and creativity of all the contributors who made it possible. What this volume attempts to convey is the almost mystical synthesis of the most private expressions and the most public of arts, the most unconscious of images and the most exposed visual media. Verse and voice combine to form vision—the epiphanies of versified and visual poets, and the inspiration that provides the wellspring of all art.

NOTES

1. Elizabeth Willis, "Christina Rossetti and Pre-Raphaelite *Noir*," *Textual Practice* 18, no. 4 (2004): 522.

2. Willis, "Christina Rossetti," 537.

3. Christina Rossetti, "Remember," in *The New Oxford Book of Victorian Verse*, ed. Christopher Ricks (New York: Oxford University Press, 1987).

4. Stacey Harwood, "The Well-Versed Movie," *Michigan Quarterly Review* 43, no. 2 (Spring 2004): 146.

5. e. e. cummings, "Somewhere i have never travelled, gladly beyond," in *A Selection of Poems* (San Diego: Harcourt Brace Jovanovich, 1983).

6. Harwood, "Well-Versed Movie," 147.

Part I

Poets on Film

Chapter One

"Besides, There's No Such Thing as Poets Anymore"

Poetic Relevance in Neil LaBute's Possession

Susan Redington Bobby

In *Imagining Characters*, A. S. Byatt and Ignês Sodré share a series of discussions on seminal works by Austen, Brontë, Morrison, and others. Concluding their conversations in "Dreams and Fictions," Sodré, a psychoanalyst, asserts, "There isn't such a thing as one reality only; several versions of reality exist, which need not be contradictory, and can play upon our mind simultaneously, enriching one's capacity to think and to imagine."[1] Sodré's observation may provide readers with a bridge that spans the gaps between A. S. Byatt's Booker Prize–winning *Possession: A Romance* (1990) and Neil LaBute's film *Possession* (2002). Heralded by some critics as a "faithful distillation"[2] while panned by others as an "honorable, interesting failure,"[3] the film nevertheless provides an alternative version of Byatt's tale. Just as Byatt herself is a fan of fairy-tale revisions, writing her own variants over the years and embedding fairy-tale motifs in much of her work, LaBute fashions a version of her tale that removes selected subplots and characters yet focuses intently on the pairs of lovers from the past and present. LaBute may remove much of the complexity of Byatt's novel, but by snipping and cutting the poetry and letters, he remains true to the spirit of her message. Furthermore, through an added scene, in which Roland wryly muses to Maud, "Besides, there's no such thing as poets anymore," LaBute privileges the Victorian lovers rather than the contemporary academics, in keeping with Byatt's narrative focus. Throughout LaBute's film, just as in Byatt's novel, the language of the past is more colorful, descriptive, and passionate, lending the "repressed" Victorian couple more credibility in terms of their ability to love

3

and be loved, while the contemporary academics find themselves unable to communicate effectively about love, incapable of feeling such sustained intense emotions, limited to imitation through the passion that only rises to the surface when they read the language of the past and walk in the footsteps of their forebears.

In Joy Gould Boyum's critical text on literature to film adaptations, she admits that "Hollywood has never been noted for its literacy. Yet from its very beginnings, it has turned to literature for inspiration and persisted in the practice of translating books into film."[4] One of the problems that plagues film adaptations is the task of distilling the "essence" of the book, because film itself is a form of art that can be held as a mirror to literature. In fact, "Far from being literature's antagonist," Boyum asserts, "film is in a very real sense a form of literature itself."[5] Similarly, Dudley Andrew's work on film theory contends that "fidelity and transformation" are integral aspects of literature-to-film adaptation. On a purely mechanical level, Andrew states, "the skeleton of the original can, more or less thoroughly, become the skeleton of a film"; this constitutes fidelity to the "letter"[6] of the film. More challenging, of course, is fidelity to "the spirit" of the literary work, the "tone, values, imagery, and rhythm."[7] Andrew admits that most argue against the success of this possibility, concurring with Boyum's comments about capturing the "essence" of the work of art.[8] Regarding the fidelity of LaBute's *Possession*, some critics argue it adheres to the spirit of the text while others claim it distills the bare elements down to almost nothing. To illustrate, A. O. Scott's review suggests that the primary difference between Byatt's novel and its film adaptation lies in the dominant pair of lovers. Scott claims that Byatt emphasizes the Victorian poets Christabel LaMotte and Randolph Henry Ash while LaBute's film features the contemporary academics Maud Bailey and Roland Michell. Scott suggests that a more literary-minded audience likely prefers the novel whereas those readers who would have likely "skipped over" the long passages of poetry in the text would prefer the film adaptation, for much of the poetry is pared down or entirely absent. Scott concludes that the film "falls far short of poetry, but it's not bad prose."[9]

Like Scott, Tamara S. Wagner also dubs the film an "honourable failure," but she admits "the mood of the novel . . . is preserved as well as most of its themes."[10] Granted, LaBute's film removes quite a bit of material. Val, Beatrice Nest, and Leonora Stern do not appear as characters and are not even mentioned by name, and every subplot in which they figure is stripped from the story. Roland is single, and the solicitor Euan, who ends up in a relationship with Val in the text, is reduced to a stock comic relief character, in his bathrobe for half his short time on-screen, offering Roland, his tenant, a beer while they talk about stolen letters. Fergus is much like his namesake in the text, though his white-blond hair is curiously absent, and Roland is an

American, not British, which requires a bit of a rewrite to include some anti-American sentiments expressed by a few characters. What remains is a much-narrowed literary detective story which uncovers an affair in the past, investigated by two soon-to-be lovers in the present, coupled with the machinations of one Mortimer Cropper, the man intent on possessing every scrap of ephemera he can that belongs to Randolph Henry Ash. While much goes missing, arguably, the mood remains. Andrew argues that "the analysis of adaptation then must point to the achievement of equivalent narrative units in the absolutely different semiotic systems of film and language."[11] Does LaBute reach the goal of equivalency between two modes of storytelling? Does the essence of the tale remain intact? The presence of poetry and poetic language makes this a reality, helping LaBute produce a variant of Byatt's novel that still points to the way that Byatt privileges the language of the past over the words of the present.

Byatt's essay "Fairy Stories—The Djinn in the Nightingale's Eye" describes how her background in fairy tale and myth informs and inspires her fiction. She explains, "My own fairy stories . . . are modern literary stories and they do play quite consciously with a postmodern creation and recreation of old forms."[12] Byatt has written several short-story collections that draw on fairy-tale and myth motifs, and she frequently alludes to fairy tales in her larger works; she even embedded fairy tales within *Possession: A Romance.* As Byatt indicates, her fairy tales have a modern twist, and as Christabel muses to her cousin Sabine, "All old stories . . . will bear telling and telling again in different ways. What is required is to keep alive, to polish, the simple clean forms of the tale which must be there. . . . And yet to add something of yours . . ."[13]

Just as Byatt plays with recasting myths and fairy tales, LaBute's script of *Possession* is both a recreation and a reimagination. Zaliewski mentions that the film had four directors, including Sydney Pollack and Gillian Armstrong, spending ten years "in turnaround," with the first scriptwriter, David Henry Hwang, penning three versions, only to have LaBute substantially alter it for the final script attributed to LaBute, Laura Jones, and Hwang.[14] In fact, looking at one of Hwang's scripts available online is instructive in viewing the process by which the story was initially conceived for film and then drastically changed, for Hwang's script closely follows Byatt's text, and yet curiously, the poetry is all but omitted.[15]

Hwang's production draft opens with Christabel's voice-over as she narrates her variant of the Brothers Grimm tale "The Glass Coffin," a fairy story about a tailor who enters a dark chamber and discovers a miniature castle and a beautiful princess with long golden hair imprisoned in glass. Christabel alters the tale to change the tailor's response to the princess who assumes he must be there to save her and marry her, for he replies that he is simply looking for fulfilling work to fuel his passion for life. When the princess laughs and reduces her glass coffin to shards, the scene shifts to a reverend presiding over the funeral of Randolph Henry Ash, reading from the Bible as Ellen places a box of her husband's effects in his grave. The scene shifts one more time, advancing rapidly into the present, to center on Roland Michell riding his bike to the British Museum. This beautifully written scene ties together the past and the present, binding it with fairy-tale symbolism that features a discovery of light within the darkness. Yet noticeably absent from this opening is any mention of Byatt's poetry.

Instead, Hwang's draft version has a decidedly Gothic feel, with Maud experiencing dreams and visions in which the ghosts of Blanche and Christabel appear, offering her clues to decipher the mystery. The séance with the Vestal Lights plays a larger role with Christabel seemingly possessed by a spirit, and weather, particularly storms filled with crashing lightning, driving winds, and rain, permeates the film settings, giving portions of the story an ominous feel. Hwang's script is reminiscent of the atmosphere of Gode's story, the original Breton-inspired myth about a woman who murders her own child, having been betrayed by her lover, which appears in a section of Byatt's novel. Unlike LaBute's final version, it does not push to the forefront the contemporary detectives, but it is so ambitious in its imitation of the novel's prose that every relationship appears equally prominent. Yet Hwang's draft does not retain the essence of the text well, for where Byatt can pull off multiple narratives and still privilege one or two stories over the others, Hwang's version seems a hodgepodge. Thus LaBute's version, though simplified, is a welcome change, for in lowering the number of subplots and characters, in focusing in on two parallel couples' relationships, and most importantly, by featuring poetic language, LaBute keeps the essence of Byatt's tale intact.

Besides stripping down the plot to its skeleton, LaBute also alters slightly the tone and emotional presence of Roland Michell. As LaBute explains, he read notes from Byatt on one of Hwang's scripts and claims she said to give Roland "more drive" and to make him different. LaBute explains, "Just seeing those notes kind of gave me the keys to the kingdom. . . . Not only did Byatt OK the change; she didn't question the humor either. She got it."[16] Arguably most of the humor in LaBute's script comes through the Americanized version of Roland Michell, played by Aaron Eckhart, who often appears silly, bumbling, and grossly informal juxtaposed with Gwyneth Paltrow's Maud, a stuffy, chilly, serious, statuesque scholar. When she offers him use of her bathroom first in her flat, he sheepishly replies, "Please, I'm just sort of a brush and flush kind of guy, so . . . forget I said that," the comment meets with a look of pure disdain from Maud. His choice of language, though, may endear him to the audience. Some reviewers and filmgoers dislike LaBute's Americanization of a lead character, but Byatt herself added two sentences to the original novel when it was published in the American edition by Random House, and those additions were meant to make Roland more accessible and attractive to American readers, particularly women, stating that he had "a smile of amused friendliness,"[17] which accurately describes Eckhart's portrayal of Roland.

Certainly Byatt's remarks on the film and her novel provide a starting point against which we may measure LaBute's efforts. Byatt explains that she "was never, to be truthful, as interested in the modern plot, except as a detective story or in the modern people's emotions. When they made the film, I think they assumed—because they were Hollywood Americans—that the story is a story about the young modern lovers, whereas actually almost all *readers* know that the story is an occluded story about the Victorian lovers, and the other two are there for finding it out."[18] Byatt points out that in her novel, the poetry of the past is "more real than criticism," having the capacity to go beyond "theory" because "it is a *thing*."[19] She adds that her contemporary critics find the concept of love to be foreign, that women have abandoned hope while men seem "desperate to re-establish a context in which romantic love has meaning."[20] Byatt explains that Maud and Roland cannot communicate about romantic love, that "[they] talk so much that [they] can't feel."[21] Finally, she asserts that the book is centered on the idea of trying "to hear the rhythms" of the Victorian era, not to "re-create" it.[22]

While many reviewers and Byatt herself seem to focus on the prominence of the contemporary academics, which they argue seems to come at the expense of the story of the Victorian lovers, I would suggest that the poetry and poetic language (or lack thereof) in the film holds the key to revealing the way that LaBute's screenplay honors Byatt's text. Perhaps those who have not read Byatt's novel will find the love story of Maud and Roland to be dominant. However, those who have read Byatt's novel might interpret the Victorian lovers' story as more prominent if they read between the lines. LaBute's screenplay does not necessarily "recreate" Byatt's novel, but it does, indeed, share its "rhythms."

LaBute's opening features Randolph Henry Ash strolling in a bucolic field, reciting lines from his poem "Ask to Embla," a flash-forward of the scene in Byatt's postscript and the beginning of the final scene of the film. The film then shifts to the present, as Ash and a Sotheby's auctioneer share the recitation of "from first to last" as the auctioneer reads the lines of "one of only two copies" surviving of Ash's poem "to his nuptial bliss." Thus the film, like the novel, privileges the poetry first and foremost, though the choice of poem is altered, as well as the scene, for Byatt opens with Roland in the London Library researching "The Garden of Proserpina." However, LaBute's choice of "Ask to Embla" is fitting because the audience is told the poem was written for Ellen, supposedly "the force that moves and holds the form," and yet later realizes Ash was writing to Christabel. In addition, LaBute's choice of ending that passage with a reference to "form" alludes to poetry underpinning the film. Therefore, LaBute splits Byatt's postscript in half and presents the first half as the opening, effectively framing the film inside its very important final textual scene.

A simple illustration of the way that LaBute contrasts the language of the past versus the present comes through when Roland speaks with Fergus about Maud. Asking whether she might offer assistance in terms of information about LaMotte, Fergus says, "She thicks men's blood with cold," a quote from Coleridge that appears in Byatt's novel. Yet Fergus supplements the poetic language with a paraphrase, explaining, "Or, if you prefer the American vernacular, she's a regular ball-breaker,"[23] a line which does not appear in the novel, likely because Roland is British in Byatt's original. While some might argue that the line was added by LaBute solely to offer a sort of "translation" for those filmgoers not inclined to appreciation of poetry, the line also contrasts the crass nature of modern-day language versus the majestic imagery in nineteenth-century verse.

Further examples of the pageantry of the Victorian poets' words lies in the various journals or letters read as voice-overs in the film that evoke the rhythm and cadence of poetry, particularly based on when the actors reciting the lines pause. One example is a portion of Blanche Glover's journal that is expressed as a couplet: "Letters, letters, letters. Not for me. / Letters I am not meant to know or see." In other cases, the lines of letters are paraphrases of Christabel's prose that sound like free-verse poetry based on the deliberate pauses inserted midsentence:

> I am a creature of my pen
> My pen is the best part of me. . . .
> I live circumscribed and self-communing
> It is best so
> Not like a princess in the thicket
> More like a spider in her web
> Inclined to snap at visitors, or trespassers
> Not perceiving the distinction until too late . . .
> Oh sir, things flicker and shift
> All spangle and sparkle and flashes
> I have sat all this long evening by my fireside
> Turning towards a caving in
> The crumbling of the consumed coals
> To where I am leading myself
> To lifeless dust, sir.

Read by Christabel, these snippets of several letters, taken together, form a poem in and of itself.

There is even an example of a jointly constructed poem from one letter in response to another, the first half up to the ellipses from the words of Ash, the second half from Christabel:

I shan't forget the first glimpse of your form
Illuminated as it was by flashes of sunlight.
I have dreamt nightly of your face
To walk the landscape of my life
With the rhythms of your writing
Ringing in my ears. . . .
I shall never forget our shining progress towards one another
Never have I felt such a concentration of my entire being
I cannot let you burn me up
Nor can I resist you
No mere human can stand in a fire and not be consumed.

During this portion of the film, viewers witness Ash and Christabel approaching one another through a crowd, oblivious to the throng of activity around them, staring intently into one another's eyes. The scene is evocative of the way poetic language permeates their inner thoughts and equalizes them as each contributes to the voice-over narration.

Additionally, LaBute takes excerpts from several poems and reshapes them to form new poetry. For instance, when Maud first enters Christabel's room in Seal Court, she tells Roland that Christabel captured the atmosphere of this family home through "dozens of poems." Maud's voice-over brings together lines from four poems in Byatt's text, "The Fairy Melusine" along with three untitled poems about fish in a pool, the dolls, and martyrdom. The excerpts, taken together, form a coherent single poem:

What are they
Who haunt our dreams and weaken our desires
And turn us from the solid face.
And in the depth of wintry night
They slumber open-eyed and bright.
Dolly keeps a Secret
Safer than a Friend
Dolly's Silent Sympathy
Lasts without end.
In no Rush of Action
This is our doom
To live a Long Life out
In a Dark Room.

The only word LaBute changes is "Drag" in line 12 to "live," but the rest of the lines are intact. This new "poem" evokes the rush of all the lines of poetry Maud is struck by as she associates the words with the objects in front of her; LaBute creates a much shorter variant of a cross section of Byatt's poems by cutting and remixing lines. It is a fascinating technique to keep the essence of Byatt's poetry in the novel intact despite the time limitations inherent in film.

Furthermore, this scene seems to bring out the first stirrings of emotion in Maud, who tears up as she looks around the room. Maud is shown as cold and emotionless until she connects the poetry of the past to the scene in the present, which points to the larger theme, that without a mystery to solve, without a set of poems to decipher and letters to read in tandem, Maud and Roland may lack the words and emotions to communicate their feelings. Despite the formidable vocabularies that each possesses, Maud and Roland seem unable to reveal their deepest emotions to one another when they must speak for themselves. Proof of Roland's inability to express himself eloquently occurs in a scene added by LaBute. The morning after Roland first stays with Maud, she finds him writing in a notebook. A close-up of the page reveals the following: "Please take back the books, the postcards, the beeswax candles, the potted plant. . . . Ungracious of me to say it, but so many gifts that are given . . ." are a few of the lines visible in the shot. Maud asks, "Are you doing your homework?" Roland replies, "No, I'm just writing stuff. Stuff for me. It's nothing." Maud asks, "You're a closet poet?" Roland replies, "Uh, more like basement, really. Just, uh fooling around." Maud looks at him with amusement and chides, "So is that what you want to be when you grow up?" Roland says with self-deprecation, "No, I'm gonna be safe and teach like everybody else. Besides, there's no such thing as poets anymore." Absent from the text, this scene is likely a revision of a mention toward the end of Byatt's novel of Roland making lists of words that he hopes will one day form poems.[24] When Maud closes the scene by asking if he'd like to see Christabel's family home, she calls Roland "poet," yet it is clear that Roland lacks Ash's talents.

In general, when Maud and Roland try to communicate about love or emotions in the film, they are nothing short of inept. They only seem to come alive when they are quoting portions of the letters that evoke poetic imagery and the poems themselves. In fact, Mick LaSalle's review states, "If 'Possession' is meant to contrast the splendor of love as practiced in the 19th century with the scratch-yourself casualness of the 21st century, it succeeds all too well."[25] La Salle is one reviewer who has picked up on the fact that Roland in particular seems caught up in the romantic majesty of the past yet unable to articulate any approximation of that atmosphere in the present, with his increasingly scruffy and unkempt appearance and stumbling attempts at romantic interludes with Maud. LaSalle explains that Roland's character represents "the fantasy of a scruffy, cuddly, sensitive stranger, a kind of modern-day Heathcliff after sensitivity training."[26]

Because Roland and Maud lack the words to woo and be wooed, they gravitate to the poetic language in the letters between Ash and Christabel and find themselves drawn to one another by their parallels to the past. Catherine Burgass states that Roland and Maud are unable to become entwined romantically for fear of losing autonomy, but they end up "driven by the narrative of the braver and more innocent Victorians."[27] When Maud reads, "I cannot let you burn me up, nor can I resist you. No mere human can stand in a fire and not be consumed," Roland replies, "You mind reading that last part out one more time?" and he listens to her raptly, as if she has written such lines for his ears only, thanking her for her recitation as he looks at her longingly. Later, lying in their shared bed in Yorkshire, Roland reads lines from Ash's "The Garden of Proserpina," and Maud replies, "I don't mind that," only seeming to find Ash, whom she calls a "soft-core misogynist," to have written beautiful love poetry once she finds that his object of affection was Christabel. In fact, the reading of these lines sets off the first physical encounter between Maud and Roland who kiss, then become uncomfortable and break away from one another.[28] Lynn K. Wells observes that Roland's perusal of Vico's *The New Science* is an apt opening for the story, for Vico wrote of the tremendous power that language possessed to both hold up a mirror to reality and to create it, themes that touch on Roland's quest in the text to discover his own poetic voice.[29] Wells asserts that the contemporary figures Roland and Maud "confirm their impressions that their own culture, for all its advances, has actually regressed into a state of paralyzing skepticism with regard to intellectual curiosity, artistic endeavor, and interpersonal relations."[30] Roland tells Maud he doesn't "allow" himself to get caught up in the epic love stories like Ash and Christabel's, because "[Roland's] antics made a lot of people unhappy, one horribly so." Maud explains that when she begins to feel affection for someone, she "go[es] cold all over . . . [for] fear of being burned up by love." It is clear in LaBute's version of the story that both Roland and Maud have become so cynical about relationships that they don't give themselves over to them completely, preferring instead to follow a line in a draft of a letter to discover a hidden love story and revel in the romance of an earlier time, finding that time more "real" and far more romantic than the present.

In keeping with Byatt's comment that men seem eager to live vicariously through the romantic idealism of the past, Roland orchestrates a confluence of the past and present in the shared letter reading scene between himself and Maud. Byatt keeps Maud and Roland separate for the initial reading of the discovered letters. The critics discover them while Sir George stands by, and immediately Sir George takes them to his wife, who reads only the first letters from Ash to LaMotte and the final two letters, leaving the rest neatly stacked in a pile and promising access only after he researches how best to proceed. Lucile Desblache argues the letters form a core function in the text, but notes that many are not presented in tandem, which is done deliberately by Byatt to enhance the fragmentary nature of the novel.[31] Yet LaBute turns the letter reading into a shared, self-contained scene in which Roland and Maud discover the letters before Sir George finds them and they take turns reading Ash and Christabel's language, forming a montage of scenes in the past and an amalgamation of poetic language in both time periods.

Furthermore, LaBute grants Roland's wish in Byatt's text, for when Maud indicates in the text that they should read the letters separately, Roland is saddened, "partly because he had a vision, which he now saw was ridiculous and romantic, of their two heads bent together over the manuscripts, following the story, sharing, he had supposed, the emotion."[32] Yet LaBute takes this fantasy and makes it reality in his refashioning of this portion of the novel, for the snippets of letters read aloud in tandem form the feel of an epic poem in and of itself. This technique of the presentation of the letters accomplishes two things: it allows for the filmmaker to use the letters as a narrative backdrop for the scenes of the Victorians to play out in a montage, and it showcases the contemporary couple's need of the romance of the past to push them into letting down their walls and opening up. But it is only through the words of others that they become emotional. This is precisely the message in Byatt's text. Byatt said, "I wanted the past to be more alive in the present than the present."[33]

Maud, too, is skeptical about romance, both in the text and in the film. In Byatt's text, when they first arrive outside Thomason Foss, Maud says that their age is "very knowing" about sex. "We know we are driven by desire," she says, "but we can't see it as they did, can we? We never say the word Love, do we—we know it's a suspect ideological construct—especially Romantic Love—so we have to make a real effort of imagination to know what it felt like to be them, here, believing in these things—Love—Themselves—that what they did mattered—."[34] In the film, Maud is walled off by coldness and skepticism toward men in general, but particularly to Roland, whose "take-what-you-want" American attitude encourages her to put up her guard immediately. And yet the promise of reading the poetry in a darkened tower room, the thrill of discovery of new words, both sends her to her room to gather note cards and to return for a moment to check her appearance in the mirror before she sits, head bent next to Roland's, immersed in a grand love story. By becoming Christabel in that scene of shared letter reading, Maud is able, for a moment, to discover what it felt like to be "Them."

While readers of the book may think the oversimplification changes Byatt's focus, it does not. The ineptness of the present-day couple sans poetry to enhance their union shows that they are weaker in terms of "romance" than the poets who preceded them. Roland's attempts to articulate his feelings are often stunningly vague, such as when he says, "Maud, I think that you are very . . . you know?" "No, I don't know," says Maud. Interestingly Maud's final comment in this scene takes the film squarely back to Byatt's intentions, when she says, "Anyway, we're getting off the track here. We came to investigate them, not us." Byatt states, "He and Maud were being driven by a plot or fate that seemed, at least possibly, to be not their plot or fate but that of those others."[35] The relationship of "those others" was true love: Ash and Christabel flamed and the flames consumed them, but evidence of their union remains through their daughter, Maud's ancestor. When the film shifts to its conclusion for Maud and Roland, it appears to end happily ever after, but taken together with the text, it may reveal a false happiness, a temporary one, for Roland and Maud apart from a literary mystery to bind them may lack the poetic language necessary to fuel their own story of true love. While some may view LaBute's final scene for Roland as evidence of their love story beginning, there is another way to interpret the scene, for there is no more mystery to solve. What remains for the couple who cannot communicate unless they possess the poetic language of others? It is fitting that LaBute places his contemporary couple in front of a roaring fire, for like Ash and Christabel, their love is perhaps destined to be short lived, evoking Christabel's prophetic proclamation, "No mere human can stand in a fire and not be consumed."

And so is there such a thing as a poet anymore? Not according to one possible interpretation of LaBute's film. There are literary critics, detectives of poetry and prose, who can sift and cut and shape the verses they discover, giving voice to the past and even redefining the words they study as mysteries are uncovered and solved. They can relive the past by tracing the footsteps of their literary forebears through clues in their poetry and letters, paying homage to the life and work of those they study. As Byatt asserts, "The 'idea' of the novel was that poems have more life than poets, and poems and poets are more lively than literary theorists or biographers living their lives at second hand."[36] LaBute's film is viewed by many as a simplified novel adaptation, a tale of two people who connect through shared academic passions, complete with a Hollywood ending as two fresh-faced contemporary academics pull their noses from their books to pledge their mutual affection. But for those who read between the lines, LaBute's film offers fidelity to Byatt's original intentions, which were to show that the poetry of the past is more alive than the words that Maud and Roland cannot find in the present, and that without such verse, this contemporary couple may emerge from their ivory towers at a loss for words.

NOTES

1. A. S. Byatt and Ignês Sodré, *Imagining Characters: Six Conversations about Women Writers; Jane Austen, Charlotte Brontë, George Eliot, Willa Cather, Iris Murdoch, and Toni Morrison* (New York: Vintage, 1997), 245.

2. Daniel Zaliewski, "Film; Can Bookish Be Sexy? Yeah, Says Neil LaBute," *New York Times*, August 18, 2002, accessed October 25, 2012, http://www.nytimes.com/2002/08/18/movies/film-can-bookish-be-sexy-yeah-says-neil-labute.html.

3. A. O. Scott, "Film Review: Poetical Flesh and Blood Proves a Strong Tonic," *New York Times*, August 16, 2002, accessed June 20, 2012, http://www.nytimes.com/2002/08/16/movies/film-review-poetical-flesh-and-blood-proves-a-strong-tonic.html.

4. Joy Gould Boyum, *Double Exposure: Fiction into Film* (New York: New American Library, 1985), 3.

5. Boyum, *Double Exposure*, 20.

6. Dudley Andrew, *Concepts in Film Theory* (Oxford: Oxford University Press, 1984), 100.

7. Andrew, *Concepts in Film Theory*, 100.

8. Andrew, *Concepts in Film Theory*, 100.

9. Scott, "Film Review: Poetical Flesh."

10. Tamara S. Wagner, "Neil LaBute's Possession of A. S. Byatt's Romance: The American Connection," The Victorian Web: Literature, History, and Culture in the Age of Victoria, November 19, 2002, accessed December 17, 2012, http://www.victorianweb.org/neovictorian/byatt/filmadapt.html.

11. Andrew, *Concepts in Film Theory*, 103.

12. A. S. Byatt, "Fairy Stories—The Djinn in the Nightingale's Eye," A. S. Byatt on Herself: Essays and Articles, May 1995, accessed December 17, 2012, http://www.asbyatt.com/Onherself.aspx.

13. A. S. Byatt, *Possession: A Romance* (New York: Vintage, 1990), 379.

14. Zaliewski, "Film; Can Bookish Be Sexy?"

15. David Henry Hwang, *Possession: Early Production Draft*, February 1996, accessed December 17, 2012, www.dailyscript.com/scripts/Possession1.pdf.

16. Zaliewski, "Film; Can Bookish Be Sexy?"

17. Mira Stout, "What Possessed A. S. Byatt?," *New York Times*, May 26, 1991, accessed December 17, 2012, http://www.nytimes.com/books/99/06/13/specials/byatt-possessed.html.

18. Margaret Reynolds and Jonathan Noakes, *A. S. Byatt: The Essential Guide to Contemporary Literature* (London: Vintage, 2004), 13–14.

19. Reynolds and Noakes, *Essential Guide*, 17.

20. Reynolds and Noakes, *Essential Guide*, 26.

21. Reynolds and Noakes, *Essential Guide*, 26.

22. Reynolds and Noakes, *Essential Guide*, 28.

23. Reynolds and Noakes, *Essential Guide*, 28.

24. LaBute additionally creates an imagist poem in the recitation of words and phrases that come to the spiritualist leading the séance with the Vestal Lights. She intones: "White earth / Valley / Waterfall / Child/Laughing / Two people / Deception / Letters / Two people / Words / Death / A Field."

25. Mick LaSalle, "Review: Desirable 'Possession'; Literary Mystery Meets Period Romance in LaBute's Latest," *SF Gate*, August 16, 2002, accessed December 17, 2012, http://www.sfgate.com/movies/article/REVIEW-Desirable-Possession-Literary-2809473.php#ixzz2FLIj6VYh.

26. LaSalle, "Review: Desirable 'Possession.'"

27. Catherine Burgass, *A. S. Byatt's " Possession "* (New York: Continuum, 2002), 31–32.

28. *Possession*, directed by Neil LaBute (2002; Universal Studios, 2003), DVD.

29. Lynn K. Wells, "Corso, Ricorso: Historical Repetition and Cultural Reflection in A. S. Byatt's *Possession: A Romance*," *Modern Fiction Studies* 48 (2002): 669.

30. Wells, "Corso, Ricorso."

31. Lucile Desblache, "Penning Secrets: Presence and Essence of the Epistolary Genre in A. S. Byatt's *Possession*," *L'Esprit Créateur* 40 (2000): 91.

32. Byatt, *Possession*, 144.

33. Reynolds and Noakes, *Essential Guide*, 20.

34. Byatt, *Possession*, 290.

35. Byatt, *Possession*, 456.

36. A. S. Byatt, "Guardian Book Club *Possession*," A. S. Byatt on Herself: Essays and Articles, accessed December 17, 2012, http://www.asbyatt.com/Onherself.aspx.

Chapter Two

Rudolph's *Mrs. Parker and the Vicious Circle*

Film Form and Parker's Poetic Legacy

Carolyn Kelley

Dorothy Parker never took herself seriously as a writer. In a 1956 interview with the *Paris Review*, she stated, "My verses are no damn good. Let's face it, honey, my verse is terribly dated—as anything once fashionable is dreadful now. I gave it up, knowing it wasn't getting any better, but nobody seemed to notice my magnificent gesture."[1] Parker's life was filled with tragedies and pain. She was orphaned by age thirteen; attempted suicide three times; had an abortion, two miscarriages, and two unhappy marriages; and she ended her life becoming what she feared most: a lonely old woman living alone in a residential hotel, like a character out of her last play, *The Ladies of the Corridor*. Despite all these personal calamities, her greatest tragedy was her woeful underestimation of her own phenomenal talent. Unfortunately, Alan Rudolph's 1994 biographical film, *Mrs. Parker and the Vicious Circle*,[2] makes the same mistake—it denigrates her magnificent talent by suggesting that her ability to suffer was her greatest artistic achievement. Rudolph's film ultimately reinforces the (false) notion that the personal events of Parker's famous life overshadowed and are ultimately more interesting and important than her writing career.

The film's discourse highlights the melodramatic events of Parker's life, such as her heavy drinking and her failed relationships with men, including her sad marriage to the drug-addicted World War I veteran Eddie Parker and her doomed love affair with Charles MacArthur. By overemphasizing these biographical events and underemphasizing Parker's role as a writer, the film perpetuates the notion that she should be remembered for what was done to her rather than for what she accomplished as a legitimate artist, and in Parker's case, as a legitimate activist as well. Rudolph admits that he sees his film as a love story between Parker and Robert Benchley, the married man with whom she shared a long and intimate, although platonic, relationship.[3] Most biographers consider Benchley the love of Parker's life, and the film speculates about why the two never tried to be a romantic couple.[4] Despite the dramatic tension resulting from the Parker/Benchley relationship, Rudolph's choice to show Parker as an unfulfilled lover instead of an artist turns the film into a maudlin melodrama instead of a meditation on what events and people helped form a great artist. Indeed, the film does not seem to believe Parker was a great artist. In addition to the sensationalistic slant, Rudolph's film takes in terms of its discursive elements, its formal elements, most obviously the black-and-white monologues dispersed throughout the film of Parker reciting her poems, also serve to denigrate her value as an artist. The events of Parker's life during the 1920s are filmed in color, and the film observes the standard narrative convention of "the fourth wall." In contrast, Rudolph films the scenes in which Parker, played by Jennifer Jason Leigh, recites her poetry in black and white, and Leigh looks directly into the camera lens. During these short scenes, Rudolph presents Parker solely as a middle-aged woman, even though Parker wrote all the poems used in the film in her thirties. By using formal strategies that isolate the recitals of Parker's poems from the film's narrative action, the film ultimately marginalizes Parker's poetry, much like scholars and critics (and unfortunately even Parker herself) marginalize her as a less-than-serious person and writer.

   In an essay that praises Parker's canny insight into male-dominated culture, Angela Weaver writes, "Biographical details such as Parker's bouts of depression and alcoholism and several failed suicide attempts continue to overshadow her literary work in the public imagination. Films such as the 1994 *Mrs. Parker and the Vicious Circle* testify to the strength and longevity of Parker's negative reputation as a celebrity."[5] Indeed, the film highlights these sensationalistic personal events that perhaps, unfortunately, define Parker's celebrity at the expense of Parker's serious accomplishments not only as a writer but also as a prolific political activist. Parker was "cited in *Red Channels* as a writer and versifier with nineteen pro-Communist credits," the subject of four anti-Communist investigative committees, investigated by the FBI, and blacklisted as a Hollywood screenwriter.[6] Rudolph inserts a scene late in the film in which a soused, sixty-five-year-old Parker tells some admirers that the director of a film she worked on "went to prison for being an American in the U. S. of A.," a statement that obliquely hints at her disgust with McCarthyism. Over the closing credits, in a scene that also takes place in 1958, Parker tells reporters that her involvement in the Spanish Civil War was "the proudest thing" she'd "ever been on." Although the film introduces a plethora of characters (thirty-six named characters have speaking parts),[7] this vast representation of the people who populated Parker's life lacks one conspicuously absent participant: Lillian Hellman. Hellman played a large part in Parker's political and professional life. She and Hellman cofounded the Screen Writer's Guild in 1933,[8] and Hellman was executrix of Parker's estate.[9] Hellman's absence could be due to the fact that the film is largely based on Marion Meade's 1988 biography of Parker, *What Fresh Hell Is This?* Meade's book presents Hellman in a bad light, possibly because she refused to let Meade interview her for the book.[10] Meade makes several catty remarks about Hellman in the biography, such as saying that Hellman was "extremely jealous" of Parker's good looks and vibrant personality.[11] Another possible, and perhaps more significant, explanation for Hellman's strange absence from the film could be because she did not figure into Parker's personal dramas, and the film concentrates on the sensationalistic events of Parker's life.

Of the nine poems Rudolph's film utilizes, only one is integrated wholly within the narrative, and this poem is the most successful inclusion of Parker's poetry in the film. Parker recites her poem "Résumé" to an audience in the diegetic world of the film. The film's last poem, "Symptom Recital," is semi-integrated into the narrative as it is heard in voice-over while Parker wanders around a muted 1926 New York City. The other seven poems are quartered off from the narrative—ripping the audience out of Parker's story and into the depths of a black-and-white-staged hell of an older and often inebriated Parker reciting her poems in a kind of oxymoronic whispery wail. In these monologues, Rudolph's camera acts like a predator, slowly creeping up on her as she speaks. By formally analyzing the poetic monologues, including when and how they are edited into the narrative, it becomes clear that the choices made in the film about Parker as a writer reflect the film's (although I believe unconscious) rejection of Parker as an artist.

The first poem, "Theory," appears during the opening credits:

> Into love and out again,
> Thus I went, and thus I go.
> Spare your voice, and hold your pen—
> Well and bitterly I know
> All the songs were ever sung,
> All the words were ever said;
> Could it be, when I was young,
> Some one dropped me on my head?[12]

On the poem's first words, "Into love," Rudolph's camera focuses on an ornate cigarette holder that pops open, revealing a stockpile of unfiltered Camel cigarettes. The cigarettes' popping up into the frame have a phallic dimension, which connect the word "love," ironically, to the many men who hurt her, by claiming to "love" her but only wanting sex. Parker said of Charlie MacArthur, the man who most profoundly broke her heart, "It serves me right for putting all my eggs in one bastard" after he remained callously unmoved by her pregnancy and subsequent abortion.[13] Rudolph holds one of these cigarettes in an extreme close-up as the camera moves up to a heavily lipsticked woman's mouth. After this mouth recites the poem's two last lines, the camera tilts up her face, stopping on intense brown eyes that stare directly into the camera. The screen dissolves to a blue title written in an art-deco-style font that reads, "Mrs. Parker," thus tying the identity of the reading lips to the main character. After a second or two, the remaining words of the title "And the Vicious Circle" appear.

This opening shot works to fetishize Parker by breaking her body up into parts: eyes and lips, thus turning her into an object rather than the subject she presumably should be in the film. Ironically, Parker spoils the voyeur's pleasure in looking at her with her direct stare into the camera—she knows that we know we look at her. Still, this direct stare, which is repeated in all seven of the monologues that occur outside the film's narrative world, imbue Parker with a vulnerability that remains unsettling. By filming her this way, Rudolph allows the audience to become intrusive and almost abusive—she shares too much intimacy with us before we have earned her trust. The audience, in essence, assumes the position of the cruel lovers who used her. She looks at us when reciting her poems in the place of the men who caused the pain that helped her craft her lines.

"Theory" explains Parker's "theory" about how she could possibly be so smart in life, yet so obtuse about men. Parker told friends that she seeks lovers who have three qualities: handsomeness, ruthlessness, and stupidity.[14] The "you" to whom Parker directs the poem can "spare" "tongue" and "pen," because she already knows the pain of love; she doesn't need to read or hear songs about it. Still, she pursues love despite all the evidence about its concluding pain, perhaps because her brain was damaged by being dropped on her head as a child. Ironically, Parker metaphorically was "dropped" by her mother, who "went and promptly died"[15] on her one month short of her fifth birthday. Perhaps the reason why she splits the word "someone" in the poem into two words, "some" and "one," reflects her attempt to distance herself from the pain of her mother's death by turning her into an object—a "one"—instead of a person.

Parker published "Theory" in her second collection of poems, *Sunset Gun*, in 1928, when she was thirty-five years old. The Parker who recites the poem in this monologue is about a decade older, which we can deduce from her hairstyle; her heavy bangs are clearly visible when the camera tilts to her eyes, and Parker only sports these bangs in the period of the film set in 1937 Hollywood. By featuring an older version of Parker reciting not only this poem but also every poem in the monologues, the poems seem more sensational; they become like carnivalesque predictions of what Parker would become—a middle-aged woman profoundly unhappy with her life and bitter and cynical about love. The use of the older Parker to read the poems feels like a party trick, not a genuine appreciation of the poems, which were all written by a younger, less-world-weary Parker, who in the 1920s still held on to her "quondam dreams"[16] of being a writer, despite her self-deprecation. By the time she reaches middle age, she is no longer in New York, but in Hollywood, turning out screenplays and resigning herself to her fate of working in a genre of writing she does not respect. In *What Fresh Hell Is This?* Meade reports that Parker "abhorred movies . . . and hoped the entire film industry would collapse, and predicted she would hate Hollywood."[17]

Because Parker disliked Hollywood so intensely, she probably would not have wanted a Hollywood film to tell her story or attempt to define her legacy, but she probably would not have been surprised that this film, which concentrates on her lurid personal life instead of her professional accomplishments, got her so wrong. In an ironic twist, this film doubles down on its Hollywoodness, or in other words, it shows the power of Hollywood as a legacy-making machine through its casting of many second-generation actors, most notably in the three leading roles: Parker (Vic Morrow's daughter, Jennifer Jason Leigh), Robert Benchley (George C. Scott and Colleen Dewhurst's son, Campbell Scott), and Charlie MacArthur (James Broderick's son, Matthew Broderick). The cast also includes Sam Robards (Jason Robards and Lauren Bacall's son) as Harold Ross, Gwyneth Paltrow (Blythe Danner's daughter) as fictional character Paula Hunt,[18] Nick Cassavetes (John Cassavetes and Gena Rowlands's son) as Robert Sherwood, and Keith Carradine (John Carradine's son) in a cameo role as Will Rogers. Hollywood cast a dark shadow not only on Parker's life, but also in the casting of this film about her life.

The film begins in medias res in Hollywood, 1937. Over opening credits, Benchley films his MGM short "Home Movies." Rudolph engages a long take that follows Benchley from filming inside the studio to his surprise encounter with Parker and her husband, Alan Campbell, outside. In the bright sunlight, Parker admonishes Benchley for his apolitical posturing—shedding light, so to speak, on one reason for their estrangement. Benchley always described his political position as "noncommittally understanding,"[19] and Parker found his lack of activism distasteful and irresponsible. As Benchley walks away, he twists his wedding ring while looking back toward Parker, a subtle gesture that refers to his choice to stay in a stale marriage instead of earlier, taking a chance on love with Parker. This gesture also reinforces Rudolph's plan to emphasize the love-story aspect of their relationship. This long take is one of many Rudolph uses throughout the film. They are not overly ostentatious, in that Rudolph does not employ difficult tracking moves or elaborate actor choreography, although this particular long take uses what Rudolph calls the "blowout effect"[20] of harsh white light hitting Benchley as he first exits the studio to emphasize the shock of his encountering Parker after many years of estrangement. Overall, however, Rudolph uses the long takes to allow much of the action to unfold in real time, like a play, which increases the film's reality effect, yet this approach also makes the cuts to the nonnarrative monologues more jarring and abrupt, which results in marginalizing these scenes and the poems recited in them from the rest of the film.

After Benchley walks away, the camera focuses on Parker now accompanied by a young film assistant who comments to her that the 1920s must have been so colorful. Parker retires to a chair to knit as the movie she presently works on continues, and she says to herself, "I suppose it was colorful." The camera tilts down to her hands and the director of the 1937 film in the diegetic world yells "Cut," and Rudolph's film cuts to a black-and-white photograph. The shot widens to show a young Parker, in color, with scissors in hand as she cuts the picture out of the newspaper. The "cut" moves us from the black-and-white 1937 Hollywood to the in-color 1919 New York office of *Vanity Fair*. Rudolph explains that he filmed the scenes after the 1920s in black and white as opposed to color because, to quote director Sam Fuller, "black and white is more real."[21] In making this choice, Rudolph matches the word "real" with "unhappy" because these black-and-white scenes show Parker in decline after the halcyon days of the Algonquin Round Table lunches of the 1920s. Rudolph suggests that Parker's life can be easily codified as 1920s equals happy and late 1930s and beyond equals sad. Yet, Parker wrote all the poems Rudolph chooses for the film in the 1920s and early 1930s, which shows Parker was well acquainted with pain, longing, and loneliness during her "colorful" decade. Having the poems performed by the older Parker implies the poems were the result of a bitter, middle-aged woman's anger at growing older, which further sensationalizes Parker by caricaturing her in this way. If the film presented the poems in color and featured their recitals during the time period in which they were composed, the film would show more respect for her as a writer by decreasing the sensationalism and the stereotyping suggested by the older Parker recitals.

Perhaps the worst offense occurs in the film's penultimate monologue, where she recites "Interior," a poem from her 1928 collection *Sunset Gun*:

> Her mind lives in a quiet room,
> A narrow room and tall,
> With pretty lamps to quench the gloom
> And mottoes on the wall.
>
> There all the things are waxen neat
> And set in decorous lines;
> And there are posies, round and sweet,
> And little, straightened vines.
>
> Her mind lives tidily, apart
> From cold and noise and pain,

And bolts the door against her heart,
Out wailing in the rain. [22]

In the narrative of the film, it is 1926, and Parker is thirty-three years old. She wakes up while staying in a guest room of Herbert and Maggie Swope's Long Island estate. She has had a dream in which both Benchley and MacArthur visit her bedroom, and both men treat her tenderly. She sits up in bed, and the film cuts to the black-and-white monologue of a fifty-two-year-old Parker reciting the poem in 1945. We can place the year as 1945, because she wears the same hairstyle she had in the 1945 scene in which she learns of Benchley's death. The scene features a sound bleed; the 1945 Parker reads the first stanza of the poem over the 1926 Parker in bed. At the second stanza, the film cuts to a black-and-white scene of the 1945 Parker also in bed. A drink rests on the nightstand. Her hair is messy, and her face looks worn and haggard. The camera starts on Parker in long-shot and very slowly moves in, until ending the scene in medium-shot. This technique gives the impression that the camera is stalking Parker, slowly creeping up on her, ready to pounce and devour her. She stares into the camera, defiant, even as she knows its intent to consume her.

Narratively, "Interior" explores the fantasy of living entirely in a world created in one's own head where "all things are waxen neat," and one can create and then control all its events. This fantasy world banishes the heart, which represents the uncontrollable elements of life, such as the pain of falling in love with the wrong person or at the wrong time, to the harsh, cold, real world, represented by the rain. Parker's use of the pronoun "her" suggests the poem is autobiographical. The men featured in Parker's dream were the two loves of her life, and both men broke her heart. MacArthur rejected the pregnant Parker, and Benchley became estranged from her and died prematurely before they could rekindle their deep friendship. Parker's dream of being visited by these two men perhaps would have precipitated her dreaming up a fantasy world in which she had total control and could lock life's heartaches, and the men who caused them, out in the "rain." Rudolph's use of "Interior" is clever, because Parker's dreaming of these two men caringly attending to her lends to the scene the same oneiric quality as this poem. Where the film falters, however, is by inserting the monologue scene of the older Parker reciting "Interior," because Parker wished for this fantasy long before middle age. To have the fifty-two-year-old Parker recite the poem, instead of the younger Parker who wrote it, suggests that having a fantasy life of living in one's mind is the prescribed province of the sad, middle-aged spinster. By buying into this stereotype, the film implies that Parker is like the fictional Tracy Lord in *The Philadelphia Story* who remains a spinster regardless of how many times she marries. The mise-en-scène of the soused older Parker alone in bed bitterly spitting out the poem to the film's nondiegetic audience highlights the lurid nature of Parker's personal decline into alcoholism and loneliness, and distracts the viewer from the beautiful, stark power of this poem.

In contrast, the only recital of a poem fully integrated into the narrative serves as the most successful and respectful inclusion of Parker's poetry in the film. Parker's recital of "Résumé" occurs at the Swopes' Long Island home the day before her dream about Benchley and MacArthur in 1926. Maggie Swope says, "Maybe Dorothy will consent to recite one of her little things for us." Alexander Woollcott says, off camera, "Please Dorothy, something bilious for dessert," perhaps to counter the sickeningly sweet patronizing voice of the hostess. Parker protests, "Well, maybe I'll just digest my little supper and sing for you later." Parker just had vented her disgust about Harpo Marx's performing his movie character "like a seal," and is obviously put out by her hostess's request. Maggie persists: "Please, one of your darling little poems." During this exchange, the camera features Maggie screen left with Parker center screen. The camera continually pushes inward slowly. Unlike the predatory feel of the camera in the poetic monologues, however, here, most likely because of the inclusion of other characters and the sunny mise-en-scène, the camera's moving in feels like a spotlight, zeroing in on a strong and confident performer. By the time Parker begins "Résumé," she is in medium-shot, alone in the frame, except for the torsos of two other male writers in attendance, F. Scott Fitzgerald and George S. Kaufman. The frame has excised the hostess in a formal move that mirrors Parker's wish to cut her out of her own mind because of her patronizing request for a "darling little" poem. "Résumé" is featured in Parker's first collection of poems, 1926's *Enough Rope*:

> Razors pain you;
> Rivers are damp;
> Acids stain you;
> And drugs cause cramp.
> Guns aren't lawful;
> Nooses give;
> Gas smells awful;
> You might as well live.[23]

The camera stays on her, inching closer until she ends up in close-up as she says the last line. She never looks into the camera, sustaining the illusion that she recites the poem only to her audience at the estate. Rudolph ends this slowly moving long take with an abrupt cut on the last word of the poem, "live," to an extreme long shot of twenty-four of the party guests, including Parker, who walks out of the shot, screen right. The dull Roger Spaulding, who is trying to seduce her, stands up, claps, and shouts, "Bravo!" The hostess also politely claps. The remaining guests, mostly members of the Algonquin Round Table, sit motionless, seemingly astonished by Parker's ghoulish poem. Parker's delivery is lively, unlike the stagey monologues in which she seems sad, vulnerable, and tired. She does repeat one gesture seen in many of the monologues; she crosses her arms in front of her body, perhaps as a way of protecting herself against the harsh reception of her poem or perhaps to protect herself from the poem's sad theme: although life is horrible, figuring out how to end life is just too complicated, messy, or painful. During her *Paris Review* interview, she tells reporter Marion Capron, "It's not the tragedies that kill us; it's the messes."[24] The poem's gallows humor also reflects Parker's own fascination with death.[25] Her choice of the title "Résumé" plays upon the idea that her attempted suicides define her, much like our own résumés define us. They represent all life's accomplishment on a few pages of paper. The poem expresses Parker's frustration with being considered another sad, slightly mad woman whose life courts more notoriety than her work, much in the same way Sylvia Plath will be defined later in the century. Parker has become fodder for what Plath will call "the peanut-crunching crowd" in her poem "Lady Lazarus."

The hostess picks Parker out of all her party guests to share a poem because she wants light entertainment, a bit of "fluff." The poem taps into Parker's anger at being considered a less-than-serious writer, both by herself and others. The title of the poem also serves as a verb—to resume—perhaps reflecting Parker's wish to resume her once-promising future as a serious writer. Rudolph's choice to feature the bodies of Kaufman and Fitzgerald, both "serious" writers who were not asked to recite one of their "lovely little things" at the party, also shows how Parker had to share the stage with male writers who were taken more seriously than she. In the film, she walks out of the frame, a move equivalent to her strutting off the stage that is the Swopes' back porch in order to demonstrate her independence—she need not wait for applause or scorn—she leaves on her own terms after performing her work. This presentation, in contrast to the monologues, features Parker reading a poem in the time period she wrote it. The film honors her work in this scene, because her recital of the poem is warm, colorful, and vibrant as opposed to the isolating coldness of the middle-aged Parker reciting her poems to a lonely viewer somewhere from beyond the world of the film. On the film's commentary track, Rudolph says the poems are the soul of the film.[26] By isolating the poems from the time period and colorful energies that went into creating them, however, the film suffocates the soul that it claims to honor. Integrating all the poems into the narrative would have provided the film with a better marrying of the artist's life and work. The film separates them and places the poems in static, sterile, and sad environments that disorient the audience, both in terms of aesthetics and chronology.

Perhaps the best example of the monologues' failure is seen in the second of the monologue poems, "The Lady's Reward."[27] This poem issues a warning to all women who follow the "rules" of playing hard to get:

> Lady, lady, never speak
> Of the tears that burn your cheek—
> She will never win him, whose
> Words had shown she feared to lose.
> Be you wise and never sad
> You will get your lovely lad.
> Never serious be, nor true,
> And your wish will come to you—
> And if that makes you happy, kid,
> You'll be the first it ever did. [28]

She cautions that playing hard to get will win your "lovely lad," but this victory will not make you happy. The poem is a feminist manifesto subtly urging women not to play games and to be cautious about what society tells them to want in a man. Rudolph inserts this monologue in a scene from Parker's life in 1919, immediately after she discovers her husband Eddie's addiction to morphine. She married Eddie without knowing him well, partially her biographers hint, because she liked the idea of him: an upper-class, handsome WASP who could provide her with a WASPy last name to replace her "ethnic-sounding" Rothschild. [29] The poem warns women not to make the same choice as she. This poem is the only one used from her third and final collection of poetry, *Death and Taxes*. A forty-four-year-old Parker (circa 1937) recites this poem, written in 1931. Parker sits with her arms propped up in front of her, as if she rests them on some out-of-frame object, perhaps her typewriter. The camera moves in a similar fashion as it does in almost all the other monologues: slowly and steadily, in one take. Like her recital of "Résumé," she crosses her arms in front of her as she speaks in a gesture of self-protection.

What makes "The Lady's Reward" monologue interesting is the fluttering of a lace curtain in the background. Usually in films, curtains move to show wind as a means of establishing verisimilitude to help convince the audience that the film is "real life," because the wind from the real world, supposedly, makes the curtains move. In this monologue, however, the curtain is distracting, because the cut from the color scene of Parker in bed with Eddie to the older Parker in black and white reciting the poem to a camera lens takes us completely out of the narrative, making the reason for the fluttering curtain, the need to show us the world of the film is "real life," unnecessary and somewhat excessive. The formal aspects of this monologue seem to be at conflicting purposes, trying to preserve verisimilitude while simultaneously destroying it, an apt metaphor for Rudolph's use of the monologues throughout the film. He wants them to preserve the soul of the film; instead, they marginalize Parker's poetic writing to the sensationalistic by jolting the audience out of the narrative. His presentation of the older, sadder Parker also denigrates the value of the poems by pulling attention away from the words and by drawing too much attention on the mise-en-scènes in which they are recited. Rudolph's film ultimately continues the cycle of underappreciating Parker's literary value.

All in all, the film *Mrs. Parker and the Vicious Circle* does not do justice to Dorothy Parker's life in terms of the activities she valued the most—being a good citizen and a good writer. By erasing Lillian Hellman from the film and all but ignoring her political activism, the film loses the political Parker. More importantly, however, Parker was an exceptional poet, a sculptor of words, who deserves better treatment and respect than afforded her in Rudolph's film. Rudolph marginalizes Parker's poetry by having the older, alcoholic Parker recite the monologue poems, by isolating these poems through black-and-white photography, and by having Parker directly address the audience. This formal marginalization mirrors the narrative marginalization of Rudolph's choice to concentrate on the sensationalistic personal dramas of Parker's life instead of her talent as a writer. These filmic choices reinforce the false idea that Parker was not a serious or gifted artist, despite the film's intentions otherwise. In a way, the film treats Dorothy Parker in the same manner that Charlie MacArthur did—the film flatters her by seeming to admire her as an artist and a person, but in the end, it does not take her seriously in either role, and it wants only momentarily to grab a piece of her colorful life and have a good time at her expense.

NOTES

1. Marion Capron, "Dorothy Parker: The Art of Fiction No. 13," *Paris Review*, Summer 1956, accessed October 18, 2011, http://www.theparisreview.org/interviews/4933/the-art-of-fiction-no-13-dorothy-parker.

2. *Mrs. Parker and the Vicious Circle*, directed by Alan Rudolph (1994; Chatsworth, Calif.: Image Entertainment, 1995), DVD.

3. Alan Rudolph, "Commentary," *Mrs. Parker and the Vicious Circle*, DVD, directed by Alan Rudolph (1994; Chatsworth, Calif.: Image Entertainment, 1995), DVD.

4. See the following biographers: Leslie Frewin, *The Late Mrs. Dorothy Parker* (Macmillan, 1986), Marion Meade, *What Fresh Hell Is This?* (Villard Books, 1988), and Stuart Silverstein, introduction to *Not Much Fun: The Lost Poems of Dorothy Parker* (Scribner Poetry, 1996). As for the film's speculation on the Parker/Benchley romance, Rudolph includes a scene in which Benchley quits his job in protest because Condé Nast fires Parker. Parker says to Benchley, "I could kiss you, but I'm afraid it wouldn't turn out right." He responds, "Are you afraid you would melt the gold in my teeth?" She replies that she is losing her husband, and "I couldn't bear losing you too." This scene reflects the theses of biographers Frewin and Meade who contend that the two never became romantically involved for fear of destroying their close friendship.

5. Angela Weaver, "'Such a Congenial Little Circle': Dorothy Parker and the Early Twentieth-Century Magazine Market," *Women's Quarterly Journal* 38, no. 2 (2010): 30, accessed December 1, 2012, doi: 10.1353/wsq.2010.0011.

6. Milly S. Barranger, "Dorothy Parker and the Politics of McCarthyism," *Theatre History Studies*, June 1, 2006, 7.

7. "Mrs. Parker and the Vicious Circle," *AFI Catalog: Film Indexes Online*, accessed October 2, 2011, film.chadwyck.com.

8. Barranger, "Dorothy Parker and the Politics of McCarthyism," 9.
9. Marion Meade, *Dorothy Parker: What Fresh Hell Is This?* (New York: Villard Books, 1988), 400.
10. Marion Meade, interview by Scott Simon, *Weekend Saturday Edition*, National Public Radio, April 22, 2006.
11. Meade, *Dorothy Parker: What Fresh Hell Is This?*, 283.
12. Dorothy Parker, "Theory," in *The Portable Dorothy Parker. With an Introduction by Brendan Gill* (New York: Penguin, 1976), 235.
13. Stuart Y. Silverstein, introduction to *Not Much Fun: The Lost Poems of Dorothy Parker* (New York: Scribner Poetry, 2001), 29.
14. Alan Rudolph, "Commentary."
15. Meade, *Dorothy Parker: What Fresh Hell Is This?*, 12.
16. A phrase from her poem "Symptom Recital," the fourth poem recited in the film, and the only one to appear as a voice-over during a narrative event in the film. Parker walks around New York City carrying her new dog Rags, a present just purchased for her by her estranged husband, Eddie. She crosses a busy street, then pauses to cry beside a tree, while an older-sounding Parker recites the poem over the movements (but no sound track) of her younger self.
17. Meade, *Dorothy Parker: What Fresh Hell Is This?*, 197.
18. According to Alan Rudolph's commentary, the fictional character Paula Hunt is a conglomeration of three actresses Marion Meade discusses in *What Fresh Hell Is This?*: Tallulah Bankhead, Helen Hayes, and Peggy Leech.
19. Donald Ogden Stewart, *By a Stroke of Luck!* (London: Paddington, 1975), 228.
20. Alan Rudolph, "Commentary."
21. Alan Rudolph, "Commentary."
22. Dorothy Parker, "Interior," in *The Portable Dorothy Parker. With an Introduction by Brendan Gill* (New York: Penguin, 1976), 215.
23. Dorothy Parker, "Résumé," in *The Portable Dorothy Parker. With an Introduction by Brendan Gill* (New York: Penguin, 1976), 99.
24. Capron, "Dorothy Parker: The Art of Fiction No. 13."
25. For instance, according to Marion Meade, Parker and Benchley decorated their shared office at *Vanity Fair* with photographs of corpses from undertaker magazines (*What Fresh Hell Is This?*, 71).
26. Alan Rudolph, "Commentary."
27. The film only uses the second half of the poem, so only the second half of the poem is quoted in this chapter.
28. Dorothy Parker, "The Lady's Reward," in *The Portable Dorothy Parker. With an Introduction by Brendan Gill* (New York: Penguin, 1976), 317.
29. Meade, *Dorothy Parker: What Fresh Hell Is This?*, 40.

Chapter Three

"A Thing of Beauty"

Art, Commerce, and Poetry in Bright Star *and*
Love and Death on Long Island

Ellen Moll

Poetry has both an elevated and a marginalized status; it is respected as among the highest of art forms, and yet its role in society seems to be fading.[1] In particular, the way that we place value on poetry continues to be a topic of debate and concern, for poets and readers alike. Contemporary cinematic portrayals of poets and poetry often show characters who struggle with the various ways that society values (or fails to value) poems, including the value of poetry in the marketplace. For this reason, it is revealing to examine two films that explore the notion of poetry as a commodity: Richard Kwietniowski's *Love and Death on Long Island* (1997), and Jane Campion's *Bright Star* (2009).

Both films avoid creating a simplistic dichotomy between art and commerce, however, and do not suggest that art must be saved from commodification. Instead, these films suggest that a poem's dual status as both art and commodity reveals the contradictory position of poetry in society, as both a marginalized and revered art form, and that this position deeply complicates the relationship between art, artist, and audience. The films further suggest that the commodification of poetry might best be understood as a series of negotiations among aesthetic, psychological, social, and economic pressures and values. Thus, the commercial is not the opposite of the artistic but rather a component of artistic production and reception that interacts with other components in surprisingly complicated ways. For this reason, these films' treatment of the commodification of poetry may also be seen as both a metacommentary on film itself, and especially on film's traditional identity

27

as a commercial art form, and as a commentary on the commodification of individuals themselves.

POETRY AS FASHION AND FASHION AS POETRY

Bright Star focuses on the relationship between John Keats and Fanny Brawne, played by Ben Whishaw and Abbie Cornish, respectively, and on Keats's career and illness during this period of their lives. Keats struggles to make a living as a poet, and his working-class status by birth and lack of income make it impossible in their society for him to marry Fanny. Although the film is loosely based on Andrew Motion's biography of Keats,[2] Campion's focus is arguably not biography but a meditation on the two characters' relationship to poetry, art, and each other. Their love and their lives are utterly shaped by his difficulties in turning his poetry into a viable commodity; their situation is made all the more poignant because the film audience knows the fame and success Keats's work will eventually have.

The film is told largely from the point of view of Fanny, a young middle-class woman who despises the fact that Keats's economic situation is preventing their happiness. Fanny starts out thinking that Keats's poetry is beautiful but incomprehensible, but through her many discussions with Keats about poetry she finds a new value in them. In the last scene, after hearing of Keats's death, Fanny recites "Bright Star" as she walks alone down a forest path, seeming to bask and mourn at each word.

The film clearly shows that Fanny, like Keats, is a Romantic spirit and an artist to be reckoned with. Fanny creates clothing and fabric keepsakes, and while she is sometimes ridiculed by other characters for her devotion to fashion, the direction and cinematography clearly indicate that Fanny's work is to be studied and contemplated the way that a poem is. The film begins with Fanny sewing, and the scene consists largely of extreme close-ups of Fanny's hands performing exquisitely delicate needlework. Throughout the film, there continue to be long, lingering shots of her work and of the finished products that she creates, notable for their beauty and precision. The film also shows that she is able to earn money for her sewing and designs, not only because of the quality of the work, but also because her designs and techniques are more fashionable than any others in the region—in other words, because her art is innovative, and because it adds something new and different to the market.

Fanny herself comments on the marketability of her work when she first meets Keats, who is staying with his friend George, another poet and a neighbor of Fanny's family. When George is dismissive and mocking of the way that she appreciates fashion—as opposed to the sublime work of poetry—and insists that she leave the two men to their poems to go back to her stitching, Fanny retorts that her "stitching has more merit and more admirers than your two scribblings put together. And I can make money from it."

Throughout the film, in fact, Campion repeatedly draws parallels between Fanny's needlework and John's poetry, suggesting their artistic similarities. For example, several scenes depict Fanny sewing her needlework as her voice, in voice-over, reads one of Keats's poems. In this way, the film reclaims or legitimizes the artistic and economic value of women's work. As Graham Fuller notes, from the opening scenes full of needles piercing cloth and linens blowing in the wind, the film is clearly set in the domestic world of women.[3] Furthermore, just as Fanny is drawn to John's poetry, Keats is moved by Fanny's gift of needlework for his brother's funeral. Thus, both Fanny and John use their art to woo the other. Again, the film claims her needlework, which is stereotypical "women's work," as an alternate or equal to the high art of poetry.

Indeed, understanding the intellectual and artistic genius of women's work has long been a feminist goal. Campion's relevance to feminist film studies has been well noted, including considerations of the way that her works disrupt Laura Mulvey's notion of "the male gaze."[4] I would argue that in this film, Campion utilizes another method of deviating from the male gaze: the film's representation of texture. The extreme close-ups of various fabrics, stitches, and sewing techniques emphasize the distinct nature of the textures in these shots. Shots linger on these textures, the lighting and the framing bringing out the miniscule variations of fabrics, and often accompanied by string music on the sound track that emphasizes the needlework's minimalist beauty. The film's cinematographic emphasis on texture—even over color or line—serves to foreground both the materiality and the artistic merit of Fanny's work and of women's work more generally. Notably, this materiality is opposed to the seeming ephemerality of the sounds of a poem, and also parallels the way that needlework has a more tangible (monetary) value in society than poems do; again, the voice-over of John's poems during the close-up shots of Fanny's needlework invites such comparisons and contrasts. While it is true that nothing much "happens" during these scenes, the scenes serve as meditations on texture, giving the audience opportunities to contemplate the artistic meaning of textures, and also to actively consider the ways that these images of textures resist interpretation and refuse to be diegetic, in ways that suggest a veering away from, if not a rejection of, the male gaze.

Through these methods, Campion creates a film that centers the artistic production of women in ways that subvert dominant understandings of canonicity and artistic valuation. It is in this context, therefore, that the film shows the highly gendered and complex social negotiations entangled in creating a work of art that is also a commodity.

The commodification of art is also seen in the film's treatment of Keats's literary career, of course. Keats scholarship has shown that his poetry was greatly influenced by his lack of financial success. Elizabeth Jones, for example, has noted that Keats's odes, especially in their treatment of ancient art objects, symbolically address the tensions of the commodification of art. According to Jones, Keats "fetishizes these cultural artifacts by presenting them as material vessels that appear to him as being empty of their former significance, and that are available to be reinvested with the desires of a poet attempting to make a living in the newly emerging cultural market," by exploring how the "subjects of the odes are commodified, and packaged for public consumption."[5] While Keats was disdainful of the need to gain popularity among the public, he also was adapting to and trying to fit his role as a "producer" taking part in the literary marketplace.

Jones also notes the way that being "fashionable" and popular were increasingly important in this time period, pointing out "the shift, in the early nineteenth century, in the status of literary endeavor from being a private act of spiritual achievement, part of the 'Grand march of intellect,' to being a cultural commodity, an act of writing something that would either stand or fall on the market; the shift reflects the reality that poetry could no longer be an end in itself, but as consumerism took hold, became a means to an end."[6] Raymond Williams has famously argued that the Romantic period saw artists emphasize their own unique status as individuals with special access to deeper understanding of life, just as artists became increasingly interchangeable as producers for an expanding consumer market.[7] Campion thus portrays a time period in which the commodification of poetry is a central literary concern, and shows the effects of this shift in the marketplace on Keats's and Fanny's life.

Because so many women were consumers, the marketplace itself became an increasingly feminine sphere in which women were prominent as both consumers and commodities,[8] and so disdain for the marketplace was also a rejection of the feminine. With regard to the literary marketplace, art was coded as masculine, commerce as its opposite.[9] Campion also presents the marketplace as a feminine sphere, and emphasizes the artistic (and arguably the feminist) value of such a sphere. The film itself is woman-centric and focused on the domestic arena. Fanny's art is portrayed as both commercially viable and artistically worthy of consideration. Keats's friend George, also a poet, mocks Fanny's concern for fashionability, at a time when poets were more than ever expected to be fashionable in their writing, but George's complaints seem driven by misogyny or personal jealousy rather than artistic integrity. Campion thus depicts the consumer market as feminine, and shows how gender and class are intertwined at multiple levels with artistic valuation, both financially and aesthetically; rejection of marketplace values in favor of an art that is pure of commodification is thus coded by the film as deeply entwined with problematic patriarchal politics. Furthermore, at the more literal level, the film encourages the audience to consider how wrong the public can be about artistic value, showing the canonical Keats unable to earn a living from his poems and Fanny creating designs that her society does not value as legitimate high art, and shows the extreme personal costs of such undervaluations. In all these ways, Campion precludes and politically problematizes the assumption that commercial value is in opposition to artistic value, or that artistic expression is somehow sullied by its participation in the marketplace; the need to successfully commodify one's art is urgent. Commodification is not naturalized or portrayed as unproblematic, however; instead, in this film, art is portrayed as the result of complex negotiations among aesthetic, commercial, patriarchal, and psychological pressures.

PASSION AND COMMERCE ON LONG ISLAND

In *Love and Death on Long Island*, a Walt Whitman poem is bestowed on a mentee as a piece of high culture, given as a gift of love, and pilfered for use in a B movie. The protagonist, Giles De'Ath, is an erudite London man of letters and professional cultural critic who becomes obsessed with Ronnie Bostock, an American film actor best known for raunchy teen comedies. Giles, played by John Hurt, is grieving for his wife of many decades who has recently passed, and the similarity of his last name to "Death" is a constant reminder of this fact (though of course the name may also subtly allude to the plot's similarity to Mann's *Death in Venice*, in which an older man becomes infatuated with a younger man). While attempting to see the latest art film, Giles accidentally wanders into the film *Hotpants College II*. He begins to leave but then is wonderstruck when he sees actor Ronnie Bostock on-screen, played by Jason Priestley. Ronnie is presumably in his twenties, but his character in *Hotpants College II* is a teenager who is being harassed by the other teens; they have humiliated him and left him lying in teenage despair on a diner counter covered in ketchup. The film then shows Giles's POV as the scene shifts from banal teen comedy to the realm of an art-lover's fantasy; Ronnie is in slow motion, and the framing and lighting shift to evoke Pre-Raphaelite paintings of tragic young swains. Indeed, Ronnie's pose now looks positively languid, and the ketchup appears like blood. The nature of the way that the infatuation begins highlights the heightened, highly staged expression of Ronnie's vulnerability and even mortality. Giles's infatuation blossoms as he gazes at the (not-) bleeding young man, an evocation of the intermingling of love and death also found in the film's title. As is typical in this film, this intermingling of love/lust and death accompanies a blurring of the boundaries between "high" and "commercial" art, categories that Giles would normally consider mutually exclusive. Also as in much of the film, the tone in this scene maintains a skillful tension between showcasing the absurdity of the situation and presenting Giles's love as sincere and sympathetic and even deeply moving. The meeting of art and commerce, in this film, is thus a combination of the ridiculous and the sublime.

This portrayal of art and commerce continues throughout the film. Giles's obsession only grows and soon he is buying teenybopper magazines (claiming of course that they are for someone else), and thus becomes passionate for the first time in the film; his obsession with Ronnie takes him out of the dreary rut of grief and apathy that he was in. Interestingly, as he becomes more passionate about life, he also becomes familiar with mainstream popular consumer culture, and thus his engagement with consumer culture has a life-affirming effect on him, despite the fact that he has spent much of his life as a tastemaker who shuns mass popular culture. Giles has never wanted a relationship with a man before, but this adaptability does not faze him; he does, however, devote considerable mental energy to finding elaborate reasons that his obsession does not mean that he has been moved by lowbrow culture, even if these justifications are only expressed to himself. Giles is a critic; his life is dedicated to elucidating the difference between great art and everything else, under the assumption that such distinctions are absolutely vital. His infatuation with Ronnie is thus the central irony of the narrative, an irony which Giles seems well aware of. Indeed, Páraic Finnerty notes that the real transgression for Giles is not his sudden interest in exploring his sexuality but his unforeseen desire for one who is associated with the mass popular culture that he so disdains.[10]

Eventually, Giles decides to go to Long Island, where Ronnie and his girlfriend Audrey live, to try to meet his idol. He runs into Audrey at the grocery store and claims to recognize her because his "niece" is Ronnie's biggest fan; of course, the meeting was not at all by chance, and his niece is purely a fiction. Audrey, however, is charmed by him and invites him to meet Ronnie, and soon Ronnie and Giles develop a friendship and somewhat of a mentorship relationship. Giles assures Ronnie that his acting talents are immeasurably beyond what his work so far has been capable of revealing, and tries to guide his view of art to become more like Giles's own. Ronnie is indeed tired of playing roles that garner so little respect and would prefer to have the type of career that would be praised by those with the cultural capital that Giles has.[11] Giles offers encouragement and flattery but also kindly criticism, claiming that he is trying to help Ronnie fulfill his artistic potential. Ronnie seems to enjoy the adulation and does want to improve his artistic credibility, but there are indications that for Ronnie, this desire is motivated by a desire for career advancement and not for a genuine preference for high art. As their relationship develops, Giles becomes more and more dismissive of Audrey, and she becomes more suspicious of Giles. When Ronnie is about to leave Long Island for an extended trip, largely at

Audrey's suggestion, Giles writes and faxes Ronnie a letter that confesses his feelings and offers Ronnie a relationship akin to that of "Verlaine and Rimbaud"—an offer to be part of an erotically and intellectually productive exchange and mentorship. He also includes Walt Whitman's poem "Now Finale to the Shore," urging Ronnie to leap forward toward his potential to his brilliant new life.[12] Ronnie reads intently, and when he is done, he appears frustrated or annoyed, although there is enough ambiguity in the performance for multiple interpretations of Ronnie's specific state of mind. Ronnie throws the multipage letter away but then changes his mind, retrieves it from the garbage, and searches quickly for something. A later scene reveals the object of his search: he has included those lines from Whitman in the newest film in the *Hotpants College* series, in which Ronnie's character must deliver a eulogy: again, the film intermingles love, death, art, and commerce, in ways that are equal parts moving and absurd.

The role of poetry in the film is particularly important to the portrayal of art and commerce. Throughout the film, Giles quotes poetry to other characters, speaking as if it were his easiest, most natural language. To Ronnie and Audrey, however, these quotations highlight Giles's education and erudition; they are markers that he, more than they, knows what determines artistic merit. They are indeed impressed and, at first, delighted with him, but more importantly, they know that they are *supposed* to be impressed with such things. In the context of Ronnie's Hollywood career, gaining the kind of cultural capital that Giles might bestow is a step toward becoming a big movie star—the pinnacle of commercial success and in some ways the epitome of the successful commodification of self. Ronnie's use of Whitman's poem in his next movie complicates these lines further, however. It is Ronnie's attempt to "elevate" the artistic merit and emotional resonance of the film, which may be equal parts career move and actorly dedication to his role. The inclusion of the poem does show that Giles has broadened Ronnie's cultural knowledge and artistic sensibilities, but there is considerable ambiguity to be found in this scene: Has Ronnie forgotten Giles and his broken heart, caring for nothing except the cultural cache that Ronnie could glean and appropriate for commercial gain? Or is including this poem a way of communicating to Giles—or to himself—something about their relationship—for instance that Giles's feelings weren't entirely unmutual, or even that in this *Hotpants College* funeral scene, Ronnie was to some extent mourning for the friendship with Giles that he no longer has? Furthermore, the poem is given by Giles as a gift to Ronnie, and as an enticement; Giles is using poetry for one of its oldest purposes, seduction. The eroticism of the language of poetry in this case makes it something that Giles uses to essentially *market* himself to Ronnie; yet, Ronnie chooses instead to use the poem to market himself to the public. It seems that Whitman's poem at the end

becomes the object through which the two main characters express, nego-
tiate, and conclude their complex relationship, with each other and with art.

The use of Whitman's poem is also significant to the film's portrayal of
sexuality. References to Whitman have been, in some contexts, a shorthand
allusion to homosexuality. Kenneth Price, however, notes that since Stone-
wall, such allusions to Whitman take on far more complex meanings, and
argues specifically that Whitman in this film "is used as part of the film's
swerve away from the death/love connection. (Whitman's 'Now, Voyager'
serves as a touchstone, indicating that Ronnie is now ready to brave the
unexpected in future journeys.) The film, unlike the novel, leaves us optimis-
tic about Ronnie, suggesting that he has benefited from his encounter with
Giles, and Giles appears ready to return refreshed to his life as a writer."[13]
Thus, it is not merely sexuality but individual personal journeys that shape
the meaning of the commodification of poetry and art, and only by interacting with a multitude of other desires, pressures, and aesthetic and marketplace considerations.

Finnerty also notes that the film signals an important shift in cinematic
portrayals of sexuality. In particular, the friendship in *Love and Death on
Long Island* is one of mutual benefit, and Finnerty argues that the film (along
with *Gods and Monsters*, which was released around the same time) signifies
a shift in the portrayal of friendships between gay older men and straight
younger men, away from representations of the danger or potential for violence in such relationships, toward a view that such friendships are opportunities for both men to expand their horizons and appreciate their relationship,
even if there is no mutual sexual desire; he states that Giles's "adventure has
reinvigorated his creativity and complicated his sense of his own sexual
identity."[14] He also notes that the film subverts stereotypes of sexuality in a
number of ways: Ronnie, the heterosexual male, "underlines the marketability of an androgynous, feminized, and passive version of American man-
hood"; Ronnie's commodification feminizes him.[15] As with the use of Whitman, sexuality again complicates the meaning of commodification in this
film.

The film therefore wryly questions the processes by which art holds power over individuals, whether intellectually, emotionally, or commercially. It
satirizes the exclusivity of high art but also explores the layered complexity
of how sexual and other desires, longing, and grief interact with various
commercial and aesthetic arbiters of value, including the marketplace, to
create meaning from works of art—meaning that is always, fascinatingly,
individual.

CONSUMING BODIES: THE COMMODIFICATION OF POETRY, FILM, AND SELF

Love and Death on Long Island clearly includes metanarrative about the tension between notions of high art and mass commerce in the interpretation and evaluation of film, particularly in its exploration about how desire relates to all of the above. Arguably, Campion's techniques, which draw attention to her filmmaking process, likewise offer commentary on the relationship between desire and aesthetics, a theme that is also seen throughout the film in the treatment of poetry and needlework. Both films thus consider the nature of cinema and filmmaking in ways that resonate with their broader themes. Specifically, the films' depiction of poetry's connection to the marketplace also serves as a commentary on the tensions and possibilities found in cinema's traditional status as both art and commerce.

One reason that poetry's commodification is a particularly appropriate topic for cinema to explore is the nature of lyric poetry. In the lyric tradition, poems are usually short, intense, self-contained, and highly subjective, which in a way makes poems more readily made into a consumable product. Additionally, these qualities make poetry uniquely suited for cinematic discussions of the commodification of literary works; more than other literary forms, a poem—not merely its narrative but the entirety of its exact language—is most easily shown on film as a product one can give or receive, buy or sell. Furthermore, the lyric poem is generally meant to be read aloud and comes from a long tradition of oral performance. For these reasons, the lyric poem is well suited for cinematic explorations of the nature of art in general and in particular for the exploration of the complex desires art—whether poetry or film—may evoke. Desire, of course, is a primary driving factor in the marketplace of supply and demand. For a work of art to be a successful commodity, it must be desired—others must want the poem, for the pleasure or the erotics of the experience, or for the cultural capital. While high art is often contrasted with popular art, and while commercial concerns are often thought to be in opposition to aesthetic concerns, these films suggest that there is no dichotomy between art and commerce. In fact, both artistic and commercial considerations interact in unpredictable ways with the vagaries, flights, and whims of human desire.

Love and Death on Long Island comments explicitly on film's status as both art and commerce. Indeed, much of the tension and irony in the film arise from the conflict between Giles's "high art" aesthetic and his amorous desire for B-movie star Ronnie, and in Giles's attempts to "elevate" Ronnie to the status of a serious actor. Giles, however, finds a great deal to admire in Ronnie's oeuvre, discovering hidden depth of potential in Ronnie's performances. As performed by Priestley, Ronnie's acting most likely appears stilted, overwrought, and unconvincing to the audience of *Love and Death on*

Long Island, but Giles appears to find a spark of hidden talent in these lackluster performances. It is apparent that Giles is eager to find a reason that his adoration of Ronnie is not merely for superficial reasons and is indeed compatible with his identity as a tastemaker. It is never entirely clear, however, why Giles is so struck with this man. Furthermore, it is during a film performance that Giles falls for Ronnie, a scene in which Ronnie's character is thrown around and emotionally wounded, chest streaked with blood-like ketchup. Is it truly Ronnie's handsome but bland looks that have made Giles fall so hard, or is it that this *Hotpants College* scene intermingled eros and death in a way that pulled Giles into its spell at precisely the right moment in his lonely, grieving life?

This ambiguity over the source of Giles's obsession, along with the fact that the *Hotpants* movie clearly parodies teen comedies that are created to make a profit with no apparent aspirations to artistic achievement, suggest that what makes art appealing to an individual is far more complex and unpredictable than Giles was prepared to believe. Finding pleasure or meaning from film is not, in Giles's case, dependent on a film's conformity to traditional definitions of artistic merit, despite what Giles would wish. A single moment of a performance in a dreadful movie may give flight to one's imagination, may evoke Pre-Raphaelite paintings more than teen movie angst, and may stir one's fantasies and desires in challenging and transformative ways. After all, Giles's obsession may seem odd, but it opens him up to new experiences and to modernity in ways that his cloistered life had previously not allowed; the *Hotpants* series transformed how Giles saw the world, which more usually is considered the goal of high art.

This juxtaposition of high and low art is also seen in the use of Whitman's poem in Ronnie's film. Again, the ambiguity of the scene is key. While ostensibly out of place in such a movie, the scene in which Ronnie reads the poem at the funeral is oddly moving, and elicits a performance from Ronnie that is far superior to any of his others that the film shows. Whitman's poem does indeed enhance the scene, but it is not clear that the introduction of the material would be helpful to the overall tone of Ronnie's film, since the genre tends to gloss over serious scenes as plot devices. Nor is it clear that the inclusion of the poem elevates the film into something else, or if it is merely appropriation of poetry (and an appropriation of Giles's devotion) for commercial purposes. Was Ronnie wise to include the poem or does it make him look ridiculous for his pretentions? Was Ronnie stealing the poem for his own use or sending a covert declaration of understanding to Giles? Was the poem used for the sake of art, for the sake of love, or for the sake of money? Again, in this film, to draw a clear line dividing art from commerce is to ignore the complicated lines entangling the characters and desires. Notably, this intermingling of "high art" with the commercial does not appear to debase or degrade the high art but rather to raise intriguing questions about the relationship between aesthetics and desire. Commodification does not empty art (poetry or film) of its meaning, but, as shown by the ambiguities discussed above, commodification is not without its artistic perils as well. In short, artistic and commercial concerns interact with artist and audience desires in surprising and often ambiguous ways. Commerce is not the death of art; commerce makes the production and reception of art infinitely more complicated.

Thus, the film's treatment of poetry parallels its discussion of film's nature as both art and commerce and subverts the notion of a dichotomy between the two. Both aesthetic and commercial considerations are based on desire and on being desired, and are therefore unpredictable and impossible to categorize. *Love and Death on Long Island* is itself an art film, one that is highly entertaining but nevertheless in a category of filmmaking that is generally distinguished from films that are thought to be primarily commercial in nature. Film is of course an enormous industry and export product, and so film studies, for example, has sometimes been in the position of explaining that cinema is indeed an art form worthy of serious academic consideration, just as painting, sculpture, and of course poetry are. In this context, it is significant that *Love and Death on Long Island* parallels the commodification of poetry to the commodification of film and, throughout the film, explores the broader relationship between aesthetics and various forms of desire. In this film, the commodification of poetry is thus used to explore film's status as both artistic and commercial endeavor, and the anxieties about cinema's artistic status its commercial nature may evoke.

In *Bright Star*, Campion explores the commodification in a different way, but arguably also suggests parallels between poetry and film. The commodification of poetry is of course key to the film's plot as well as its treatment of desire. The two main characters both want what society has told them not to want: each other. Their relationship is impossible precisely because Keats's poems are not considered valuable enough on the marketplace to give Keats an income that would support a family. The film at once suggests that successful commodification of art is desirable and a way to reveal oneself and one's genius to the world, and that it is deeply unjust that such commodification is necessary. *Bright Star* thus complicates the notion of the commodification of poetry in ways that contrast interestingly with *Love and Death on Long Island*.

Clearly, in *Bright Star*, the market can be wrong, particularly in the way that the market serves as an arbiter of taste and artistic merit. The audience knows Keats's poetry, by reputation at the very least, and knows that today, Keats is as canonical a poet as there is. Keats's lack of funds and fame during his own lifetime, however, prevents him from marrying Fanny and possibly contributes to his poor health, and thus he dies while his love for Fanny is unconsummated. Just as the central irony of *Love and Death on Long Island* is about art's status as commodity (or, more precisely, Giles's lifelong devotion to highbrow culture juxtaposed with his newfound obsession with a star of lowbrow films), in *Bright Star*, the central irony is that Keats cannot find a sufficient market for his poetry, despite the fact that the audience knows the renown that Keats's work will find after his death. This knowledge, along with the film's portrayal of the tragic consequences of Keats's failure to turn his poems into viable commodities, problematize any dismissal of the marketplace as unimportant to art; the plot encourages the audience to feel a sense of injustice at John's failures and at the unconsummated love of Fanny and John, thus creating a desire to see commercial success match his artistic achievement, as if it were only right and natural for financial gain to follow artistic brilliance.

At other times, however, the film resists the supposition that great poetry could or should be thought of in commercial terms. In fact, poetry is often portrayed in unearthly terms, including in the title of the film, a quote from a Keats poem. Poetry takes on a quasi-mystical or transcendent quality in scenes where Fanny is moved by Keats's poems. In one notable scene, butterflies invade Fanny's room, creating a fabric of wings that surrounds her in a scene that evokes magic realism. The connection of poetry to some greater plane—to mysteries unknown—suggests of course that poets should not strive, first and foremost, to be easily accessible. As a product that the public consumes, however, an inaccessible poem might bring difficulties to the poet; the film emphasizes both the difficulties of reading Keats's poems and his commercial struggles so often that it is difficult not to wonder if the two are connected. Fanny even comments on how difficult Keats's poems are to understand, even as she marvels at the beauty of their language, but the film does not seem to encourage the audience to judge her for her struggle or to judge Keats for writing poems that are such a struggle. In fact, Fanny asks Keats to tutor her in poetry so that she might understand better, and it is through their discussions of poetry that their relationship deepens, intellectually and emotionally. Again, Fanny is entrenched in the marketplace—she loves fashion and has her own reasonably successful business—and so in a sense, Keats is sharing his work with one who comes from the world of commerce as opposed to his world, the world of letters. Yet, just as in *Love and Death on Long Island*, it is impossible to disentangle the reception of poetry from the individual desires and relationships that shape the meaning of these poems for these characters.

This seeming conflict between accessibility and mystery, however, seems to be addressed in a key moment in the film's portrayal of poetry. Keats explains to Fanny that a poem is not to be understood or taken in as if it were a message or as if it were for some specific purpose. Instead, Keats suggests, "A poem needs understanding through the senses. The point of diving in a lake is not immediately to swim to the shore; it's to be in the lake, to luxuriate in the sensation of water. You do not work the lake out. It is an experience beyond thought. Poetry soothes and emboldens the soul to accept mystery." There is mystery in poetry, but the mystery is an invitation; anyone can potentially find oneself utterly immersed in a poem.

This description of poetry is an apt description of Campion's filmmaking style as well. Although there may indeed be social commentary in her work, her films often include scenes that invite the viewer to dwell on the images on-screen and to contemplate their symbolism without necessarily trying to "work out" the meaning, as in Keats's metaphor of the lake. In this film, there are such scenes depicting fabrics and needlework, gardens, linens, and other props that evoke the feminine sphere, often with a voice-over of Keats's poems. These scenes are rarely essential to the main action of the film but instead allow the audience to "luxuriate in the sensation" of light reflecting off white lace, for instance, or the darkness of a forest path. Keats's description of the nature of poetry thus also serves as an especially apt description of the experience of watching *Bright Star*, and the scene in which Keats espouses this philosophy of art and poetry therefore suggests important resonances between cinema and poetry.

It is reasonable, therefore, to ask how the film's treatment of the commodification of poetry might resonate with film's status as commodity and as art. Campion is a successful filmmaker and is one of the most critically acclaimed and commercially successful filmmaker from her home nation of New Zealand. Due to the nature of distribution (particularly in the predigital age but still to some extent today), a filmmaker must usually be perceived to have commercial potential in order to reach an audience, even a small one. The status of an art film that is ostensibly a feminist love story about a famous author, written and directed by an internationally acclaimed director, is itself an example of how the production and reception of film involves a complexity of desires and varying aesthetics. Campion, however, clearly has a reasonably large audience for her films. It is particularly interesting to note, then, that the film deromanticizes the idea of a poet toiling in obscurity until his early death. Their love is tragic and perhaps idealized, but John's inability to achieve commercial success and the solitude that results is not depicted as a symptom of his genius but as the cause of the end of his poetic production. There are indeed real tensions between art and commerce, but the film suggests that to devote oneself wholly to one and not the other is tragically naïve, a sentiment highly appropriate for a successful and acclaimed filmmaker such as Campion.

Both *Love and Death on Long Island* and *Bright Star* thus resist the urge to position artistic and commercial concerns as dichotomous opposites, and suggest that art's status as consumer product creates situations that are rich with irony and highly dependent on individual reception. Furthermore, both films parallel the commodification of poetry, which society clearly gives the status of high art, with film's existence as a highly commercialized form of art. This parallel suggests that film's status as a commercial industry does not undermine its status as art, but rather that art, human desire, and the market-place interact in specific, highly individualistic, sometimes problematic but often potentially transformative ways.

Significantly, both films also suggest that the commodification of art—both poetry and film—bears similarities to the commodification of individuals. The lyric poem is, of course, often thought of as an expression of self, and Romantic poetry particularly emphasized the individual. It is therefore significant that these films consider not only the ramifications of the commodification of poetry but also the ramifications of the commodification of self. Both films, in fact, suggest parallels between the two processes in ways that resonate with the themes discussed above.

In *Bright Star*, marriage is clearly portrayed as an economic arrangement as well as a union based on love, and one that must be in the families' best interests. It is an old saw that such arrangements turn women into chattel, and while I do not wish to debate the intricacies of such a claim here, it is significant that in Campion's film, it is also the male of the relationship who is treated like a consumer product by this practice. Keats struggles and large-ly fails to turn himself into a renowned poet whose work gains acclaim and financial gain, and he wants to be recognized as a great writer; in modern terms, he is trying to brand himself. His failure to commodify his poems and his own public image as a poet in turn make him an unsuitable match for Fanny. Thus, as both a poet and as a potential husband, Keats cannot be sold, and the two failures are irrevocably linked. The fact that Fanny must marry based on social and family expectation and financial considerations, at the expense of her own agency and desire, also highlights the way that marriage to some extent makes her a product to be consumed. Thus, the depiction of their unconsummated relationship in Campion's film critiques the way that gender and class commodify individuals, and allow the market to regulate human desire. And while poetry's commodification is portrayed with ambiv-alence, the portrayal of the commodification of human beings, and their bodies and desires, appears to be strictly condemnatory.

Love and Death on Long Island, on the other hand, depicts the commod-ification of the individual in a way that parallels the film's treatment of the commodification of poetry. Ronnie is a pinup boy; he is sold on posters and in teenybopper magazines as an object of lust and fantasy. His face, body, and public persona are all fetishized in the mass media that Giles explores as he pursues his devotion to Ronnie. His career success quite explicitly de-pends on his ability to be seen as a desirable consumer product.

While Ronnie does wish for a career that makes him less of a commodity (though his dreams of being an A-list movie star with serious roles would perhaps mean merely a less aggressive commodification of self), his status as consumer product is not portrayed as entirely negative. His status as commodity has given him fame and the means to afford a life of leisure and a spacious, well-lit home that visually contrasts with the small but book-filled darkness of Giles's home. Furthermore, with the way that Priestley portrays Ronnie's film acting, the audience is left doubting his prospects for a broader career, despite Giles's certainty to the contrary. But Ronnie's status as consumer product is also largely responsible for his relationship with Giles, which, though it ends, opens up both men to interactions and ideas that they were previously closed to. Furthermore, when Giles consumes Ronnie-related products, he finds resonances with high-art parallels, which may seem humorous but serve to call into question the processes by which artistic achievement is judged. For all these reasons, Ronnie's commodification does not appear to be something destructive to him or to his artistic sensibilities; in fact, it is what potentially spurs him to a richer life as an artist by exposing him to the ideas and poetry of Giles's world. The film thus suggests a wry pragmatism with respect to the commodification of the individual; its benefits or harm are largely ambiguous, and its motivations have elements of both the sublime and the absurd. This description could apply equally well to the commodification of Whitman's poetry at the end of the film; the consumer product, whether the individual or the individual expression found in the lyric poem, is part of a complicated web of meanings and desires that cannot be described by the simple dichotomy of art versus commerce.

In summary, in these films, the marketplace is neither a purely sullying force nor a panacea; the marketplace is a tangled web of desires and interaction points among producers and consumers of poetry and other arts. The commodification of poetry is revealed to be multiply interwoven with the processes by which gender, sexuality, and class shape the lives and desires of individuals. The commodification of poetry in these films also provides a way for the films to address cinema's status as among the most commercial of art forms. Furthermore, the commodification of poetry—and of film—resonates with the portrayal of the commodification of the individual in these works. In all these ways, these films suggest there is no great divide between art and commerce; to understand the relationship between art and commerce, one must follow innumerable threads of valuation and desire, passing through heady explorations of the passionate and the absurd, the psychological and the political, the pragmatic and the idealistic. In these films, the marketplace is the site of negotiation of the boundaries between self and other, enacted through the work of art. Whether in the works of Whitman or Keats, Campion or Kwietniowski, such negotiations are never simple.

NOTES

1. ˙An example that demonstrates worries about the status of poetry in society is the fact that the Poetry International Foundation has felt the need to offer a lecture series on the "Defence of Poetry," http://www.poetryinternationalweb.net/pi/site/collection/article_item/int_article/368.

2. Andrew Motion, *Keats* (Chicago: University of Chicago Press, 1997).

3. Graham Fuller, "Too Late for Antique Vows," *Sight and Sound* 19 (2009).

4. Feona Attwood, "Weird Lullaby: Jane Campion's *The Piano,*" *Feminist Review* 98 (1998); Carol Jacobs, "Playing Jane Campion's Piano: Politically," *MLN* 109 (1994); Laura Mulvey, *Visual and Other Pleasures* (Bloomington: Indiana University Press, 1989).

5. Elizabeth Jones, "Writing for the Market: Keats's Odes as Commodities," *Studies in Romanticism* 34 (1995).

6. Jones, "Writing for the Market."

7. Raymond Williams, "The Romantic Artist," in *Culture and Society: 1780 – 1950* (New York: Columbia University Press, 1983), 30–48.

8. Mary L. Roberts, "Gender, Consumption, and Commodity Culture," *American Historical Review* 103 (1998): 821; Orrin Wang, private conversation, December 12, 2012. Many thanks also to Orrin Wang for his many helpful suggestions about consumer culture in the Romantic period.

9. This sentiment is echoed also by Hawthorne's famous invective against the "damned mob of scribbling women" and their commercial success.

10. Páraic Finnerty, "The Englishman in America: Masculinities in *Love and Death on Long Island* and *Father of Frankenstein,*" *Genders* 51 (2010): 9.

11. John Guillory, *Cultural Capital* (Chicago: University of Chicago Press, 1995). Guillory develops the term from Pierre Bourdieu.

12. While the film is adapted from Gilbert Adair's novel of the same name, the use of Whitman is specific to the film.

13. Kenneth Price, *To Walt Whitman, America* (Durham, N.C.: Duke University Press, 2006), 67–69.

14. Finnerty, "Englishman in America," 18.

15. Finnerty, "Englishman in America," 19.

Chapter Four

This Aura Sucks

Narrative Cinema and Popular Poetry Criticism in
So I Married an Axe Murderer

Liz Faber

Imagine a poet. He's twenty-something, wearing all black, sitting in a kitschy coffee shop, drinking a cappuccino. When he reads his poetry, he stands in front of a microphone on a small stage in the corner of that coffee shop. He speaks with his Ginsbergesque New York "poet voice," accenting certain syllables by raising his voice and gesturing wildly with his hands. And, most importantly, he looks out at you—the audience—as you watch him perform. Of course, the content of his poems are beside the point, as long as they "authentically" reflect his look and performance style. He is, in short, the icon of a Beat poet.

Now imagine a Beat *poem*.

This is a slightly more difficult task and, from a pop culture perspective, likely coincides with the image of a Beat poet. In Thomas Schlamme's 1993 romantic comedy *So I Married an Axe Murderer*, the Beat poet is Charlie Mackenzie (Mike Myers), the typical image of 1990s Beat-chic, and through-out much of the film, his poetry is dependent on his image. In the film, Charlie is a twenty-something poet who wears all black, hangs out in a coffee shop, and performs a series of poems for open-mike night about his ex-girlfriends, all titled "Woman, Woman, Woman." These performances simul-taneously parody what the Beat image has become and reinforce a distance between the audience and the poet that maintains the focus on the poet, rather than his words. Later in the narrative, however, Charlie performs a new poem called "This Poem . . . Sucks" on a rooftop in an attempt to win back his newest girlfriend, Harriet (Nancy Travis). Not only does the scene juxtapose the earlier ones by taking the poem itself seriously, but it also provides insight into a new way of allowing a mass audience to move past the spectacle of the poet image in order to critically examine the meaning of the poem. Thus, in this chapter, I will briefly trace the history of the poet image over the last fifty years, particularly the shift toward a "Beat-chic" in the 1990s and examine ways in which scholars, poets, and audiences alike have largely ignored the role of the *poem* in favor of the role of the *poet*. I will then analyze the scene in which Charlie performs his typical "Woman, Woman, Woman" poem, followed by a juxtaposition of its empty imagery with the seriousness of "This Poem . . . Sucks" in order to show how the film not only sutures its audience in through typical Hollywood-style editing, but also, and as a direct cause of this editing, dispels the performative aspects of the poet/ spectacle and provides access to the meaning of the poem. In turn, I argue that the meaning of the poem itself further critiques the poet/spectacle, thereby doubly proving its own point. By thus blending cinema and poetry histories—via *So I Married an Axe Murderer*—I hope to reexamine the relationship between poetry and narrative cinema as vital, cultural media that can— and should—work together.

POETRY DOESN'T SUCK, THE POETIC IMAGE DOES

Before turning to the ways in which *So I Married an Axe Murderer* refocuses audience attention away from the poet, I'd like first to explore the historical and theoretical context in which the film is situated. In the early twentieth century, American modernist poets such as T. S. Eliot and Ezra Pound sought to "depersonalize" poetry by shirking the Romantic connection between poem and poetic personality and taking a more scientific approach to the linguistic contemplation of the world around us.[1] Interestingly, though, these poets simultaneously achieved a sort of cult status—what Joseph Epstein has described as a "religious aura"—that, for many academics, became the ultimate image of the poet.[2] After World War II, however, with the rising acceptance in avant-garde circles of surrealism across artistic media and the psychoanalytic ideas of Sigmund Freud, poetry shifted its focus back toward the self. Yet, even such poetry was still mainly read in academic circles and performed on college campuses. By the 1950s, however, the Beat generation of poets, including Allen Ginsberg, Jack Kerouac, and Gregory Corso, sought to bring poetry into the popular consciousness. And, to a large degree, they succeeded, predominately as a result of the Beat philosophy of existing somewhere between the weary everyday and the greatness of spirituality. Even the term "Beat" arose from street culture, immediately placing it outside academic circles.[3]

Despite the Beats' success in bringing printed poetry to the popular consciousness, poetry was quickly demonized in mainstream exploitation films of the late 1950s and early 1960s. Through films such as *The Beat Generation* (Charles Haas, 1959), *A Bucket of Blood* (Roger Corman, 1959), *The Rebel Set* (Gene Fowler Jr., 1959), *Beat Girl* (Edmond T. Greville, 1959), and *Hallucination Generation* (Edward A. Mann, 1966), the image of the Beat poet was solidified as equivalent to both the Bohemian philosophy of the Beat generation and the presentational form of their poetry, regardless of the meaning of the poems themselves. As Jack Sargeant has pointed out:

> The representation of Beatniks allowed filmmakers to appropriate, and parody, a collective mainstream fantasy version of "Beatnik culture" manifested via the lifestyle and accoutrements of the goatee beard–wearing "drop-out": bongo drums, poetry, jazz, parties, weird slang, existential angst, artistic pretentions, drugs, and, to a lesser extent, their beliefs in Buddhism, communism, and free love. The themes associated with the Beatniks in the public eye would also guarantee a salacious audience, anxious to witness—and vicariously enjoy—the exploits of the "bizarre new youth culture," as long as they were granted the salve of moralistic tongue clicking by the film's closing credits.[4]

Although avant-garde/experimental filmmakers of the time were equally inspired by and in conversation with the Beat generation of poets[5] in a way that, I argue, denied the establishment of a spectacle of poetic authenticity, there was, nevertheless, still a widespread fascination with the Beat poet himself that led to the common conflation of a poet's authentic identity and the meaning of his poetry.

By the late 1980s, the image of the Beat poet remained in the popular consciousness, but poetry—and poets—had receded back into academic circles. In 1988, Joseph Epstein wrote his now infamous essay, "Who Killed Poetry?," in which he diagnosed two problems with contemporary poetry.[6] First is the poet himself (at the time, Epstein listed Robert Penn Warren, Richard Wilbur, Seamus Heaney, Allen Ginsberg, and John Ashbery) who tends to become well known by name, but his work is rarely read because his image as a poet overshadows his work. Second is the contemporary shift from epic poems—long narratives told in poetic verse—to lyric poetry—short poems that contemplate a single moment or image. According to Epstein, the loss of narrative in poetry is what has ultimately caused readers to become less interested in the poem and more invested in the image of the poet.[7]

In response to Epstein's essay, nearly everyone in American poetry circles began seeking new ways to open poetry to a mass audience, resulting in two major events in the early 1990s. The first was the rise of slam poetry competitions, instigated by poet Marc Smith in the working-class bars of Chicago. These competitions are essentially open-mike poetry readings in which the audience judges each poem.[8] While such efforts did, indeed, bring poetry to a wider—and, importantly, nonacademic—audience, slam as a genre openly conflates the poet with the poem through an emphasis on identity performance:

> Because NPS [National Poetry Slam] rules ensure that at slams authors are also always performers and vice versa, audiences commonly conflate the voice of the poem with that of the author. Through the sheer format of the competition, audiences are encouraged to see slam performances as confessional moments in which the "I" of the poem is also the "I" of the author-performer. . . . [T]here is a hyperawareness of self among slam poets and audiences, one that manifests itself most commonly through the author's performance of identity.[9]

Thus, slam *did* bring poetry back to a mass audience; however, it simultaneously made every competitor into someone performing the role of poetry, and in turn, every reader of poetry became, in actuality, a reader of poetic identity.

The second major result of Epstein's article was the publication of Dana Gioia's important response, *Can Poetry Matter?* In this book, Gioia defines poetry as "the art of using words charged with their utmost meaning."[10] When scholars in the latter half of the twentieth century analyzed a poem, they located these meanings: hence, we know meaning is there, if hidden behind the poet's image. Yet, Gioia provides only two reasons why poetry matters: first, language is powerful, and poetry can help us harness and understand how to use language in its most powerful form; and second, all forms of art are becoming marginalized to the point that artists are finding it difficult to locate an audience outside of academia and small, avant-garde communities.[11] While I agree wholeheartedly with the first point, the second again focuses attention on where the *artist/poet* fits into society, rather than what his or her art can do. Even in his more recent book, *Disappearing Ink*, in which Gioia reconsiders the role of poetry in the rapidly changing print culture, he continues to conflate the societal place of the poet with that of his poetry:

> The end of print culture raises many troubling questions about the position of poetry amid these immense cultural and technological changes. What will be the *poet's place* in a society that has increasingly little use for books, little time for serious culture, little knowledge of the past, little consensus on literary value, and—even among intellectuals—little faith in poetry itself?[12] (emphasis mine)

Here, Gioia implicitly argues that the poet's place is equivalent to the role of his or her poetry, and, even more problematically, that this place is disappearing as a result of a general loss of appreciation for high culture. Yet, at the same time, he recognizes the continuing problem in more popular forms of poetry, including slam in particular, but also rap/hip-hop and other forms of popular music—as well as, I would add, today's newest musical stars, most notably Lady Gaga's radical creation of an empty superstar icon—of focusing only on the performance of the poet as a means of judging and deriving meaning from a poem, rather than examining the lyrics of the poem itself.[13]

Thus, there has been a long-standing tension among academic poetry circles, the avant-garde, and pop culture that has sought to provide a mass audience access to the vital function of poetry. Yet, the spectacle of the poet has, throughout the twentieth century, consistently gotten in the way. This "aura" of the poet, as Epstein calls it, is not unique to poets, however. Walter Benjamin, in his seminal 1936 article, "The Work of Art in the Age of Mechanical Reproduction," argued that works of art such as paintings have an aura that constructs a sort of "cult value" because they are rare and inaccessible to the general population. This value is expressed both socially and monetarily and maintains an intellectual power structure that makes it difficult for everyday people to glean meaning from artworks.[14] Reproducing the artwork—especially through the cinema—decreases the value of the "original" because everyone can see it.[15] Of course, poetry is also infinitely reproducible, as it may be printed and reprinted in any number of books; yet, the singularity of an author's performance, not to mention the singularity of the author him- or herself and the fact of the decline of print culture, renders poetry significantly less accessible than movies. Even songs—poetry of the twentieth century—are infinitely reproduced every day on the radio and You-Tube and downloadable quickly and cheaply from the Internet. Yet, again, songs are generally associated with a singular singer or band; cinema, on the other hand, is created and performed by a multitude of voices, personalities, and images. Further, while academic/avant-garde art—and I add poetry to this—tends to be seen as elitist by the general population, with film, to use an overused phrase, everyone's a critic: everyone knows how to "read" and respond to a movie, even in the most rudimentary ways.[16] In fact, we are socially encouraged to do so, because the cinema is specifically created for the masses. We have to be taught to read poetry at some point in school; meanwhile, we all go to the movies and manage to talk about them. This is, of course, not to say that film history and analysis are not important parts of any school curriculum. Visual literacy is an absolutely vital part of learning to think critically and analyze the hypermediated world around us; however, most people not only have a broader access to films than poems, but because the cinema is still treated as "just entertainment," on the whole, more people are likely to engage with them, see them, memorize them, talk about them, and so forth.

So in 1993, when *So I Married an Axe Murderer* (hereafter, *SIMAM*) was released, it was situated in a time of simultaneous crisis and invention. Rap and slam were becoming popular, and poetry was moving outside of academia. Just five years earlier, while Epstein had invoked Walter Benjamin's sense of "aura" in describing the modernists, the solutions offered after Epstein only magnified the aura of the poet, to the point of total performativity; meanwhile, *SIMAM* actually seems to have played out Benjamin's assertion that film can degrade the aura of a work of art and allow access to meaning for a mass audience. Yet from 1993 to the present, *SIMAM*, which parodies the image of the poet while offering a mode of critical access to poems, was overlooked by poets and scholars alike. And so, I would like to turn now to the ways in which the film demonstrates both Benjamin's solution to the aura (cinema itself) and Epstein's (narrative).

THIS POET . . . DOESN'T MATTER

In many ways, *SIMAM* is a typical Hollywood film, relying heavily on continuity editing and the general conventions of romantic comedy. Nowhere is the 180-degree line broken, and each instance of editing effectively hides the apparatus of the camera. Generically, the film follows the typical romantic structure of "boy meets girl, boy loses girl, boy gets girl back." The fact that boy (falsely) suspects girl to be an axe murderer provides the comedic twist. On top of this, it significantly parodies the Beat-chic image that had become firmly set in audiences' minds by the time of its release. Yet, in combining such parody with typical editing and narrative techniques, it actually allows the audience to be sutured into the narrative and, through a process of juxtaposing the earlier "Woman, Woman, Woman" poem with the later "This Poem . . . Sucks," it defies audience expectations, thereby encouraging serious, critical access to the meaning of this latter poem.

Throughout the first half of the film, Charlie performs his "Woman, Woman, Woman" poem in a coffee shop several times. In these scenes, the audience in the coffee shop is clearly seen, thereby distancing the film's audience from Charlie's performance and positioning him as the spectacle/object of our gaze. In other words, we don't just see Charlie perform; we see other people watching him. Furthermore, because these poems are repeated several times as a formula for performance, the audience is conditioned to conflate Charlie's Beat persona—fake New York accent, unlit cigarette, accompanying jazz music—with his poems. In this way, *SIMAM*—at first—reinforces the performative image of the Beat poet through editing and mise-en-scène.

The meanings of the "Woman, Woman, Woman" poems also rely on formulaic, pop-culture iconography that reinforces Charlie as a poet icon.

Before turning to the poems themselves, however, I should note that, because they were written specifically for performance on-screen, the lines always already coexist with the image. In this sense, the shots also function as lines of the poems and create meaning as much as the words themselves. Additionally, as with all traditional narrative films, the audience is meant to "read" the entire film at once, including dialogue, cinematography, editing, and so forth. Thus, I've transliterated each poem from the film here as they are both heard and seen in the film: the spoken dialogue is in regular typeface, while the other cinematic elements are in italics. In the spirit of recognizing plural authorship (rather than singular performative authorship), I should also note that the poetry in the film was written by the screenwriter, Robbie Fox; yet, without the performance of the actors, the cinematography, the editing, and the direction, the poems would exist solely on a page written by Fox. It is the very combination of arts that allows access to critical meaning of the poems in *SIMAM*.

So when written, the first incarnation of "Woman, Woman, Woman" is as follows:

1. *Medium tracking shot of Charlie walking onstage as audience in foreground claps and snaps for him*
2. Jazz trio begins playing
3. *Camera rests on medium shot of Charlie holding unlit cigarette, standing in front of a microphone*
4. Woman
5. Image of a woman is projected on small screen behind Charlie
6. Wo-man
7. Whoa
8. Man
9. *Silence; jazz music begins with Charlie's next line*
10. She was a thief
11. You gotta belief
12. She stole my heart and my cat
13. *Close shot of projected image of woman holding a cat*
14. *Wide medium tracking shot of Charlie, over audience members' shoulders*
15. Betty
16. *Projected image changes to Betty Rubble from the television cartoon* The Flintstones
17. Judy
18. Josie and those hot pussycats
19. *Silence until Charlie's next line*
20. *Projected image changes to* Josie and the Pussycats *from the cartoon of the same name*

21. They make me horny
22. Saturday mornie
23. Girls of cartoo-ins
24. *Wide shot of coffee shop audience*
25. Won't leave me in ruins
26. *Medium shot of Charlie in front of the microphone*
27. I want to be Betty's Barney
28. Close medium shot of Charlie
29. Silence
30. Hey, Jane, get me off
31. This crazy thing
32. Close shot of Charlie
33. Called love
34. Jazz trio continues
35. *On last beat of music, in medium shot, Charlie blows out a candle*
36. Audience applauds

From the very beginning, the combination of the music and the fact that we watch Charlie situate himself onstage establishes this poem as a performance. In addition, the fact that Charlie's performance exists only during his poetry performance (to this point, Myers has been speaking in his natural Canadian accent, and Charlie the character apparently does not smoke) add to the spectacle image, as each element is a part of the performance. When Charlie begins to recite the lines, the images projected behind him echo his words, further solidifying the link between the poet's words and the image he's presenting. Then, in the shift from talking about a photographed woman to hand-drawn cartoons, Charlie claims that he "wants to be Betty's Barney" (a reference to the *Flintstones* couple Betty and Barney), thereby calling on pop-culture iconography to align himself with a character, rather than a real-live man who has just gone through a breakup. And finally, in the last lines, he speaks as a cartoon character, referencing the *Jetsons* line, "Jane, get me off this crazy thing," thereby finally positioning himself as a complete spectacle. To close the poem, he blows the candle out in an allegorical gesture that turns his breakup into nothing more than a performative motion. In the second performance of "Woman, Woman, Woman," much the same happens, except the poem is about Harriet, and Charlie can't bring himself to blow the candle out at the end. Rather than dispelling the image of the poet, though, the film's audience again identifies with the coffee shop's audience, who react to the performance with confusion, indicating that Charlie has screwed up his own formula.

About halfway through the film, these primary audience expectations are challenged when Charlie performs "This Poem . . . Sucks." Immediately, the audience is sutured into the scene in a way that allows them to identify with, rather than objectify, Charlie. As the scene begins, we hear the same jazzy music as the earlier poetry performances; but immediately, the audience's expectations are denied, as the camera focuses on the jazz trio playing on a rooftop, rather than the coffee shop. As Charlie enters, then, we notice he is looking somewhere off camera, inciting us to identify with him and his gaze as we desire to see what he sees. In the reverse shot, we see an empty window, followed by Harriet's entrance. Thus, the object in this scene is no longer the poet, but rather Harriet.[17] In this way, then, the distance established at the beginning of the film through identification with the coffee shop audience has now been diminished. It's important to note, too, that, since Charlie is a fictional character performing poetry written solely for this film, he carries no tie to a "real" poet outside the diegetic film world. Hence, in identifying with him as he performs "This Poem . . . Sucks," we can truly be sutured into the narrative of the film in order to look past the spectacle of the poet—both Charlie and the real Beat poets whom he references—and focus on the meaning of the poem.

The poem's meaning also deconstructs the performative spectacle of the poet. Just as in the "Woman, Woman, Woman" poems, it's important here to also consider the audiovisual aspects of the performance to be as much a part of the poem as the lines themselves. So when transliterated into text, the poem reads as follows:

1. High, wide shot of trumpet, snare drum, and standup base playing on building rooftop
2. Enter Charlie carrying small poetry notebook and unlit cigarette
3. *Close-up shot of Charlie*
4. Harriet
5. Harri-
6. Et
7. *Wide medium shot of Harriet's window as she enters and leans on sill*
8. Hard-hearted harbinger of haggis
9. Beautiful
10. Bemused
11. Close shot of Charlie
12. Bellicose butcher
13. Untrust-ing
14. Two trumpet notes
15. Unknow-ing
16. Two trumpet notes, then silence from band
17. Unlov-
18. Ed?

19. Music begins again
20. Tighter medium shot of Harriet at window
21. Medium three-shot of Charlie, drummer, and trumpeter
22. He wants you back! He screams into the night air like a fireman going to a window that has no fire
23. Trumpet growls
24. Charlie nods at Harriet in recognition of trumpeter
25. Medium shot of Harriet, who looks impressed
26. Except the passion of his heart
27. Two-shot of Charlie and drummer
28. I am lonely
29. Drum flare; silence
30. It's really hard
31. Five trumpet beats; silence
32. This poem
33. Sucks.
34. Band continues as Charlie approaches Harriet

While the cadence and jazziness of "This Poem . . . Sucks" is similar to "Woman, Woman, Woman," and the camera does cut back and forth between Charlie and his audience, the overall meaning has clearly changed. Audiovisually, Charlie holds the same unlit cigarette and speaks in the same fake accent, but this time, since the scene is taking place on an empty rooftop instead of on a coffee-shop stage, the staginess of these aspects of Charlie's performance become jarring. Why should he stage his performance when, quite literally, he has no stage? Furthermore, unlike in the earlier performance, he now reads from his notebook, thus denying any possibility that his words are authentically flowing from his poetic soul.

The dialogue further calls attention to the falseness of his performance. The first part of the poem, a description of Harriet—this time without the projected image—serves to solidify her as the object of Charlie's gaze. Further, the cadence of "Harriet / Harri-et" mimics the cadence of the first few lines of the "Woman, Woman, Woman" poem; yet here, the juxtaposition of a particular woman—Harriet—with that of the abstract "woman" again jars the audience out of their expectations and calls attention to Charlie's false performativity. The second part of the poem is a description of empty imagery—"a fireman going to a window that has no fire." This directly parallels Charlie's position under Harriet's window, again making him the active non-spectacle and her the image/object.

The first major turn in the poem comes with the two declarative statements—"I am lonely" and "It's really hard." Here, Charlie begins to assume an active role as speaker of the lines, rather than a passive spectacle whose lines must coincide with the image presented. And finally, the last two lines—"This poem / Sucks"—fully dispels any remaining elitism or conception of a perfect poetic image by engaging in a self-reflexive evaluation. In the very last word, then, Charlie drops back into his natural accent, thereby completely dropping his performance and ending the poem as himself.

SO IT SUCKS . . . NOW WHAT?

As I've shown, twentieth-century poetry has been plagued with the problem of the poet spectacle, from the modernists, through the Beats and contemporaries, and well into more recent slam poets, rappers, musicians, and so forth. In resituating poetry within a fictional, narrative context, though, *SIMAM* succeeds in deconstructing the spectacle of the poet by suturing the audience into the narrative in a way that allows them to focus instead on the meaning of the poem. And, to make things more interesting, *SIMAM*'s main deconstructive poem—"This Poem . . . Sucks"—simultaneously uses its meaning to both reinforce and dispel the falseness of a poet's performative identity.

Yet, this is just one film, made twenty years ago. Since its release, slam has grown and fizzled, rap/hip-hop has gotten flashier and more prominent than even slam, and new artists like Lady Gaga have taken performativity to an all-new height; meanwhile, literary poetry seems to have receded even further into academia, such that more people know the names of poets, rather than their poetry. (Maya Angelou is a particularly salient recent example, as she is widely known as an actress in addition to being a poet.) So where can we go from here? *SIMAM* provides an important case study in the ways poetry may be used in narrative film as a gateway to a more widespread understanding of different forms of poetry. In many ways, though, quotes from movies, not to mention television, music, and the Internet, have become a form of cultural currency that has displaced the oral and literary traditions of poetry that the Beat generation sought to rekindle. Poetic lines certainly still have the power of describing the human condition, from the profound to the mundane, through concrete imagery and the creative use of language. And yet, the spectacle of celebrity in other, more widely available media continues to diminish the accessibility of poetry for the general population. Even other films that feature characters reciting poems within the diegesis, such as *Dead Poets Society* (Peter Weir, 1989) or *Shakespeare in Love* (John Madden, 1998) reinforce the greatness of the poet (Keats, Byron, and others in the former and Shakespeare in the latter) rather than the meanings of the poems.

But, of course, film as a medium unto itself is becoming just as lost in the hypertextual digital age as poetry did in the age of mechanically reproduced film. Yet, the elasticity of poetic language lends itself to hypertext culture quite well; YouTube, Netflix, Hulu, and a variety of other digital media sites, not to mention the range of platforms through which media can be consumed, have allowed for the rapid convergence of media, blending text, image, sound. Now, more than ever, cultural meaning is created and sustained within and between texts, among creators and consumers. This intertextuality, hypertextuality, and transtextuality of meanings has opened a space for poetry that moves beyond the spectacle of the author. And so, in reconsidering *SIMAM*, I hope to open a dialogue among scholars, poets, and mediamakers that could result in a new form of collaboration which breaks free of the twentieth-century fascination with the spectacle of the poet. Not only can we reconsider poetry within the mass medium of film, but we can also begin, once again, to consider poetry itself *as* a mass medium in collaboration with other media. In doing so, then, we can begin seeking a democratized, culturally reproducible place for the art—rather than the artist—in the hypermediated twenty-first century.

NOTES

1. Christopher Beach, *The Cambridge Introduction to Twentieth-Century American Poetry* (Cambridge: Cambridge University Press, 2003), 49.
2. Joseph Epstein, "Who Killed Poetry?" *Commentary* 86, no. 2 (1988): 13.
3. Jack Sargeant, *The Naked Lens: An Illustrated History of Beat Cinema* (n.p.: Creation Books, 2001), 5.
4. Sargeant, *Naked Lens*, 222–23.
5. For more on these conversations, see Daniel Kane, *We Saw the Light: Conversations between the New American Cinema and Poetry* (Iowa City: University of Iowa Press, 2009) and Susan McCabe, *Cinematic Modernism: Modernist Poetry and Film* (Cambridge: Cambridge University Press, 2005).
6. Just three years after the publication of "Who Killed Poetry?," Dana Gioia wrote in his response article, "Can Poetry Matter?" (*Atlantic*, May 1991, http://www.theatlantic.com/magazine/archive/1991/05/can-poetry-matter/305062/) that "no recent essay on American poetry has generated so many immediate responses in literary journals. And certainly none has drawn so much violently negative criticism from poets themselves. To date at least thirty writers have responded in print. The poet Henry Taylor published two rebuttals."
7. Epstein, "Who Killed Poetry?," 18–19.
8. Susan B. A. Somers-Willet, *The Cultural Politics of Slam Poetry: Race, Identity, and the Performance of Popular Verse in America* (Ann Arbor: University of Michigan Press, 2009), 5.
9. Somers-Willet, *Cultural Politics of Slam Poetry*, 32–33.
10. Dana Gioia, *Can Poetry Matter? Essays on Poetry and American Culture* (St. Paul, Minn.: Graywolf, 1992), 20.
11. Gioia, *Can Poetry Matter?*, 20–21.
12. Dana Gioia, *Disappearing Ink: Poetry at the End of Print Culture* (St. Paul, Minn.: Graywolf, 2004), 5.
13. Gioia, *Disappearing Ink*, 8.
14. Walter Benjamin, "The Work of Art in the Age of Mechanical Reproduction," in *Media and Cultural Studies: Key Works*, ed. Meenakshi Gigi Durham and Douglas M. Kellner (Oxford: Blackwell, 2006), 22.
15. Benjamin, "Work of Art," 20–21.
16. Benjamin, "Work of Art," 30.

17. Admittedly, such a playing out of the typical use of male gaze is problematic in its own right. But for the purposes of identification with, rather than objectification of, Charlie the poet, it is absolutely vital that we identify with his gaze on Harriet.

Chapter Five

Star/Poet/Director

Poetry and Image in Guru Dutt's Pyaasa

Carrie Messenger

Guru Dutt's 1957 hit film *Pyaasa* (*Thirst*) puts a poet, a prostitute, and a publisher's wife in a love triangle, asking audiences to triangulate voices, bodies, and capital. The selling of bodies and poetry could potentially lead to big business for the characters, but nobody in the triangle except for the publisher's wife ends up with any kind of financial success. The movie *Pyaasa* itself, though, was a financial success, an artistic vision that managed to sell tickets even as the audience was asked by the film's final images and song sequence to turn their backs on the world around them. What was the audience thirsting for that *Pyaasa* delivered? *Pyaasa* has anarchic undertones unusual in a mainstream film. I argue that Dutt's anarchic vision asks the audience to consider a world where verse, voice, and vision are deliberately fragmented. Bollywood films are much less invested with the continuity of Hollywood demands, but within the world of Bollywood cinema, *Pyaasa* is still unusual, pushing Bollywood conventions as far as they can go.

The poetry within *Pyaasa* creates an alternative narrative within the film, ultimately transcending the main narrative of the film itself. But song sequences usually serve this function in Bollywood cinema, allowing for diegetic and nondiegetic sequences that comment and contrast to the main line of action, and, in fact, can become so important that a clear vision of what is the main line of action is blurred. If the narrative is also running a counternarrative, or counternarratives, the Bollywood tradition of playback singers who sing the songs while the actors lip-synch them further breaks down the possibility of a single, embodied poetic voice. The poet who is singing onscreen is not only an actor and not the poet who wrote the verses, but also not the actual performer of the lyrics we are hearing, either. The fact that Guru

Dutt is both lead actor and director of *Pyaasa*, but not the writer of the poetry, adds yet another level of complication. Dutt is the poet of the image, not the lyric. The movie fragments the poet, separates the singer from the song.

Even the narrative of the main plot keeps coming back to poetry, back to the songs, while constantly trying to separate Vijay the character from his work, his poetry. Vijay loses his girlfriend Meena to a society marriage with a wealthy publisher, Mr. Ghosh. Meena is played by Mala Sinha, and the publisher by the actor Rehman. Vijay meets a prostitute, Gulabo, who has bought his manuscript sold off by his family for scrap paper, but who comes to appreciate Vijay's poems as poems. Gulabo is played by Waheeda Rehman (no connection to the actor playing Mr. Ghosh). After Vijay lends his coat to a man who is later run over by a train, everyone thinks Vijay has committed suicide and his posthumous poems become a huge hit. When Vijay crashes his own death anniversary celebration, only Gulabo is glad to see him, and he sings a song urging the audience to burn and blow up the world around them, an invitation to fragmentation.

The film's cinematic audience is directly addressed by the song at the end, but all the way through the film, we have two stand-in figures for our interactions with Guru Dutt/Vijay. Meena and Gulabo are not just Vijay's love interests. They are his two biggest fans, from very different periods of his life, the era of his college success for Meena and the era of his destitute failure for Gulabo. These women are his readers. Part of the movie's structure elevates Gulabo the prostitute over Meena the society wife, but the movie always works to link them through dialogue and image.

After Mr. Ghosh the publisher finds out about Meena's past with Vijay, he tells her, "My wife's no better than a streetwalker." Dutt cuts immediately to Gulabo being thrown out of a car by a customer who refuses to pay. She runs into Vijay, who calls her his wife to save her from a cop. Mr. Ghosh calls his wife a streetwalker; Vijay calls a streetwalker his wife. *Pyaasa* is full of these upside-down moments. When Meena runs into Vijay after their class reunion at Mr. Ghosh's office in front of the elevator, she tells him after they talk, "I forgot I was on my way up," and we see her as social climber. As the elevator doors close on her, the bars are reminiscent of the end of *The Maltese Falcon*, with Mary Astor on her way down. Gulabo is seen over and over again on the stairs, running up and down to catch Vijay. Her social mobility seems to be of another kind altogether.

Meena and Gulabo have only one scene together. The camera starts with Meena. We see Gulabo as the camera focuses on the title of the poetry file, "Shadows." (It's fitting that Vijay's manuscript is called "Shadows," an echo of movies themselves as the play of shadow and light.) As we enter the office, we see Gulabo's reaction shots and the delivery of her dialogue. We only cut to Meena for lines of dialogue. We are seeing Gulabo through

Meena's eyes. Yet the sympathy of the spectator lies with Gulabo. Gulabo backs up to the bookshelves and is in the front of the frame, and then Meena is back in the forefront as she shakes Gulabo. The prostitute is visually identified with books and poetry throughout this scene. As the scene ends and Mr. Ghosh has accepted Vijay's manuscript, Gulabo's image is superimposed over the printing press at work, and then we see her hugging the book the way she used to hold the file of Vijay's poetry.

Gulabo sees poetry; Meena and Mr. Ghosh see a publishing opportunity. Sudresh Mishra highlights the importance of the exchange of capital in his reading of *Pyaasa*. For him, Gulabo and Vijay's true friends are able to "distinguish between the aesthetic-affective worth of his poetry, its use value, which they refuse to disengage from the embodied subject, and the abstract exchange value that others calculatedly seek in it."[1] Gulabo has given the Ghoshes a gold mine. Mishra points out, "Gulabo, who makes a living by trading her sexual labor for money, has his manuscript published at her own expense and without claiming royalties. The disembodied, alienating, and spectral character of exchange value is made manifest in the sensational reception of *Parchaiya* (*Shadows*)."[2] If nothing else, the business dealings of the Ghoshes seem to be very shady indeed. Meena's relationships always come back to exchange value. Gulabo, although she makes the book happen, makes *Shadows* cast its shadow, is the character who shadows over the printing press, and refuses to be directly involved in the exchange of capital. She pays for the book to be printed, rather than be paid by Ghosh.

Although the love triangle here of Gulabo/Meena/Vijay is certainly linked to writer/publisher/reader, or embodied subject/capital/alienated subject, there are more triangles at play that allow for intertextual readings of the film. The love triangle in *Pyaasa* is also a reworking of the themes of *Devdas*, a Bengali novel by Saratchandra Chattopadhyay filmed over and over and over again by Indian filmmakers, most famously in 1935, 1955, and eventually 2002 and 2009. This echo of *Devdas* would have been something contemporary audiences would have been aware of, and certainly something audiences today are still conditioned to respond to because of the continuing popularity of the *Devdas* films. In fact, Guru Dutt himself made a movie about making a version of *Devdas*, his *Kagaaz ke Phool*, in 1959, casting himself as the director and using Waheeda Rehman, his Gulabo, again as the romantic lead. *Pyaasa* and *Kagaaz ke Phool* are companion pieces, movies that take up the same triangles, the same spaces between life, art, and the reader/spectator. In *Devdas*, Devdas can't be with either his childhood sweetheart or his prostitute girlfriend because what he loves most is the bottle. In *Pyaasa* and *Kagaaz ke Phool*, poetry and movies take the place of alcohol, although they are ultimately just as addictive and destructive.

The triangle of Meena/Vijay/Gulabo recalls the triangle in *Devdas*, but it also would bring up in many Indian spectators' minds the gossip around the triangle of Guru Dutt, actress Waheeda Rehman who plays Gulabo, and playback singer Geeta Dutt, Guru Dutt's wife. Shoma Chatterji points out: "In addition to evoking mythological hypertexts, Guru Dutt's casting decisions resonate for Indian audiences who are aware of his much-touted affair with the actress who plays Gulabo."[3] The characters are Krishna/Radha/ Meera, deities and mythical figures, and Devdas/Paro/Chandramukhi, prominent literary characters (the Indian Romeo and Juliet) but also Guru/Geeta/ Waheeda, the star, his wife, and the ingénue. Geeta Dutt sings for both female leads in *Pyaasa*. The characters share more than their love for Vijay, more than their scene of confrontation in the publisher's office. *Pyaasa* features song sequences where the voice of Guru Dutt's actual wife is channeled through the body of the lover, both through Gulabo and through Meena, a tension that disembodies the voice at the same time that it also creates the strange embodiment of an idealized creation, a Frankenstein, the best of both of these women as well as Geeta Dutt's voice.

When Vijay and Gulabo meet, she is singing his poetry to him, the poetry from the file she bought for scrap paper, perhaps the most potentially flattering scenario and meet-cute moment of any poet and reader. Because it is Vijay's poetry Gulabo, who is both Geeta Dutt and Waheeda Rehman in those scenes, is singing, Vijay is embodied within the figure of Waheeda Rehman on-screen as well. But Vijay's poetry is not Guru Dutt's; Guru Dutt is the screenwriter, but not the writer of the lyrics and poetry, which were written by Sahir Ludhianvi. So the voice of the poetry is split by the two of them, poetic voice and poetic image, evocative of how the voice of song is split by Geeta Dutt and Rehman, the audio and the image.

This fragmentation is not, the way it might be in an independent American film or European art house production, a gesture toward a break with continuity systems, but rather, a fragmentation that is at the heart of the Bollywood system. Lalitha Gopolan argues that Bollywood cinema constantly draws attention to its fragmented nature. Playing on Tom Gunning's term "Cinema of Attractions," her book on Bollywood is called *Cinema of Interruptions*. These interruptions include both the elaborate song sequences worked throughout the three-hour-long Bollywood films as well as the intermission interval, which, according to Gopolan, "obviously upsets the image of the dream chamber, but by not acknowledging its presence we fail to see it as a punctuation that binds and disperses narrative energies in Indian popular cinema."[4] These interruptions have their advantage, for, as Gopolan writes, "Just as continuity in classical Hollywood narrative offers us both pleasure and anger, in this cinema, too, we find pleasure *in* these interruptions and not *despite* them. Indian cinema is marked by *interrupted pleasures*."[5] I'd like to add the fragmentation of the character of Gulabo into Geeta Dutt/Waheeda Rehman, or the character of Vijay into Guru Dutt/Mohammad Rafi, his playback singer, as another kind of interrupted pleasure, the very kind of interrupted pleasure that Hollywood, as *Singin' in the Rain* explores, will go to great lengths to smooth over, even while Debbie Reynolds's voice is dubbed over as she sings for Jean Hagen, a playback singer being used for a character playing a playback singer. *Singin' in the Rain* is from 1952, the same decade as *Pyaasa*. Gopolan's idea of a cinema of interruptions, of stirring or even waking from the dream chamber in opposition to Hollywood's constant dreaming, allows me to read *Pyaasa*, a film where both content and style are pointing toward fragmentation and artifice, as a kind of constantly interrupted pleasure. We know that Waheeda Rehman isn't singing, and that Guru Dutt isn't singing, but we don't care. We're only partly dreaming. Dutt wants us to wake up, but he keeps on giving us lullabies to listen to. When Vijay wakes up in the hospital, it's because he hears somebody reading his poetry, and then he sees somebody reading his book *Shadows*. The sound is his verse; the book is alienated from him. For Vijay, the sound and image don't match, and he wakes up. Dutt is pointing the way for us, too.

Of course, there are moments in *Pyaasa* where sound and image do match. Corey Creekmur finds the movie to be unusually balanced, triggering an almost physical response in the viewer: "When the camera moves in and out throughout *Pyaasa*, it seems to replicate the physical act of breathing, or the opening and closing of the heart's valves. In the original sense of the eventually denigrated term, *Pyaasa* is a true melodrama, a narrative that not only (like most films) is accompanied by music, but which finally blends cinematic style and music to the point where they cannot be isolated."[6] I would agree with Creekmur that the sound and image cannot be isolated, and I find his image of the lungs and heart a beautiful one, but I find myself interrupted in all of *Pyaasa*'s key song sequences. Dutt wants us to always think about sound and image together, but because they can't be reconciled. Vijay the poet at the end of the film denies that he is Vijay; he backs away from any kind of claim to be the authentic poet, the author of his verses. Dutt the director backs away from a mimetic cinematic vision. If we watch the camera's movements and synch it to our own breathing, like the stars lip-synching to the playback singers, the camera makes us hold our breath, make our hearts skip a beat, so we are always reminded of the gaps and fractures in the world Guru Dutt gives us.

The song sequences are at the heart of the cinema of interruptions, and in *Pyaasa*, they are almost always about poetry, highly self-referential. During the song sequence "Aaj sajan mohe ang laga lo," after Vijay saves Gulabo from the police officer, which Ravi Vasudevan explores at length as a moment of *darsanic* practice, where he argues "the relation between devotional voice, devotee, and object of devotion determines the space of the scene"[7] the devotional voice in question is that of Geeta Dutt's. The song begins with Gulabo the character gazing at a devotional singer who is "singing" Geeta Dutt's song; later, Gulabo moves on to gaze at Vijay. Vasudevan explores the meaning of Muslim actors such as Dilip Kumar and Nargis taking part in Hindu devotional rites, specifically *darsanic* practice, stating, "An oral history might uncover nothing less than a parallel universe of concealed identities."[8] Gulabo is played by the Muslim actor Waheeda Rehman, and Devdas has been played by the Muslim actors Dilip Kumar and Shahrukh Khan. The movies create a parallel universe of a national cinema where everybody worships the same gods. The world of the playback singer, I would argue, offers another partially concealed, partially revealed universe, one that echoes the far more charged questions of religious identity and national identity. Playback singers become stars in their own right. The Indian audience has been able to divorce the image from the sound. Famous playback singers give concerts and record compilations of their greatest hits. They might not be part of *darsanic* practice during the film, but they have a world of *darsanic* opportunities outside.

Darsanic practice, according to Vasudevan, allows Bollywood to use a cinematic gaze that comes out of a different tradition than Western films. Vasudevan, working with Laura Mulvey's theory of the gaze in "Visual Pleasure and the Narrative Cinema," argues that the gaze in Indian popular cinema can be a mutual one, a cinematic space where women can sometimes own the gaze themselves, through the Hindu concept of *darsana*. In *darsanic* practice, as Vasudevan describes, "the devotee is permitted to behold the image of the deity, and is privileged and benefited by this permission, in contrast to a concept of looking that assigns power to the beholder by reducing the image to an object of the look."[9] Vasudevan goes on to analyze scenes between Gulabo and Vijay, and I agree with his interpretation of the possibilities for mutual gazes in *Pyaasa*. In the scene between Meena and Gulabo, though, I wonder which one of them gets the gaze, which one of them is assigned power by the film. Are we looking at Gulabo through Meena's eyes, or feeling Gulabo's sensation of being looked at?

What happens to the *darsanic* when women are looking at each other? Who is authorizing the gaze here? Is it Guru Dutt the director in the moments when it isn't Guru Dutt the actor? Who authorizes us to look as audience members? Vijay Mishra's book *Bollywood Cinema: Temples of Desire* takes up the question of audience and authority through the lens of desire and the star/fan relationship. In his reading of *Pyaasa*, he offers an assessment of Gulabo as audience stand-in. For him, "*Pyaasa* must be read . . . not through the thematizations of the hero as poet but through the manner in which it reads the marginalized Indian woman. With all his Romantic limitations—Waheeda Rehman as Gulabo is both far too attractive and her sensibility is far too labored—Guru Dutt nevertheless makes the relationship between stars and audience much more complex."[10] Mishra picks up Vasudevan's idea of mutual gazes and inserts the audience into the equation. If Rehman is too attractive, too labored in her sensibility, it's all the more flattering for us.

Vijay's number one fan is Gulabo. She's much more glamorous than the actual audience, but when we see her on the screen, we get to be her. The *darsanic* gazes she shares with Vijay can be read as authorizing gazes from the star to all of us through her. But his former number one fan was Meena. Is Meena the figure of the bad reader? The bad fan? The audience that needs to be punished? The nonmarginalized Indian woman?

I find I need to think about Meena to make sense of Vijay the poet/hero/star and Gulabo the adoring audience. Meena turns her back on Vijay and his poetry, but the movie keeps turning back to her, through the flashbacks and repeated scenes of confrontations. Meena is given the chance to deny Vijay over and over, in their college days, when Vijay comes to work for her husband, and finally when she looks away during the poetry reading at the death anniversary. The film is structured around her refusals. Meena is the character who gets to sing two duets with Vijay, not Gulabo, putting Meena in a position of sharing a poetic voice, of getting to be seen as a fellow poet alongside Vijay, her college classmate. Gulabo performs Vijay's words, but never her own.

In the flashbacks, Meena is Vijay's equal, but in the film's present, Meena is the publisher's wife. She is necessary for the poems to become a book. She stands for the capitalism that Vijay turns away from, but that Guru Dutt, when *Pyaasa* becomes a box office hit, gains from. His next film, *Kagaaz ke Phool*, was a flop, and Dutt didn't direct again, although he continued to act and produce before his suicide in 1964. So *Pyaasa* is the rare critically acclaimed film appreciated in its own time, as Vijay within the film is appreciated (minus the fact his success is posthumous!), a perfectly balanced moment of the artist star giving his audience exactly what they wanted to gaze at when they wanted to do their gazing.

One of the unusual features of Guru Dutt's cinematic style, whether the film succeeded or failed at the box office, is a literal gaze, the regular use of unusually large close-ups. Guru Dutt's use of black and white is gorgeous; light is almost a character in his films. His cameraman V. K. Murthy, in Nasreen Munni Kabir's BBC program *In Search of Guru Dutt*, said that when he would work with other directors, they would say, "I want Guru Dutt's style. Use a 75mm, or a 100mm lens," bigger than anyone else was using.[11] These lenses allowed for some of the extremely large close-ups in *Pyaasa*, like the ones of only Dutt's eyes and nose during the song sequence where Vijay roams the lanes of brothels, asking us to look at the desperate situation of poverty and prostitution with him. In the middle of the song sequence, there's almost a mini silent film as a dancer is forced to dance instead of tending to her sick child. Instead of intervening, Vijay leaves. He does nothing, but Dutt forces us to look at the image of the mother, and then, increasingly, at the image of Vijay in closer and closer close-up. These close-ups fragment Vijay's face, potentially interrupting the *darsanic* moment, but they end up making the eyes themselves appear all the more intensely, to reduce the whole film in those moments to nothing more than eyes gazing back at us.

If Vijay/Guru Dutt is authorizing his audience with his benevolent gaze, a Bollywood star gazing down upon us all, in gigantic, riveting close-ups, what is Dutt authorizing us to do? Where is our admiration of Vijay/Guru Dutt supposed to take us? Vijay's song at his own death anniversary is a challenge to the current order. This song, "Yeh Duniya Agar Mil Bhi Jaye To," became a hit, still played on the radio today. Vijay sings, in the words of the poet Sahir Ludhianvi, "What is this world to me, even if I can have it?" He goes on to sing, "Burn it! Blow it asunder!" He's ready to destroy the world. It's the most riotous poetry reading ever. When he sings, "This world belongs to you, you keep it," I keep thinking he's singing to us, the movie audience, that the world of the film is ultimately ours. He's leaving us this husk of a film while he goes off somewhere else, a better world. It's a gift, even if it's not one we asked for, even if we'd rather have one of his earlier, lighter films. If Vijay is turning his back on poetry, Dutt seems close to turning his back on cinema itself.

Everyone in *Pyaasa*'s two love triangles is at the death anniversary: Mr. Ghosh and Meena and Vijay, as well as Vijay, Meena, and Gulabo. They are introduced in order, first the triangle of Vijay's first relationship with Meena, then the triangle of his relationship with Gulabo. The image throughout the song sequence is intimately linked to the song, with editing choices highlighting the question of which came first, the image or the song? Is the image cut for the song, or the song written to reinforce the image? The song sequence draws unusual attention to the tension between image and sound. Corey Creekmur writes that the final song sequence "elevates the film to an astonishing musical and dramatic crescendo, as slight head movements by all the major characters in the film match rising musical figures as Dutt cuts rhythmically among their close-ups. As the song builds from a whisper to a scream, Mohammed Rafi's steady voice breaks as Vijay's supposed admirers mutate into a rioting mob."[12] Rafi's voice is fragmenting; so is the social fabric around Vijay. The movie, too, is breaking down at the plot level. Meena and Mr. Ghosh do not get their comeuppance. Meena's tortured gaze at Vijay (at one point she even covers her eyes with her hand) suggests that she still loves him, but she doesn't change. She stands by the choice she made long ago. Mr. Ghosh doesn't lose the money he made off Vijay's book, or get in trouble with the law for keeping Vijay's friends from finding him in the hospital when he was presumed dead. We might worry that Gulabo will be trampled by the crowds, but she isn't. We might think she will be rewarded for her loyalty, brought up to the stage, but that doesn't happen, either. She can't reach Vijay. She's kept as distant as Meena and Mr. Ghosh. As Gulabo tries to approach Vijay, he's dragged off the stage by Mr. Ghosh's henchmen. The riot starts when they turn off the lights, cutting off both image and song at once. It's as if the two need each other to function. The film's final scene immediately following the "Yeh Duniya" song sequence feels like a wish fulfillment for Gulabo and the audience rather than any kind of conclusion to the questions raised by the riot and the song urging us to destroy the world we can't have. Vijay shows up at Gulabo's building; she rushes down the stairs to him. They walk off hand in hand, to a place where, Vijay says, "I won't have to go any farther." Where is that place? How much further *can* he go, after what has already happened at the anniversary reading? Sudresh Mishra reads the end as a gesture toward a utopia, but one that can't work outside of the movie, something behind India under Nehru and its economic order. He writes, "What the last scene signals is a coming community, selfless and utopian, where forms of work, association, and affection are impossibly emancipated from the law of the commodity."[13]

If there is a community here, it is one made up of only two, the poet and the fan, the star and the audience, the film's director and his lover, the rescuer and the prostitute. The film's final image, with Gulabo and Vijay going off hand in hand to "Where I won't have to go any farther," can be read as romantic and sentimentalized, an echo of the Little Tramp and the Gamin walking off at the end of *Modern Times*, but it also can be read as suicidal. Gulabo and Vijay walk off into a fog. They don't seem to be on a road, and Vijay certainly has a death wish. What space is left for poetry, or cinema, let alone the world itself, is in question. The world is ours. We keep it. They're gone.

NOTES

1. Sudresh Mishra, "News from the Crypt: India, Modernity, and the West," *New Literary History* 40, no. 2 (2009): 334.
2. Mishra, "India, Modernity, and the West," 334.
3. Shoma Chatterji, *Subject: Cinema. Object: Woman* (Calcutta: Parumita Publications, 1998), 170.
4. Lalitha Gopolan, *Cinema of Interruptions: Action Genres in Contemporary Indian Cinema* (London: British Film Institute, 2002), 21.
5. Gopolan, *Cinema of Interruptions*, 21.
6. Corey Creekmur, "*Pyaasa Thirst*," in *The Cinema of India*, ed. Lalitha Gopolan (London: Wallflower, 2009), 112.
7. Ravi S. Vasudevan, "The Politics of Cultural Address in a 'Transitional' Cinema: A Case Study of Indian Popular Culture," in *Reinventing Film Studies*, ed. Christine Gledhill and Linda Williams (New York: Oxford University Press, 2000), 147.
8. Vasudevan, "Politics of Cultural Address," 157.
9. Vasudevan, "Politics of Cultural Address," 139.
10. Vijay Mishra, *Bollywood Cinema: Temples of Desire* (New York: Routledge, 2002), 114.
11. Quoted in Nasreen Munni Kabir, *Guru Dutt: A Life in Cinema* (Delhi: Oxford University Press, 1996).
12. Corey Creekmur, "*Pyaasa*," http://www.uiowa.edu~incinema/pyaasa.html.

13. Sudresh Mishra, "India, Modernity, and the West," 335.

Chapter Six

Chicken Poets and Rough Poetry

Figuring the Poet and His Subject(s) in Independent Chinese Cinema

Qi Wang

Contemporary Chinese cinema, and especially its independent sector that blossomed from the early nineties on, has featured a subtly persistent figuration of the poet. From its fictional characterizations in *Night Rain in Bashan* (*Bashan yeyu*, dir. Wu Yigong and Wu Yonggang, 1980) and *Chicken Poets* (*Xiang jimao yiyang fei*, dir. Meng Jinghui, 2002) to the various degrees of invocation of real poets in independent documentaries such as *Shi Zhi* (*Shi Zhi*, dir. Jiang Zhi, 1999), *Nightingale, Not the Only Voice* (*Yeying bushi weiyi de gehou*, dir. Tang Danhong, 2000), *Dream Walking* (*Mengyou*, dir. Huang Wenhai, 2006), *Rough Poetry* (a.k.a. *Low-Class Poems, Xialiu shige*, dir. Zhao Dayong, 2008), *Poetry and Disease* (*Shi yu bing delücheng*, dir. Geng Jun, 2011), and *Believe in the Future* (*Xiangxin weilai*, dir. Yu Xiaoyang, 2011), the poet as a cinematic trope evolves across a range of moving image texts and contexts, reflecting an intriguingly changing attitude to the (ir)relevance of poetry in a speedily capitalizing China. How are the poet figures represented in these diverse cinematic texts? How does their presence encourage a matching adjustment or innovation in film language? And how do such character figurations and aesthetic configurations give form to an informed refiguring of contemporary Chinese cultural psyche? Focusing particularly on *Chicken Poets* and *Rough Poetry*, this chapter aims to provide an analysis in those directions and hopes to shed light on a facet of the contemporary Chinese cinema culture that has so far remained underexplored. [1]

Chicken Poets is the only film by Meng Jinghui, contemporary China's most accomplished director of avant-garde theater. [2] Mixing hilarity with poignancy, it tells a metaphoric tale about the choices facing creativity and integrity in contemporary China that beset none other than a poet figure who is caught between idealist commitment and commercial success. Yunfei is a published young poet who finds himself in a seemingly hopeless writing block. Coming to seek support from Chen Xiaoyang, his friend who has given up on writing poetry and become a businessman, Yunfei soon slips into Chen's project of running a chicken farm and producing fancy black eggs with allegedly higher nutrition value. In the meantime, Yunfei starts a relationship with Fangfang, a young woman who falls in love with his poetry and who herself as a dreamer wants to become an air stewardess despite her condition of color blindness. To impress Fangfang, Yunfei cheats in writing and relies on a poetry CD-ROM that a mysterious seller forces upon him one night. By simply following the programmed instructions and merely typing in titles, he has poems spewing out of the computer onto a printer without any further human labor. Yunfei becomes an instant success. Immediately put to commercial use, his verse becomes promotional material for supermarkets and home decoration products, while he appears in television talk shows, playing with fancy but empty words to cash in on fame. Fangfang breaks up with him in disillusionment. Soon the chicken farm gets shut down because of discovery of a chicken virus. Chen has already run away, dumping the failure on Yunfei's shoulders. Realizing how far he has deviated from his true purpose in life, Yunfei shaves his head like the Russian poet Vladimir Mayakovsky (1893–1930), a figure that is apparently his key inspiration throughout the film, and declares his resolution to truly commit to poetry by choosing, above all, a completely different way of living. He has the chicken farm destroyed and leaves the place behind him.

The film's critique of commercial philistinism that captivates a fast-capitalizing China is quite obvious. As a country that started its search for a more sustainable form of socialism (with capitalistic characteristics) on the basis of the insufficiently processed trauma of Maoism and the Cultural Revolution, China operates in a postsocialist mode whose essential character is tension and contradiction, torn between a desire for success and recognition in the contemporary global world and a vague, self-denying nostalgia for the utopian dream that socialism once provided illusory food for (but fatally betrayed with its devolution into Maoist autocracy). Admitting his creative depletion from the very beginning of the film, Yunfei finds himself in an embarrassing and scary position as if caught in an in-between void. One brief scene of him getting hysterically stuck in a dysfunctional elevator that stops between two floors clearly signifies his discomfort and fear of being in such a nonplace. This pathological condition of claustrophobia is an inversed expression of his desire to break through into the open. As if to respond to that desire of his, Fangfang as the persona of the poet's conscience tends to be identified with open spaces. For instance, her professional dream of being an air stewardess points to a life up in the air and, as I shall illustrate a bit later, crucial scenes about her subjectivity take place in an open field.

The structure of *Chicken Poets*, while following a rather consistent overall narrative flow of Yunfei losing himself and then finding himself, demonstrates at the same time (and especially in some local places) an utterly poetic pattern that manifests a motif of *repetition with variation*. The poet figure, for example, has at least four variations: Yunfei, Mayakovsky, Fangfang, and Chen. Yunfei is the protagonist who undergoes an actual change in character whereas the other three remain constant on their respective iconic, idealist, and corrupt planes. Mayakovsky, whose image is twice juxtaposed with Yunfei's own (at the beginning of the film and after his poem CD-ROM fails to work), emits a soul-penetrating gaze at the young poet, the logic of their implied relationship realized by the shot/reverse shot structure in editing. The dialogic parallel—or repetition—between Mayakovsky and Yunfei is suggested by the intense similarity of their presentation: both face the camera, Mayakovsky staring from a black-and-white photographic image in which the only background is a monochromic whitish wall, and Yunfei, dressed in black, sitting against a monochromic background of blue. The visual grammatical unit that connects their gazes is a red tomato, a prop that is also identified with Fangfang as she always eats it and has a tomato-like flashing toy at bedside. As the only colorful and kinetic highlight, the red tomato is thrown at Yunfei, flies across and beyond the frame, its reddish juice dripping on the photographed face of Mayakovsky in a third shot. In the first appearance of this sequence at the very beginning of *Chicken Poets*, Yunfei's voice of reading "A Cloud in Trousers"—Mayakovsky's famous poem of 1915 expressing a new, revolutionary kind of poet identity—suggests his identification with the iconic poet whose soul-penetrating gaze seems to offer inspiration and encouragement. Its second appearance, however, follows Yunfei's horrified realization that the poetry CD-ROM he has been relying on in producing fame-bringing, profit-producing poems expires (as it is only a test copy). This changed context renders the same sequence of Yunfei and Mayakovsky in a renewed Kuleshov effect: this time Mayakovsky's gaze—no longer supported by Yunfei's passionate poem-reading voice-over as at the earlier moment—appears rather like a scolding response to the young poet's situation, pressing him to face the fatal falsity in his poet identity. Quite fittingly, Fangfang breaks up with Yunfei right after this sequence (without actually knowing that Yunfei has been cheating in writing). As the communicative connection between Yunfei and his poetic conscience (i.e., Mayakovsky), Fangfang functions just like that attacking red tomato on the narrative level with her constant admonitions that Yunfei should forget about business and continue writing poetry.

Starting with the monochromic photographic image of Mayakovsky, the duo of black and white becomes a color motif in the film, forming a layer of imagistic and poetic formation that visually piques Yunfei for his lost dream of being a poet. In this sense, Fangfang's condition of color blindness, while having little narrative importance in pushing forward the story or the fate of the central protagonist Yunfei, is a fitting dramatic design that echoes a series of black and white conditions in the film. Matching in color and emotional tonality with the image of Mayakovsky, important scenes of Fangfang's subjectivity—such as her first date with Yunfei and her breakup with him— are presented in a sepia-toned black and white. When eventually Yunfei chooses to return to his poetic calling, he appears, with his head newly shaven like that of Mayakovsky, also in black and white. In the meantime, black and white offers a visual filter through which to suggest the presence of poetry (or of a kind of augmented alterity) and to ridicule the capitalistic economy and consumerism that the antipoet Chen pursues. For example, three pairs of men, all dressed in black or white, greet Yunfei or Fangfang with identical gestures or movements (e.g., eating a banana, turning their heads to look) at various points without any imaginable contribution to the narrative. As the film's primary setting, the chicken farm—essentially a spacious yard house—is equipped with white-painted architecture and black chickens (producing black eggs) raised on its ground.

At an earlier point of the film, a sequence qualifying as a ciné-dance number cuts together Chen and a row of anonymous young men, all dressed in black. Across a total of twenty-five shots and ninety-nine seconds, this sequence relies on three sets of visual enactment (e.g., shot framing; color palette; acting) that each contain three main elements in themselves: the shots alternate between long shots, medium shots, and close-ups; the limited palette is composed of black (e.g., costume, eggs, chicken), white (e.g., wall, tablecloth), and yellow (e.g., oil, cocktail); and the movements of the human figures are egg cracking, egg cocktail mixing, and drinking. Such a limited number of visual and kinetic elements are edited to the rhythm, or rhyme, of three primary sounds: a persistent string music tune, the sound of egg cracking (plus imitative sound effects), and the sound of egg cocktail mixing (particularly that of hitting the bowls with chopsticks), all to be summarized by the sound of guzzling down the cocktail. The resulting rhythm, musically as well as visually, is of a well-controlled sort that operates within a system formed of the number of three in its varied renditions. On top of that, the sequence's average shot length (ASL) is 3.99 seconds, an ASL that verges on the editing rhythm between contemporary mainstream film editing and a music-video-influenced commercialized experimentalism.[3]

Compared to this swift and confident montaged choreography of business and consumption, the activities of Fangfang and Yunfei (when the latter is not yet absorbed in the chicken business) tend to defy edited choreography or montaged rhythm, which essentially is a kind of mechanic poetry. Thus interestingly, although editing is also used in presenting Fangfang and Yunfei, its manipulative power of constructing a fancy whole out of disparate fragments tends to give way to repetition to reinforce the integrity of the characters' subjectivities. During what might be their first date, Fangfang and Yunfei stand by the roadside, apparently observing the traffic. In voice-over we hear her asking him what colors the cars are. Unlike the neat match between image and sound in the black egg dance scene accomplished through crafty editing, here we hear Fangfang's voice but see them standing in silence. Four tracking shots pass by the two with their positions and expressions staying practically unchanged, producing the impression that these shots are repetitions of the same moment. When they are standing in the field, the camera movement, whether that of zooming onto Fangfang or panning past them and across the field, is quite slow and reserved, allowing the characters to speak about themselves, him about his claustrophobia, her about her color blindness.

Rather than fancy editing, single shots or takes with rich connotations—reminding one of (but not yet as elaborate as) the many poetic long takes in the cinema of Andrei Tarkovsky—tend to be used to communicate important moments and changes in Fangfang and Yunfei. For example, following their first date at which Fangfang gets to share her inner world with Yunfei, a sepia-toned black-and-white shot shows her walking in slow motion along a puddled road with reflections of shiny clouds, holding what most likely is a volume of poetry (and possibly either by Yunfei or Mayakovsky). The composition of this shot is diagonal, dialogic, and layered: Fangfang walks toward the front left along the puddled road that stretches along a diagonally framed fence while a plane—a symbol of her dream that is indeed her poetry—flies across the screen from left to right in a doubled manner: it flies in sky as its reflection flies in the puddles. In the background supporting this symbolic dialogue between subject, object, imagination, and poetry is an expanse of clouds with silver linings that also becomes partially reflected in the puddles. The soundscape of this otherwise silent shot is no other than the impassioned voice of Mayakovsky reading his poem, "A Cloud in Trousers." Layers of images and meanings are presented in a single and extended moving image. Later at their breakup, Fangfang sings a poignant song that is essentially a love poem, one that is about color and love (i.e., he is color to her). She is seated in a tracking shot and finishes singing the entire song in a single take lasting about two minutes. To add to the already surreal or subjective visual effect of her bursting into song and moving across the cinematic space while remaining seated the whole time, a deliberation of slow motion is achieved by having the actor of Yunfei (Chen Jianbin) chase after her in movements at reduced speed (while she moves at normal speed).

Do such aesthetic choices—specifically the temporal differentiations between fast-paced montage (in presenting the materialistic chicken business) versus slower and fuller takes (in presenting the world of poetic minds)—

signify that poetry, at least in the context of *Chicken Poets*, is to be kept as integral as possible and to be as free from mechanical intervention as possible? If we assume a positive answer to that question, then Meng Jinghui, who returned to theater and rarely touches cinema again after the making of *Chicken Poets*, seems also to attach an integral quality—one that is perhaps more theatrically than cinematically informed if the latter is (narrowly) understood as a mechanical manipulation of time and space—to the voice of the poet.

In crucial scenes of Yunfei and Fangfang such as those analyzed above, their voices or voice-overs provide important evidences of their interiorities and anchor their images. In contrast, presentations of Chen's chicken business tend to rely on fancy montage that not only dissects sound from image but also manipulates that dividedness to construct an illusion of a mechanically renewed integrity. Apart from the black egg dance number previously analyzed, early in the film a publicity sequence plays a pastiche on familiar socialist media (in this case, official documentaries about agricultural development) and applies the eulogizing voice of a female broadcaster to promote Chen's "technologically innovative," "peasants-enriching" business of raising black chickens. Whereas the voices of Mayakovsky, Yunfei, and Fangfang belong to themselves, Chen's voice is not heard in this publicity sequence. Instead, his facial and oral movements are choreographed in such a manner as to match with the high-pitched, authoritative-sounding female voice as if he were a puppet. As Yunfei explains in a voice-over, Chen is always the quickest to adapt to demands of the times and has in turn been a poet (when poetry was in fashion in the eighties in China) and a businessman of all sorts (from the nineties on when China entered a full-fledged market age, leaving behind it a complicated past including the Cultural Revolution and then the Tiananmen Incident in 1989). As a poet turned businessman who casts the past behind rather too conveniently in pursuit of materialistic profit, Chen no longer has poetry or anything of spiritual essence to offer. That is perhaps why his voice gets erased and replaced by that of state and capital. In contrast, Mayakovsky, Fangfang, and eventually Yunfei have a voice and a meaning to share with the world.

The sound of Mayakovsky's reading "A Cloud in Trousers" is featured in at least two places: in the slow-motion shot in which Fangfang walks across a puddled road with a volume of poetry in hand, and toward the end of a long take in which Yunfei reads a poem—the only moment we actually see him do so in the film—walking past the chicken farm facilities that are being destroyed in the fire in the yard. The poem that Yunfei is reading is one about poet identity by the turn-of-the-century Italian twilight poet Sergio Corazzini (1886–1907):

Why do you call me poet?
I am no poet
I am but a weeping child
I have only tears to offer to the silent world
Why do you call me poet?
My wretchedness is the wretchedness of everyman
My happiness was of the simple kind
So simple that I could only confess it
With embarrassment
Today I think of death
I am ill indeed
And each day I die a little
As do all things
So I am not a poet
Poets must lead a different life[4]

As Yunfei finishes reading this poem, the voice of Mayakovsky seeps in. As if he were hearing, accepting, and joining Mayakovsky's inspiring verse and voice, Yunfei responds by reciting lines from "A Cloud in Trousers." The camera, which has hitherto observed Yunfei in a tracking medium shot, zooms in onto him as he now looks straight at the camera. An encounter between gazes, voices, and subjectivities is thus achieved within this single shot, evoking a compressed and mutually enriching identity of the poet(s).

Rough Poetry is a jewel of an experimental film of forty-eight minutes by independent filmmaker Zhao Dayong who is reputed for his documentaries *Street Life* (*Nanjing lu*, 2006) and *Ghost Town* (*Feicheng*, 2008). Despite its claim to be fictive, *Rough Poetry* has a peculiar documentary feel due to its employment of nonprofessional actors and the close parallel existing between the creative and presentational circumstances of the featured poems. Shen Shaoqiu is a former policeman turned poet; his pen name is Dian Qiu Gu Jiu whose literal meaning "exchanging expensive furs for wines" readily connotes a poet figure who cares more for abandon and freedom than materialistic possessions. Shen plays a barely concealed version of himself in *Rough Poetry* as a policeman who writes poems. In the film, this policeman gathers together some convicts and shares with them his works (which *are* poems previously written by Shen). The rest of the cast, despite their unstated real identities, all speak a heavily and variedly accented Mandarin that strongly reminds one of the millions of provincial migrants roaming around China (especially in its coastal south that is more economically developed) for better opportunities in life. Some of them unfortunately end up in jail because of the challenging circumstances of a rootless life. The minimalist mise-en-scène that supports this thinly disguised cast from the real world is an emphatic version of the prison: all the figures are placed inside a tremendous iron cage that is in turn placed in a barren indoor space with grayish walls and a concrete ground, lit by a single hanging lamp. Within such a space that is at once open and closed and of a double interiority (inside a cage that is inside an unidentified place), the policeman asks—or, due to the obvious power imbalance, perhaps even demands—the convicts to read his poems.

Shen's poems are of a particular kind—"low poetry" (*di shige*)—that is replete with crude images and profane words about animals, death, excrement, sex, trash, and violence. In a comprehensive discussion on the subject, Zhang Jiayan, a renowned independent scholar of contemporary Chinese poetry, understands such a subversive recourse to "the low and the ugly" elements in Chinese society, human existence and language itself as being born out of a burning desire to shatter and break away from familiar poetic discourses that eulogize a deeply problematic official ideology, conventional aesthetics, and familiar moral corruptions.[5] Practitioners of the low poetry— of which Shen Shaoqiu, the impersonator of the policeman, is an important member and proponent—necessarily rebel with a counterstrategy that defies approval, beauty, carefulness, cleanness, and correctness and instead aims at blaspheming, discrediting, and disgracing those positive familiarities in order to provoke awareness and even change.[6]

The longest poem featured in the film is one called "We make flowers" (*Women zuohua*). Descriptive of prison life that involves making paper or plastic flowers as one form of assigned labor (that brings some profit for the prison), the poem speaks in first-person plural of the suffocating and hopeless life of incarceration:

> we plead guilty we are human trash and waste
> we plead guilty we were born cheap and puny
> we plead guilty mice's blood run in our vessels
> we plead guilty although words are not tattooed on our faces
> we plead guilty we have dark sultry eyes
> we plead guilty we don't understand what a true crime is[7]

The reader of this poem is a pretty woman who seems to have entered jail on account of involvement in organized crime. As she reads the poem, looking not exactly comfortable at first but increasingly absorbed, the camera inspects her in a fluid medium to close-up shot. Consisting of thirty lines and five stanzas, "We make flowers" has a neat and strict cadence that organizes a series of disparate images of prison life and personal expressions about prisoners' subjectivities—for example, "whose shitting stinks so strongly right next to me"; "in order to see our friends and family"; "we were born cheap and puny"; "we took drugs because we wanted to forget this hateful world"—around three behaviors: "we make flowers," "we plead guilty," and "we go on sleeping." In terms of both narrative content and their positions in the form of the poem, these repeated behaviors are obviously presented as the result of enforcement, incarceration, and restriction. More specifically, the phrase "we make flowers" ends each line of the first two stanzas and begins each line of the fourth stanza; "we plead guilty" begins each line of the third stanza; and "we go on sleeping" ends each line of the fifth stanza. Apart from the uniform sentence structure, the number of characters used in each line and stanza is strictly under control as well. Each line of the first three stanzas contains sixteen characters (including a colon), while each line of the last two stanzas contains nineteen characters (including a colon), resulting in a rhythm that is not only audible from the repetition of the same phrases ("we . . .") but also amazingly visual as each stanza looks like a wall of character-bricks with a vertical bar (formed from the colons) running straight through them. The verbal and imaginative space of the poem is also accessible as a visual one. [8]

However, rather than creating a comparably neat and carefully choreographed image of this experience and expression of prison life—such as what Fritz Lang famously did with modern workers' life in *Metropolis* (1927)—or crafting a cinematic dance number comparable to the black egg sequence in *Chicken Poets*, director Zhao Dayong eschews simulating the textual control of the original poem and seems to be more interested in the dynamic— perhaps even the possibility of subjective or imaginative breakthrough that poetry, here freshly translated and thoughtfully realized through cinematography, might bring to a life of incarceration and restriction. His camera dwells on, lingers around, flows past, and comes back to the female inmate who is also the poem reader, functioning more like a listener, like the others in the cage, to the reading, rather than a director. Visibly handheld and looking up close, the camera seems to flow between the partially framed figures as both an observer and participant in this moment of poetic sharing. Perhaps unsurprisingly, like in *Chicken Poets* when the reading of a poem is featured, a longer take uninterrupted by editing is used in order to keep the completeness of the poem and its delivery.

Throughout *Rough Poetry*, the position of the camera (or filmmaker) is never quite specified except that it is outside the cage. As is demonstrated by the scene above, this does not mean that the camera is a noninvolved outsider to the people or activities in the cage. As a matter of fact, at a rather early point in the film, an intense two-minute take shows in close-up the silent, confrontational gaze of a male inmate who seems to detect the camera in the half dark. The unusual length of this close-up shot engages the filmmaker as well as the viewer in a sustained communication with this rather disconcerting gaze from within the cage. That moment of "coming face-to-face" between the camera and the characters—or subjects as the inmates are essentially the subjects of the film as well as the featured poems—receives an extended treatment at the end of the film: nine silent shots show the faces of all the characters, each lasting one to two and a half minutes. Even though the status of these figures' realness is not for sure (except the poet Shen who is the real author of these poems whether on-screen or offscreen), juxtaposing them sequentially (along with that of the poet) seems to suggest their comparability and connection.

Until this point of intense silence (but not stillness, as we see minute movement on the human face, such as that of the eyelids, throat, and even emotions and tears), the soundscape of the film is a subtle polyphony shared by distinct strata of poem reading (e.g., by the poet, the woman convict, and two male inmates), ambient noises of the people laughing, conversing, or moving about in the cage, and a faint darting sound of an unidentifiable origin. In contrast, the ending of *Rough Poetry* is a sequence of intensely silent moments. Looking at the camera, the faces bear expressions of a reduced and complicated kind. At the same time expressionless and expression-full, comfortable and awkward, suggesting much yet explicating little, they invite all and no interpretations, creating an unspeakably rich moment that would best be understood as poetic. This moment of poetry arrives after poems are read and now dwells on the silent and the suggestive, allowing and encouraging the viewer to participate in it with empathy and imagination— two crucial capacities of a poet or purposes of poetry—with due respect and gentleness. At this point, the actual identity of the inmate-characters becomes perhaps much less important because our interested investment in these faces in front of the camera is rather unambiguously focused on their physical, momentary, and real qualities as surfaces of lived lives rather than as fictional characters or even documentary subjects. These faces, while being very specific and individual, become at the same time immensely suggestive and essentially poetic. Whereas it is necessary for Yunfei to live a completely different life than offered by success in a consumerist economy in *Chicken Poets* in order to realize his poetic potential, *Rough Poetry* illustrates the possibility, however restricted and momentary, of finding poetry and deliverance in a life where a physical walkout seems least possible.

NOTES

1. An earlier related discussion of the influence of traditional Chinese poetry and painting on cinema is provided by Catherine Yi-yu Cho Woo, "The Chinese Montage: From Poetry and Painting to the Silver Screen," in *Perspectives on Chinese Cinema*, ed. Chris Berry (London: British Film Institute, 1991), 21–29.

2. Meng Jinghui (b. 1964) has directed over thirty theatrical plays since 1990. Some of his most successful works were also originally scripted by him in collaboration with others or written by his creative partner (also wife), Liao Yimei, e.g., *I Love XXX* (*Wo ai XXX* , 1994), *Rhinoceros in Love* (*Lianai de xiniu*, 1999) , and Amber (*Hupo*, 2005). Scholarly studies of his works in English have only recently begun. See, for example, my analysis of *I Love XXX* in Qi Wang, "Writing against Oblivion: Personal Filmmaking from the Forsaken Generation in Post-Socialist China" (unpublished doctoral dissertation, University of California, Los Angeles, 2008), 109–26. Also see Yuwen Hsiung, "Emotion, Materiality, and Subjectivity: Meng Jinghui's *Rhinoceros in Love*," *Asian Theater Journal* 26, no. 2 (Fall 2009): 250–59. A discussion of *Chicken Poets* can be found in Rossella Ferrari, "Disenchanted Presents, Haunted Pasts, and

Dystopian Futures: Deferred Millennialism in the Cinema of Meng Jinghui," *Journal of Contemporary China* 20, no. 71 (2011): 699–721.

3. It is interesting to bear in mind here David Bordwell's calculation of an ASL of four to six seconds in a sensation-driven, post-1960s Hollywood cinema, which might be a sign of capitalism's recent and latest development. In their computer-generated visualization of the temporal patterns in visual media (and especially in American, French, and Russian cinemas from 1900 to 2008), Lev Manovich and Jeremy Douglass use the data provided by Cinemetrics, an interactive website devoted to the measurement and analysis of film editing, and also note a general pattern of decreasing ASL in the history of American cinema, arguing that the changes in the cinematic rhythms reflect changes in the American society's historical and cultural patterns. See http://www.cinemetrics.lv/bordwell.php; softwarestudies.com/cultural.../ visualizing _ temporal _ patterns .pdf.

4. http://www.pennilesspress.co.uk/poetry/italian_twilight_poets_chris.htm.

5. Zhang Jiayan, "Chinese Low Poetry Tide" (zhongguo di shichao), http://blog.boxun.com/hero/2007/xwziwj/149_1.shtml.

6. Shen Shaoqiu's short poem "Sunflower" is written on the wall behind the cage (my translation):

My whole life
Is after light
Yet once I ripen
My neck will be broken

Next to the poem is a playful declaration: "Love live the pretty women!," an obvious pastiche of familiar Chinese revolutionary slogans such as "Long live Chairman Mao!," "Long live the Chinese Communist Party!," and "Long live our motherland!"

7. This is my translation of the third stanza. The entire poem is accessible in Chinese at http://tieba.baidu.com/p/132328931.

8. For a look at the physical form of the poem in Chinese, see http://tieba.baidu.com/p/132328931.

Part II

Poetry as Film

Chapter Seven

"Some Are Born to Endless Night"

The Blakean Vision of Jim Jarmusch's Dead Man

Hugh Davis

In Jim Jarmusch's 1995 postmodern Western *Dead Man*, Johnny Depp plays an accountant named William Blake who undergoes a journey to and through the land of the dead accompanied by a Native American spirit guide named Nobody, who mistakes Blake for the English Romantic poet of the same name. Although critics usually mention the superficial references to the poet—Nobody quotes lines from Blake's poetry throughout the film, for instance, and there are a number of visual references to specific poems— there is surprisingly little criticism on the ways that Blake's poetry informs *Dead Man* both thematically and structurally. In a recent article entitled "William Blake and *Dead Man*," Troy Thomas discusses the film as a broad adaptation of Blake's work and argues that it "thoroughly interiorizes Blake's ideas within the framework of a postmodern Western that resists decoding even as it uses the English poet's writings in a constant point of reference and inspiration."[1] While this is certainly an accurate description of the film, Thomas also acknowledges the inherent difficulties in adapting poetry for the screen and points to the ways that *Dead Man* both appropriates allegorical figures from Blake's work and transcends them, thereby making the film something different than a straight adaptation. In this essay, I would like to offer a complementary reading of the film by framing the relationship between *Dead Man* and Blake's poetry as less one of adaptation, in which Jarmusch translates Blake's allegories into a different medium, than of inter-textuality, in which the film and the poems interact in a way that allows the interplay of ideas to become more complex through a chain of associations. While Thomas is mostly concerned with the ways that Blake's major allegorical works such as *The Four Zoas* and *The Book of Urizen* inform the film's

overarching themes of "materialism, innocence, and spirituality,"[2] I will focus on two early scenes—William Blake's conversation with the train's fireman and his interaction with the reformed prostitute Thel—in order to demonstrate how individual lyric poems, primarily from *Songs of Innocence and
of Experience*, serve as key intertexts for *Dead Man*, helping to shape the
film's meaning without necessarily becoming part of its allegorical apparatus.

    In general terms, Blake's poetry is centered on the reconciliation of oppo-
site states of matter, being, and spirit; as he writes in "The Argument" to *The
Marriage of Heaven and Hell*, "Without Contraries is no progression. Attraction and Repulsion, Reason and Energy, Love and Hate, are necessary to
Human existence."[3] Jarmusch adopts this basic logic and uses it to structure
Dead Man, establishing early on a dialectic of opposition that is not only
thematically central to the film but that also is embodied in its form. For
instance, at the beginning of the film, Depp's character travels by train from
Cleveland, Ohio, to an undisclosed territory in the Wild West to take a job in
the town of Machine. At one point during the long, tedious, and otherwise
virtually silent rail journey he is joined by the train's fireman (played by
Crispin Glover), who engages him in conversation, speaking the film's first
lines of dialogue:

> Look out the window. And doesn't this remind you of when you were in the
> boat? And then later that night, you were lying, looking up at the ceiling, and
> the water in your head was not dissimilar from the landscape, and you think to
> yourself, "Why is it that the landscape is moving, but the boat is still?"[4]

On first viewing, this speech makes little sense, as it seems to refer to an
event to which the audience has not been privy; even Depp's Blake doesn't
know what he's talking about. However, on subsequent viewings, the audience knows that the fireman is describing the end of the film, when the
protagonist is cast adrift in the Pacific Ocean in a Makah burial canoe, his
journey through the land of the dead complete. Jarmusch thus collapses the
distinction between beginning and end, dislocating the narrative from a simple linear progression and placing it on a spiritual temporal plane where
before and after are not only of no consequence but are one and the same.
The fireman's confusion of past ("you were in the boat") and present ("you
think to yourself") tense accomplishes the same goal, inviting the viewer to
think about time as simultaneously whole or, in Blake's terms, to hold "Eternity in an hour."[5]

    Furthermore, the fireman's white face is covered in soot from the furnace,
which invokes both Blake's chimney sweep—"A little black thing among the
snow"[6]—and "The Little Black Boy," who cries "My skin is black / but Oh
my soul is white."[7] His use of the word "ceiling" also echoes Blake, whose

Bard informs the Earth that "The starry floor / The watry shore / Is giv'n thee till the break of day";[8] in this instance, the ceiling invoked by the fireman is both the top of the sky and the floor of heaven, a line of demarcation (like the boundary between land and water) that seems insurmountable from the human perspective but is illusory from the divine, an idea that is given visual form at the end of the film when Nobody sends Blake back "through the mirror at the place where the sea meets the sky," a place that finally fades into the same blackness from which the film—itself black and white—emerges. This opening speech by the fireman, then, establishes the theme of reconciliation of opposites that will continue throughout the film, whether in the initiation of the "stupid white man" into Native American spirituality; the fusion of human and animal (the Raccoon People, Nobody as bear) and male and female (Iggy Pop's cross-dressing Sally Jencko); the mirrored image of the sun and moon in the bald heads of the twin marshals, whose deaths come at the moment when William Blake the accountant and William Blake the poet become one ("Do you like my poetry?"); the union of life and death (Cole and Nobody kill each other simultaneously; Cole, like death, eats his own parents, his own source of life); the fact that Nobody is half-Blood and half-Blackfoot, a cross between two warring tribes; and so on. Even the two main characters' stories move in parallel but opposite directions: as Nobody paddles Blake down the river toward the Makah village at the end of the film, he sees the remnants of his own story—burning village, skeleton from the Blake engraving, elk brother—moving backward to its beginning.

While Jarmusch uses the fireman to introduce the theme of contraries in his first speech, the conversation that follows extends the fundamental idea to the uncanny and the relationship between orality and literacy and then to the nature of the sign itself. The fireman asks Blake, "Where is it that you're from?," and Blake replies "Cleveland" and then adds, "Lake Erie," to which the fireman echoes, "Erie." In keeping with the fireman's emphasis on opposition, Blake's answer is significant in that "cleave" is a Janus word, that is, a homograph that is also an antonym: a word that has two opposite meanings, in this case both "to adhere to" and "to split." Also, by emphasizing that Blake is from "Erie," a word that the fireman keeps repeating back to him ("Do you have any parents back in Erie?"; "And do you have a wife in Erie?"), Jarmusch is invoking its homonym "eerie," which in turn introduces the idea of the uncanny, which, according to Sigmund Freud, is the feeling of experiencing a situation as simultaneously strange and familiar, as in the phenomenon of déjà vu. Freud begins his essay "The Uncanny" by discussing the German word *heimlich*, which "on the one hand it means what is familiar and agreeable, and on the other, what is concealed and kept out of sight";[9] in other words, "*heimlich* is a word the meaning of which develops in the direction of ambivalence, until it finally coincides with its opposite *unheimlich*."[10] For Freud, this doubleness of *heimlich* is an important clue to what is happening when one experiences uncanniness and leads to a brief overview of the double in literature, the development of which he identifies, following Otto Rank, as having originated as "insurance against the destruction of the ego," the soul having emerged as the first double of the body in the primitive imagination, but evolving in the adult psyche into an "uncanny harbinger of death."[11] Indeed, he observes, many people experience the uncanny "in the highest degree in relation to death and dead bodies, to the return of the dead, and to spirits and ghosts."[12] What strikes Freud as most significant about literary representations of a doubled self, though, is their similarity to a type of pathological cognitive dissonance that allows one to "treat the rest of the ego like an object" through a kind of "self-observation."[13] Although Freud discusses other aspects of uncanniness such as repetition and coincidence, he ultimately brings all the disparate threads together in defining the uncanny as "something which is secretly familiar, which has undergone repression and then returned from it."[14] In other words, the feeling that one has when one experiences the uncanny is both strange and familiar because it recapitulates the structure of the psyche: a conscious ego catching a glimpse of the repressed id, which, though hidden, is nonetheless present. One is one's own double then, and seeing one's reflection out of the corner of one's eye can be profoundly disconcerting to the conscious self, precisely because the double is the one that is real.

In *Dead Man*, there are a number of doubles: in addition to those defined by Blakean opposition, as discussed above, the three bounty hunters are mirrored by the three trappers; the federal marshals who discover Blake's campsite are twins; and the skulls, rocking babies, and coffin makers that Blake observes while walking through the town of Machine at the beginning of the film and the Makah village at the end are eerily similar. John Dickinson and the priest at the trading post are also doubles: both pull a gun on Blake; both tell lies; and both hate Native Americans, as Dickinson, who is more concerned with retrieving his "very spirited and valuable horse" than he is avenging his son's death, draws a clear distinction between "men and Indians," and the priest sees Nobody as a subhuman pest fit only to be exterminated. Moreover, Dickinson has a stuffed bear in his office, and there is a bear hide in the rafters of the trading post, the head of which hangs down in front of the priest; both contrast with Nobody, whom Blake mistakes for a bear mating in the forest, as a symbol of life and procreation as opposed to death and stasis—embodied by Dickinson's posed bear, a mere simulacrum of life (needless to say, taxidermy is almost always uncanny).[15] Dickinson and the priest are both fathers (one literal, one titular) who try to kill Blake, a detail that Freud would certainly approve of, since the Oedipal drama is what leads to the repression of the id in the first place. The fact that this primal scene is repeated, with the "father" winning the first encounter and the "son" the second is also significant, not only for the psychological and spiritual progression that it represents but also because repetition, "the unintended recurrence of the same situation"[16] and particularly of events that seem to be meaningful in some hidden way, constitutes for Freud a primary source of the uncanny.

The most important double in the film is William Blake: even though the accountant has initially never heard of the poet, they are nonetheless doubles who eventually become one; or rather, William Blake the poet is that part of himself that William Blake the accountant has repressed and, guided by Nobody, must acknowledge and integrate into the self in order to achieve psychological and spiritual wholeness. However, any discussion of knowledge or repression or progress is problematic, as William Blake, in either incarnation, is from the very beginning of the film, as the title indicates, a dead man. Although the film operates on a number of levels, and the same scene can resonate in different ways depending on the frame through which it is viewed, the key to understanding Blake's journey is the realization that, even though he arguably "dies" several times in the film—once when he is shot, perhaps when he lies down with the fawn, and certainly at the end— Blake is, in fact, dead the entire time, the fireman as Charon having ferried him by rail to the land of the dead. The film depicts a journey both to and through the underworld, then; his death is both a consummation (an end that is also a beginning) and a preparation for what lies beyond. In this way Jarmusch gives concrete form to the uncanny, which accounts for the film's overwhelming sense of otherworldliness: Blake is both dead and not dead; he is his own ghost; like each of us when our doubles look back, he haunts himself. Similarly, Nobody is somebody in the sense that he is Blake's spirit guide, but he is also nobody in the sense that he has no existence apart from Blake (either one or both), coming into the film when Blake is shot and dying along with him at the end (or, rather, both dying on shore and accompanying him in the canoe in the form of his image on a locket).

After a discussion of Blake's parents and fiancée "in Erie" in the opening scene, the fireman then asks why he has "come all the way out here, all the way out here to hell." Blake answers that he has a letter from Dickinson Metal Works assuring him of a job, but when he shows it to the fireman, the fireman replies, "I wouldn't know, because I don't read, but I'll tell you one thing for sure: I wouldn't trust no words written down on no piece of paper, especially from no Dickinson out in the town of Machine. You're just as likely to find your own grave." Just as with the themes of opposition and doubling, Jarmusch here uses the fireman to introduce another important idea, both for William Blake the poet and the film: the relationship between the written and spoken word. In the "Introduction" to *Songs of Innocence*, Blake writes as follows:

Piping down the valleys wild
Piping songs of pleasant glee
On a cloud I saw a child.
And he laughing said to me.

Pipe a song about a Lamb;
So I piped with merry chear,
Piper pipe that song again—
So I piped, he wept to hear.

Drop thy pipe thy happy pipe
Sing thy songs of happy chear,
So I sung the same again
While he wept with joy to hear

Piper sit thee down and write
In a book that all may read—
So he vanished from my sight
And I pluck'd a hollow reed.

And I made a rural pen,
And I stain'd the water clear,
And I wrote my happy songs
Every child may joy to hear. [17]

While this poem superficially seems to have little to do with *Dead Man*, it actually encapsulates several concepts that are fundamental to both Blake's poetry and the film while offering a clear example of intertextuality between the two media. First of all, the poem is set in the "valleys wild," which represents a typical Romantic valorization of the natural world, in this case associated with inspiration by the muse of innocence, which Jarmusch shares, identifying the Machine of industrial civilization with hell in the film and equating spiritual renewal with a return to nature. Next, the muse instructs the speaker to "pipe a song about a Lamb." For Blake, as in the poem "The Lamb," the lamb is Christ, who, though innocent, is sacrificed for our sins. However, Christ is also the Good Shepherd, which makes each Christian ("Every child") the lamb as well. In *Dead Man*, Nobody is explicitly equated with the lamb, as he is not only shown during the flashback being taken to England in a cage next to one but he also shepherds Blake on his spiritual journey and even dies for him at the end.

The poem also encapsulates the reconciliation of opposition that constitutes the basic structure of both Blake's poetry and the film: the child on the cloud laughs at first, then weeps, and finally "[weeps] with joy." The same pattern of thesis-antithesis-synthesis is apparent in the way that the song (as well as the poem) manifests itself: the child instructs the poet first to pipe, then to sing, and finally to write. At first, music, which flows through the piper's hollow pipe, is revealed truth unmediated by language; the Blake engraving (for the title page of an 1808 edition of Robert Blair's 1747 poem *The Grave*) that appears during Nobody's flashback depicts the same idea in the form of an angel blowing a trumpet into a skeleton's ear in order to bring the dead (or, in the Christian formulation, the living who are spiritually dead) back to life (as one must metaphorically die to be born again). For Blake, however, since the world is corrupted by sin, the Word of God must fall into language in order to be received by mankind; therefore, the child instructs the piper to sing. When he does, the child cries tears of joy. The song is about the Lamb, and the child laughs at first because Christ incarnate came into the world but then weeps because He was crucified. But, since the crucifixion led to the resurrection, it was actually a triumph rather than a defeat, so the child "[weeps] with joy." Just as the fall into language parallels the crucifixion, the transformation of death into transcendence occurs when the child instructs the poet to "sit thee down and write / In a book that all may read." In the pattern of reconciliation of opposites established by the poem (lamb + shepherd = Christ; life [incarnation] + death [crucifixion] = resurrection; laugh + weep = weep for joy), then, writing functions as the synthesis of the antitheses piping and singing, the Truth as revealed through unmediated revelation and the truth as translated into the spoken word, which "Every child" must paradoxically "read" in order to "hear."

While writing would seem to represent the same type of synthesis as the resurrection in the logic of the poem, its status as a vehicle for spiritual truth is actually more ambiguous, an idea that both Blake and Jarmusch emphasize. For instance, in order to write his "happy songs," the poet must pluck a "hollow reed" and stain "the water clear." The hollow reed, which symbolizes inspiration, the conduit through which unmediated revelation flows, must now be "pluck'd"; in being transformed into a "rural pen," it can fulfill the poet's function but is no longer alive. Similarly, the water must be "stain'd" in order to be legible on the page, but just as the spirit has to be made flesh to be redeemed, it is no longer pure. Jarmusch directly alludes to this poem in the scene in which Cole Wilson, Conway Twill, and Johnny "The Kid" Pickett stop in their pursuit of Blake and Nobody to read a "Wanted" poster. Or, rather, "The Kid" reads it, since Twill is illiterate, and then is killed by Cole. As Cole watches the blood from his head wound "[stain] the water clear" in a puddle, he announces that "The Kid" is just "a Navajo mud toy now." Instead of depicting a child who serves as the muse of innocence transmitting "happy songs," Jarmusch completely inverts the poem, here punishing "The Kid" for being able to read and then laughing so hard that he almost cries (Cole, in fact, asks, "You gonna shed tears for us?" before killing him).

Writing, for Blake, entails a type of paradoxical relationship to the truth, then: both dead and alive, the written word is not the Word, but it is also (for most) the only way it can be known. In *Dead Man*, writing is even more suspect: not only does the fireman abjure reading, but he explicitly states, "I wouldn't trust no words written down on no piece of paper" and goes on to equate the written word with deception and death. (Although the words he speaks to Blake are true, the accountant is unable to understand the message; hence the need, as with the song, for its translation into a different medium, which is the film itself.) Similarly, the mise-en-scène of the trading post is dominated by chains, traps, dismembered animals, and signs on which the priest has written out various Bible verses, most of which have to do with death and destruction. As the priest is the film's most loathsome character, the fact that he is so closely associated with the written word is telling. When Nobody evokes Blake's poem "The Everlasting Gospel," reciting, "The vision of Christ that thou dost see / Is my vision's greatest enemy,"[18] he is clearly commenting on the priest's misappropriation of scripture in having read and even transcribed it but having completely failed to understand its meaning.

Of course, one of the problems with the written word is its polysemous nature; the status of virtually any text (as opposed to direct revelation) as a medium of truth is complicated by the fact that it can interpreted in multiple ways, not all of which are immediately apparent. As Blake writes a few lines after those quoted by Nobody in "The Everlasting Gospel," "Both read the Bible day & night / But thou readst black where I read white."[19] Interpretation is a central thematic concern in *Dead Man*, as the protagonist's spiritual progress depends on his learning to read signs, both literally and figuratively. According to Ferdinand de Saussure, the father of modern linguistics, a word (more precisely, a sign) does not bear a one-to-one correspondence with the thing it ostensibly names; rather, the sign is composed of two parts: the signifier ("tree") and the signified (the concept it names: a tree is that leafy thing that is bigger than a bush). For Saussure, signifiers are arbitrary and differential; they have no inevitable relationship to the concept they name, and they are meaningful only within the language system that contains them.[20] In *Dead Man*, Jarmusch presents a number of unstable signifiers that either contain multiple meanings, change over the course of the film, or fail to signify anything beyond themselves. The title itself is an unstable signifier, in that it is not completely clear what "dead" is supposed to mean, since the protagonist (who in my reading is already dead) to all appearances seems to be very much alive. In the same way, several characters over the course of the film ask Blake if he has any tobacco, and he replies, with various levels of incomprehension or annoyance, "I don't smoke." The joke is that he doesn't understand that tobacco is a common sacrament in Native American religion, its smoke serving to carry prayers up to the heavens, and whether or not he smokes—a white man's way of thinking in which tobacco is merely a commodity to be consumed—is irrelevant. Just as when he thinks his coin will buy a fifth of whiskey but the bartender hands him a pint, he has to adjust his expectations; only when he realizes the true meaning of the question, which is something like "Are you ready to go to the place where all the spirits came from and where all the spirits return?," can he make the voyage. In fact, Blake and Nobody's last conversation revolves around precisely this point. Looking up from the burial canoe, Blake says, "Found some tobacco." Nobody explains, "The tobacco is for your voyage," and Blake replies, "I don't smoke." Although the words are exactly the same as all the previous times he has discussed tobacco, their meaning is completely different, as he now understands his earlier cluelessness. A perfect example of polysemy, "I don't smoke" is a signifier (not unlike the word "cleave") that signifies multiple, even contradictory, meanings. Not only is this final evocation of the phrase a nice bit of postmodern irony, but it also recalls the fireman's question from the initial monologue, when he asks, adopting Blake's perspective, "Why is it that the landscape is moving, but the boat is still?" Here, Jarmusch is pointing out that what seems to possess one type of objective reality—the words are identical—can be transformed through subjective experience.

Clearly, Jarmusch is highly attuned to the inherent instability of the sign and in *Dead Man* builds on the ambiguity and polysemy exhibited by the poetry of William Blake to interrogate the nature of the sign itself. When Blake first comes to Dickinson Metal Works, he asks a worker for directions to the office, and the worker points to a sign that reads "Office." Through this visual pun Jarmusch is alerting the viewer that signs and signification are important, as the sign in this case is not the thing it names but does point the way to it. Similarly, when Blake is in her room with Thel, a former prostitute who now attempts to make a living selling paper flowers, she hands him one of the flowers and, after telling him she would like to enhance it with a drop of French perfume, asks, "What does it smell like?" He answers, "Paper," to which she responds, "Well, it is paper." Here, the paper flower is an empty signifier; since it does not point beyond itself, it cannot function as a sign, at least not in a way that Blake can understand. Within the larger context of the film, however, the paper flower, meaningless in itself, signifies the necessity for Blake to learn to read signs, or more specifically to recognize a signifier when he sees one, which is the theme of his interaction with Thel as a whole and which is a model for the viewer, who (through the Blakean intertext) is also being instructed how to read. As Depp's Blake says of the flowers, "They really are something"—but what?

After Blake discovers that his expected job at Dickinson Metal Works has been taken and that he has cut all ties to his previous life in the East for nothing, he meets Thel outside the local saloon, where he has gone to drown his sorrows. In one of the more obvious references to Blake's poetry in the film, Jarmusch takes her name from "The Book of Thel," an allegory of innocence in which the title character is a virgin who, invited by "the Clod of

Clay,"[21] wants to taste the world of experience but then flees from it when she gets too close. In Blake's formulation, spiritual growth can only occur through the dialectic of innocence and experience, in which the fall from innocence into experience is a necessary condition for the reconciliation of, as the subtitle to *Songs of Innocence and of Experience* has it, the two "contrary states of the human soul"[22] into a higher innocence that transcends duality. By rejecting the world of experience, Thel keeps her innocence, but for Blake this repudiation of the world leads not to salvation but to spiritual sterility. Without experience, true innocence remains an abstraction.

Jarmusch's Thel is obviously fallen; it's not an accident that Depp's character first notices her after she's been thrown down in the muddy street by a grotesque former customer, and his drunken "We liked you better when you was a whore" reveals everything the viewer needs to know about her backstory. What is important in this image of Thel lying in the mud, a soiled blossom among the other scattered flowers from her basket, however, is that it constitutes a visual allusion to Blake's poem "The Sick Rose," which reads as follows:

> O Rose thou art sick.
> The invisible worm,
> That flies in the night
> In the howling storm:
>
> Has found out thy bed
> Of crimson joy:
> And his dark secret love
> Does thy life destroy.[23]

On the simplest level, this poem is about the "invisible worm" of sexual sin and its resultant guilt, whose gnawing at the rose of life corrupts its beauty, leading to disease and death. For Blake, though, the sin has less to do with sex—which he sees as healthy and life affirming, the body being merely the portion of the soul perceptible to the senses—and more to do with the fact that it is "dark" and "secret"; in other words, what makes sex sinful is the law—whether biblical injunction or social more—that proscribes it and forces it out of the light and into darkness. In "The Garden of Love," for instance, Blake writes:

> I went to the Garden of Love,
> And saw what I never had seen:
> A Chapel was built in the midst,
> Where I used to play on the green.
>
> And the gates of this Chapel were shut,
> And Thou shalt not. writ over the door;
> So I turn'd to the Garden of Love,

That so many sweet flowers bore.

And I saw it was filled with graves,
And tomb-stones where flowers should be:
And Priests in black gowns, were walking their rounds,
And binding with briars, my joys & desires.[24]

The garden of love—the Garden of Eden before the fall—is the site of playful innocence until the chapel is built; then the "sweet flowers" of beauty and freedom give way to pain and "binding" and death. Specifically, the written commandment "Thou shalt not" is what causes the transformation: for Blake, the law precedes the sin—in fact, creates the sin, as there is no sin without the law—not the other way around. Jarmusch emphasizes this point in the trading post, where, as mentioned earlier, writing is equated with sin, deception, and death, and the fact that the priest has tobacco for the white man but not for the Indian also reflects the way that religion (what worship becomes once it is written down) distorts God's love, which should be freely available to all. Once the concept of sin is introduced by the "Priests in black gowns" (like those who operate trading posts and deal in infected blankets), love is corrupted. No longer a liberating joy, sexual desire binds (not unlike Thel's corset), punishes, and enslaves the soul; this is why the rose is sick. As Blake explains in "Earth's Answer" from *Songs of Experience*: when the voice of the Bard calls on the Earth to rise out of darkness and be reborn, the Earth replies that she can't, as love, which was once "free,"[25] has now become its own opposite: "cruel, jealous, selfish fear."[26]

This perversion of love—cruelty, jealousy, and selfishness can be seen as corrupted forms of love; in fact, St. Augustine defined all sin as a perversion of love—is evident in the next scene, when Thel's ex-boyfriend Charlie surprises her and Depp's character in bed. He has brought her a present, clearly expecting a reunion, but his anticipation turns to sadness and then jealousy as he realizes what has happened. Charlie's love, which is quickly transformed into a type of possessiveness that will not allow Thel to belong to anyone but him, becomes a source, not of delight, but pain. As Blake writes elsewhere, "He who binds to himself a joy / Does the winged life destroy."[27] Like the "invisible worm" of "The Sick Rose," he has found out Thel's "bed of crimson joy," and it results in their mutual destruction. Similarly, even though she obviously still has feelings for him, Thel twists her love for Charlie into something more like hate; rather than allow him to leave, she can't resist the line "I never really loved you anyway," which is calculated to inflict maximum emotional damage. As Blake writes in "The Clod & the Pebble," this is the type of love that

. . . seeketh only Self to please,
To bind another to its delight,
Joys in another's loss of ease,

And builds a hell in heaven's despite.[28]

Sadly, Charlie's response—shooting her through the heart—seems inevitable in this situation; in Blake's fallen world, love is so corrupted that it leads inexorably to death.

What happens next, though, further extends and complicates the Blakean message, underscoring the real significance of this scene. After Charlie kills Thel, Blake returns fire with Thel's revolver, eventually hitting Charlie in the throat. He then gathers his clothes and climbs out of Thel's second-story window, knocking the paper flowers off the windowsill as he falls into the street, taking Thel's place in the mud surrounded by soiled flowers. By beginning and ending this episode with this image of flowers in the mud—the sick rose—Jarmusch presents the corruption of love through a Blakean lens—whether expressed through desire, regret, jealousy, or hate—as the true sign of the fallen world. However, just as the meaning of "I don't smoke" changes throughout the film, the repetition of this image reveals a new level of significance. Unlike Blake's Thel, who never moves beyond a state of innocence, Jarmusch's Thel, having fallen from innocence into experience, is able finally to transcend the opposition between the two states, at least partially, as her last act is one of self-sacrifice in throwing her body in front of Depp's character in order to protect him before Charlie fires. In freely giving her life for another, she embodies Blake's other type of love in "The Clod & the Pebble":

> Love seeketh not Itself to please,
> Nor for itself hath any care;
> But for another gives its ease,
> And builds a Heaven in Hell's despair.[29]

By reconciling the light of love and its dark doubles of sexual sin and cruelty—the sacrificial clod and the selfish pebble—Thel fulfills several functions. For one thing, like the fireman, she serves as a way for Jarmusch to embody the idea of transcendence through a Blakean reconciliation of opposites, a motif that plays out in numerous ways throughout the film. More importantly, she initiates Depp's character into the world of experience, here exemplified by sex and death. When he falls from her second-floor window into the muddy street, he is replicating her earlier fall, both literally and symbolically. While this tumble provides a bit of comic relief, serving both to break the tension of the scene and remind us that our hero is a tenderfoot badly equipped for the role of gunfighter, by having a meteor flash across the sky as he does so, Jarmusch is actually punctuating the scene with a final reference to Blake the poet.

In "The Tyger," from *Songs of Experience*, Blake addresses the problem of evil in the world by creating a counterpart to "The Lamb" of *Songs of Innocence*. If the lamb represents the God of love and mercy, the tiger is the

God of wrath. In a series of questions that have no answers, Blake asks "what hand or eye" could have "framed" the tiger's "fearful symmetry":[30]

> What the hammer? what the chain?
> In what furnace was thy brain?
> What the anvil? what dread grasp
> Dare its deadly terrors clasp?
> When the stars threw down their spears,
> And watered heaven with their tears,
> Did he smile his work to see?
> Did he who made the Lamb make thee?[31]

In the reference to chains and furnaces, Blake is connecting the Industrial Revolution to the fall from the garden—to sin and death—a critique of civilization that Jarmusch reflects in Dickinson Metal Works, which manufactures the chains that hang in the priest's trading post and bind everyone in the modern world. The next stanza contains an even more pointed question, though. Blake invokes the fall of the rebellious angels and demands to know if God approved; after all, if He is omnipotent, He could have easily forestalled Satan's challenge to His throne and prevented the advent of sin and death. In challenging God in this way, Blake aligns himself with the figures of Icarus, Prometheus, and Satan in the poem—all of whom fell from heaven in one way or another—to emphasize that he expects to be damned as well for blasphemy. But Blake embraces the sin, accepting the medieval concept of the felix culpa, the fortunate fall, which states that original sin is good because it paved the way for Christ to redeem the world. Depp's character's fall from Thel's window, then, is of this sort: the meteor is "the stars throwing down their spears" and a sign that the fall is fortunate—precisely because he can now "die" from his wound and begin his journey to death in order to transcend it.

Of course, Blake cannot see his fall as fortunate at this point; after all, he is still wearing his glasses—the symbol of the rationality he needs to read the written word but not to experience the more direct revelation that occurs after Nobody steals them from him. In other words, he can still only see the paper flower and not smell its perfume, which in this film is that of tobacco smoke. In this scene, as in the earlier scene with the fireman, Jarmusch alludes to Blake's poetry both directly and indirectly in order to introduce a series of ideas that will resonate throughout the film. Blake is concerned with a few major concepts—innocence and experience, opposition and unity, freedom and bondage—and treats them over and over again, both in the relatively simple lyrics in *Songs of Innocence and of Experience* and the more complex allegories such as *The Four Zoas*. However, rather than merely repeating the same ideas in different words, with each new iteration Blake reveals deeper connections and complexities between and among the figures of his spiritual and political landscape, triggering a series of associations that both generate and replicate the process of understanding. In *Dead Man*, Jarmusch follows much the same course, providing the key for decoding at least one aspect of his multivalent text but resisting being limited by it. Ultimately, rather than an adaptation of Blake's poetry, the film represents a synthesis of the very different media of poetry and film into a form that transcends what either can do individually. In this way, Jarmusch reconciles two contraries, creating new possibilities for approaching Blake's poetry as well.

NOTES

1. Troy Thomas, "William Blake and *Dead Man*," *Adaptation* 5, no. 1 (2012): 60.
2. Thomas, "William Blake and *Dead Man*," 61.
3. William Blake, "The Argument" to *The Marriage of Heaven and Hell*, in *The Complete Poetry and Prose of William Blake*, ed. David V. Erdman (New York: Anchor, 1988), 34. All subsequent references to Blake's poetry are from this edition.
4. *Dead Man*, directed by Jim Jarmusch (Miramax, 1995), DVD. All quotations from the film are from this DVD.
5. Blake, "Auguries of Innocence," 490.
6. Blake, "The Chimney Sweeper," 22.
7. Blake, "The Little Black Boy," 9.
8. Blake, "Introduction" to *Songs of Experience*, 18.
9. Sigmund Freud, "The Uncanny," in *The Norton Anthology of Theory and Criticism*, ed. Vincent B. Leitch (New York: Norton, 2001), 933.
10. Freud, "Uncanny," 934.
11. Freud, "Uncanny," 940.
12. Freud, "Uncanny," 940.
13. Freud, "Uncanny," 940.
14. Freud, "Uncanny," 947.
15. All this is in addition to Sally Jencko's version of the "Three Little Bears," in which the bears kill Goldilocks, scalp her, and make a sweater out of her hair.
16. Freud, "Uncanny," 941–42.
17. Blake, "Introduction" to *Songs of Innocence*, 7.
18. Blake, "The Everlasting Gospel," 524.
19. Blake, "The Everlasting Gospel," 524.
20. Ferdinand de Saussure, "From *Course in General Linguistics*," in *The Norton Anthology of Theory and Criticism*, ed. Vincent B. Leitch (New York: Norton, 2001), 963–65.
21. Blake, "The Book of Thel," 5.
22. Blake, *Songs of Innocence and of Experience*, 7.
23. Blake, "The Sick Rose," 23.
24. Blake, "The Garden of Love," 26.
25. Blake, "Earth's Answer," 19.
26. Blake, "Earth's Answer," 18.
27. Blake, "Eternity," 470.
28. Blake, "The Clod & the Pebble," 19.
29. Blake, "The Clod & the Pebble," 19.
30. Blake, "The Tyger," 24.
31. Blake, "The Tyger," 25.

Chapter Eight

Into the Woods

William Shakespeare's A Midsummer Night's Dream
and Peter Weir's Dead Poets Society

Nichole DeWall

In his analysis of Peter Weir's *Picnic at Hanging Rock* (1975) and *Dead Poets Society* (1989), film scholar Jonathan Rayner stresses the importance of attending to the visual and literary allusions in both films: "The sources quoted in [*Dead Poets Society*] from Whitman and Thoreau to Tennyson and Shakespeare," Rayner writes, "require as close an analysis as the references to the visual arts in *Picnic*, and the poems included elucidate the undertones of *Dead Poets* just as allusions in *Picnic* extend the film's debate on individual and national determination."[1] Rayner's analysis of the literary allusions in *Dead Poets Society* is important, particularly the connections that he makes between the film, Thoreau's *Walden*, and Whitman's *Leaves of Grass*. Shakespeare's play, however, is largely beyond the scope of Rayner's discussion, and the passing (and sometimes parenthetical) references that he makes to the play only begin a conversation about the ways that *A Midsummer Night's Dream* informs the thematic and formal concerns of the film.

Shakespeare's pastoral comedy, in fact, forms a subtext throughout *Dead Poets Society* that extends far beyond the brief staged scenes that appear in the film. The film's themes of transformation, destruction, and renewal are also found in *A Midsummer Night's Dream*. Like Theseus's Athens in the play, Welton Academy's commitment to the civilizing properties of order and tradition is seen as ultimately misguided. In the woods, characters in both the play and film experience the dreamlike intoxication of poetry and the cruel chaos that can occur when the imagination is unleashed. The Puck-like Mr. Keating (Robin Williams) disrupts the worlds of the unsuspecting adolescents. The film, however, offers a more realistic and complicated depiction than the play of what happens when these characters wake up to reality, and brings into relief the generic distinctions between comedy and tragedy. As this chapter demonstrates, not only is *A Midsummer Night's Dream* integral to our understanding of Weir's film, *Dead Poets Society* should be included in any scholarly consideration of the history of Shakespeare on film.

Dead Poets Society traces the stories of seven boys at Welton Academy, a prestigious Vermont preparatory school. The boys' existence at Welton is dictated by the school's strict and traditional curriculum. When brand-new faculty member, Mr. John Keating, uses British and American poetry to inspire the boys to "seize the day" and follow their dreams, each boy goes on a journey of transformation and self-definition. Mr. Keating also encourages the boys to revive the Dead Poets Society, a secret poetry organization that he formed when he himself was a Welton student. Most transformed by Mr. Keating's methods is transfer student (and younger brother of Welton Academy's most recent valedictorian) Todd Anderson (Ethan Hawke), whose shyness and fear of public speaking paralyze him both inside and outside of the classroom. The other boys rebel in their own ways, too: Charlie Dalton (Gale Hansen), for example, adopts the name "Nuwanda," seduces women, and publishes an unauthorized editorial in the school newspaper; Knox Overstreet (Josh Charles) pursues Chris Noel, the girlfriend of the star football player at the local public school; Neil Perry (Robert Sean Leonard), a senior honors student, plays Puck in an off-campus production of *A Midsummer Night's Dream* without obtaining the permission of his domineering and controlling father. After his father discovers his transgression and forbids him from acting, Neil commits suicide. The school blames Mr. Keating for Neil's death, and he is forced to leave Welton and teaching forever.

Although the poetry of American writers like Walt Whitman enjoys the most on-screen treatment, *A Midsummer Night's Dream* appears frequently throughout the film. Neil is seen often coming to and from rehearsals with his script in his hand. Early in the film, we observe a rehearsal from Neil's perspective in which the actors who play Lysander and Hermia block a scene from the first act of *A Midsummer Night's Dream*. Many of the boys' story lines build up to an extended play-within-the-film sequence that falls toward the end of *Dead Poets Society*. It is opening night, and the boys accompany Mr. Keating to Neil's performance at Welton's local sister school. Knox's story line is resolved this night when Chris Noel agrees to accompany him to the play. During the production, Neil recites the "merry wanderer of the night" speech in which Puck describes the practical jokes that have earned him a reputation as a "shrewd and knavish sprite" (2.1.43, 33).[2] In the next shot, Neil looks on from the wings as Lysander and Hermia discuss sleeping arrangements in the forest. Back onstage, Neil's Puck sprinkles dew over

Titania and Bottom. The final lines from *A Midsummer Night's Dream* that appear in the film are also the final lines of the play: Neil stands alone onstage and delivers Puck's "If we shadows have offended" epilogue (5.1.418) to his father who stands menacingly in the back of the auditorium.

A Midsummer Night's Dream was an even more pervasive presence in Tom Schulman's original screenplay.[3] One scene not included in the final shooting script describes Neil in an early rehearsal as his Puck plays tricks on the lovers in the forest. During this rehearsal, Neil holds a jester's stick that he frequently carries around the campus at Welton. Todd and Neil spend a good deal of time in the original screenplay rehearsing Neil's lines, and Neil even attempts to recruit Todd to work behind the scenes on the production. During the final play-within-the-film sequence, Todd mouths Puck's lines as Neil speaks them from the stage. In addition, Charlie's original story line revolves around the female student who plays Hermia in the play, Ginny Danburry. Ginny is the younger sister of Chet Danburry, and when Charlie attends *A Midsummer Night's Dream* at Henley Hall, he instantly falls in love with Ginny and "sits absolutely enraptured by her" for the rest of the performance.

It is clear, then, that *A Midsummer Night's Dream* informed Schulman's writing process and vision for the film, despite the fact that a substantial amount of the play's on-screen time was eliminated in the final cut. The structure of the film parallels the structure of Shakespeare's pastoral comedy, particularly in its juxtaposition of an orderly, civilized setting and a natural, potentially terrifying one. Both Shakespeare and Weir use the exposition phases of their works to establish Athens and Welton as spaces of order, reason, and tradition. In Shakespeare's Athens, the ancient seat of Western reason and civilization, Theseus has just returned in triumph with his reluctant bride, Hippolyta. Theseus is the mythical character associated perhaps most closely with reason and order. Hippolyta, queen of the all-female Amazonian warriors, has been conquered by Theseus's masculine, phallic power: he has "woo'd [her] with [his] sword, / And won [her] love, doing [her] injuries" (1.1.16–17). In four days' time, he will use the ultimate mechanism of civilization to domesticate the savage Hippolyta: heterosexual marriage. When Egeus, the conventional *senex iratus* of ancient Greek comedy, storms into the scene "full of vexation" (1.1.22) and invokes the "ancient privilege" (1.1.41) of Athens to marry off his young daughter Hermia to his choice of suitor, Theseus complies immediately. In this scene, Theseus is unwavering in the face of the lovers' protests: "To you your father should be as a god," he says to the distraught Hermia. Theseus's harshness in this scene triggers the lovers' flight into the Athenian woods, a green space where the "sharp Athenian law / Cannot pursue [them]" (1.1.161–62).

Like Shakespeare, Weir takes pains to establish his "Athens," Welton Academy, as a space that values tradition, order, and the gradual and deliber-

ate passage of time. The film begins during preparations for the opening
convocation of the new school year. It is 1959 and, as headmaster Mr.
Nolan (Norman Lloyd) makes clear during his opening remarks, this convocation
ritual has been going on for one hundred years. These are not the boisterous,
exhilarating, behind-the-scenes shots that we experience later when the curtain closes on Neil's *A Midsummer Night's Dream*. Rather, the preparations
here are predictable, even tedious. The camera hovers over a mural that
depicts cherubic young men who look up to an allegorical figure of liberty.
The link between the past and the present is made when the camera slowly
pans down to a young boy who is being fussed over by his mother; she
tightens her young son's tie as though symbolically initiating him into the
strictures of Welton Academy. Clearly, this is a rite of passage for this new
initiate, and one that his older brother has been through before him; the
brothers quickly pose for a picture in a two-shot. An elderly alum who will
pass the "light of knowledge" from his candle to the younger generation of
students receives instructions. An oil painting of a distinguished gentle-
man—perhaps a past academy president or founder—supervises the preparations from the wall above them.

For the older male students at the academy, this convocation ritual is
familiar. The senior students who have been selected to carry Welton's ban-
ners chat idly, presumably catching up with one another after their summer
break. These boys have clearly done this before. One older student opens the
case to his bagpipe with ease and begins to assemble his instrument knowingly. The boys' dress indicates a strict hierarchy: with the exception of the
bagpiper who wears a traditional Scottish Balmoral bonnet, the older boys
have earned the right to go without head coverings. In contrast, the younger
boy wears a beanie; his slightly older brother wears a straw boater hat. The
link between past and present that has been made visually by Weir is reinforced textually when Mr. Nolan asks the older boys to stand and answer the
"same question" that was asked "one hundred years ago": "What are the four
pillars?" The older boys stand at attention and answer, "Tradition, Honor,
Discipline, and Excellence." The camera cuts to the face of a bewildered
young member of the incoming class who looks around as if confused. The
viewer assumes that it is only a matter of time until this young boy becomes
fully incorporated into this rule-bound and orderly world.

Weir continues to develop Welton as a space of order and tradition beyond this opening convocation sequence. Most notable is his repeated use of
the schoolmaster's desk as a symbol of power and tradition throughout the
film. During a montage of classroom scenes on the boys' first day of classes,
for example, the large and imposing desk is visible in nearly every shot. The
desks in these scenes are extensions of the teachers' control over their students. Even in non-classroom spaces at Welton, the desk is used as a symbol
of authority: during study hall, for example, Latin teacher Mr. McAllister

barks orders from behind his desk and the boys immediately fall into line. In contrast, the desk is conspicuously absent or unattended in interior spaces in which Welton's students enjoy more freedom. There is no desk in the student lounge, for example, where the boys dress more casually and attempt to listen to forbidden rock 'n' roll music.

The boys seem to recognize the desk as a symbol of power, as well. For example, when Neil forges a letter from his father that will allow him to participate in *A Midsummer Night's Dream*, he types the letter at the desk in his dorm room as if imitating his father's authority. Returning from rehearsal one night, Neil notices Todd sitting forlornly in Welton's courtyard. Todd's parents have sent him the same desk set for his birthday that they sent him last year. Neil's participation in the play has emboldened him, and he encourages Todd to hurl the desk set off the rooftop and into the night sky. Neil does this to comfort Todd, but as the desk set falls in pieces to the ground, it also marks Neil's continued separation from the strictures of Welton.

What marks Mr. Keating as different from the Welton Academy establishment is his spatial relationship to his classroom desk. Most often, Mr. Keating sits, stands, or leans on it—or moves it out of the way altogether. Mr. Keating only sits behind his desk once, and that is to parody teachers who use the location as a seat of power and authority. This second classroom scene begins with Mr. Keating sitting at his desk at the front of the classroom; it quickly becomes clear, however, that he is playing the part of a traditional teacher only to mock it. He asks Neil to read the preface to their textbook and the camera pans across the faces of the boys: some are engaged, some are distracted. The camera cuts back to Mr. Keating, who is clearly fidgety and uncomfortable behind the desk. He looks impishly out at the boys, whistles slowly, and rises from his desk chair to stand at the chalkboard. The class soon realizes that this was all an elaborate setup: Mr. Keating instructs the boys to rip out their textbooks' prefaces and throw them in the wastebasket. From this point on, he will only use his desk to disrupt the vertical relationship between student and teacher that is a hallmark of Welton's educational system. Later, Mr. Keating defiles the sacred space of his desk by having the boys stand on it while he looks up at them from a crouching position on the floor. The boys will mimic this exercise in the final scene of the film when in defiance of Mr. Nolan they stand on their desks in a show of support for Mr. Keating. As Peter McLaren and Zeus Leonardo write in "Deconstructing Surveillance Pedagogy: *Dead Poets Society*," "By making the familiar strange, Keating begins the rudiments of a lesson on the unnaturalness of classroom settings, that is, its hierarchical spatial organization and centralized arrangement."[4]

With Neil as their leader, the boys decide to flee from Welton and the repressive presence of desks. On the night of their first Dead Poets Society meeting, Weir includes an extended sequence that traces the boys' journey from Welton to the woods. As in *A Midsummer Night's Dream*, the woods in *Dead Poets Society* are not entirely comforting and peaceful; their wildness holds mystery, terror, and potential cruelty. Before they reach the outdoors, the boys travel through many of Welton's interior spaces that Weir uses in the opening convocation sequence. This time, however, the camera traces the boys' shadows as they glide across the mural that opens the film and the Gothic arches of the chapel's ceiling. To build suspense, Weir intercuts shots of the boys' flight with shots of residential dean Dr. Hager who, suspicious of their absence, shines a flashlight down the hallway toward the boys' vacant bedrooms. The boys whisper in hushed voices; a hooting owl is heard; the score is dissonant and haunting.

According to a published interview, the boys' journey into the woods was an especially significant part of the film for Weir. He expanded the sequence dramatically from the few lines that it occupied in Schulman's original screenplay.[5] He cloaked the sequence in fog to add to the forest's mystery: "Part of the appeal of fog is that it isolates and obscures and it's full of secrets," he says.[6] Working with his wife, production designer Wendy Stites, Weir made the boys' dark, hooded capes in this scene evoke a sense of the secret and forbidden: "It wasn't just a run to the cave. It's a very particular journey and they're wearing particular clothing, which led to the hooded coats and things. And I was trying to link it all to the secret societies that go back to meetings in caves."[7]

The boys' retreat into the woods offers them at least temporary release from Welton's oppressive and restrictive atmosphere. Poetry intoxicates and transforms them. The film encourages us to view these transformations as positive: during their exhilarating encounters with poetry in the cave, the camera closes in on the boys' faces, which glow with inspiration and awe. They become daring and bold: Knox calls Chris Noel and agrees to attend her party; Charlie publishes an inflammatory article in the school newspaper; Neil auditions for *A Midsummer Night's Dream*. Their transformations come at a price, however, and the pain of reentry into civilized society for them is disorienting, bewildering, and sometimes violent. Many of the boys are physically harmed as a result of their rebellion: Knox receives a bloody nose and death threat from Chris Noel's boyfriend Chet Danburry; Charlie receives a paddling from Mr. Nolan; and Neil, of course, ultimately kills himself with his father's revolver.

The forest in *A Midsummer Night's Dream* is a place of transformation and potential violence, as well. For many years, playgoers expected to see Shakespeare's Athenian wood portrayed as an idyllic green world where sprites and fairies engage in harmless pranks. Since William Dieterle and Max Reinhardt's dark and often terrifying 1935 filmic adaptation of the play, however, scholars and directors have recognized the more anarchic and destructive aspects of Shakespeare's text. After all, the pastoral space that greets the lovers in *A Midsummer Night's Dream* is being destroyed by a civil war between the king of the fairies, Oberon, and their queen, Titania. Oberon lays claim to a changeling boy whom Titania has taken into her care; their quarrel results in a series of disruptions in the natural world. Titania explains in her monologue at the beginning of act 2 that the rivers are flooding, the crops are rotting, the air is awash in contagious diseases, and the seasons are inverted in the forest:

> Therefore the winds, piping to us in vain,
> As in revenge, have sucked up from the sea
> Contagious fogs which, falling in the land,
> Hath every pelting river made so proud
> That they have overborne their continents.
> The ox hath therefore stretch'd his yoke in vain,
> The ploughman lost his sweat, and the green corn
> Hath rotted ere his youth attain'd a beard;
> . . . .
> Therefore the moon, the governess of floods,
> Pale in her anger, washes all the air,
> That rheumatic diseases do abound:
> And through this distemperature we see
> The seasons alter: hoary-headed frosts
> Far in the fresh lap of the crimson rose,
> And on old Hiems' thin and icy crown
> An odorous chaplet of sweet summer buds
> Is, as in mockery, set: the spring, the summer,
> The childing autumn, angry winter, change
> Their wonted liveries. (2.1.88–95, 103–113)

The conflict between patriarchy and matriarchy that is suppressed and redirected in Athens through the marriage of Theseus and Hippolyta has here been left unchecked. Because the characters who play Theseus and Hippolyta in the Athens scenes often double as Oberon and Titania in the forest scenes, the viewer is encouraged to think of these two worlds as inversions of one another.

To obtain the changeling boy, Oberon orders Puck to drop a love-in-idleness potion in Titania's eyes that will make her fall in love with whatever she spies upon waking: "Be it on lion, bear, or wolf, or bull, / On meddling monkey, or on busy ape" (2.1.180–81). Titania becomes enamored with Bottom, a weaver and aspiring actor who rehearses with his fellow rude mechanicals nearby. By this point in the play, however, Puck has transformed Bottom into a half man / half ass, so Titania actually dotes on a grotesque minotaur. In many productions, Titania's passionate (and sometimes sexual) relationship with Bottom is exploited for comic effect. However, their relationship is also cruel and humiliating for Titania. Oberon recognizes his perverse treatment of her and even begins to take pity on her; he releases her from the "hateful imperfection of her eyes" (4.1.62). During Titania's "imperfection," however, Oberon has stolen the changeling boy, an action that violates Titania and her relationship with the boy's deceased mother.

The lovers, too, experience the forest as something exhilarating and potentially terrifying. Lysander and Hermia, the two lovers whom Theseus forbids from marrying, flee to the forest to escape the strict and punishing laws of Athens. At first, the lovers seem to enjoy their time in this wild and uncivilized place. In a scene that appears in rehearsal in *Dead Poets Society*, Lysander playfully suggests to Hermia that they sleep in the same space: "One turf shall serve as a pillow for us both; / One heart, one bed, two bosoms, and one troth" (2.2.47–48). Hermia refuses and the couple quickly falls asleep. While asleep, Puck mistakes Lysander for Demetrius, the young Athenian suitor who has pursued Hermia into the forest. Lysander awakes and becomes enamored with Helena, the long-suffering former fiancée of Demetrius who, spaniel-like, has chased Demetrius into the forest, as well. Demetrius has also received a dose of the potion, and both suitors quickly redirect their affections toward Helena.

As a result of Puck's recklessness, the two female love-objects, Hermia and Helena, suffer extreme psychological and emotional distress in the forest. Hermia awakens from a nightmare in which a snake attempts to feast upon her heart while Lysander watches:

> Help me, Lysander, help me! Do thy best
> To pluck this crawling serpent from my breast!
> Ay me, for pity! What a dream was here!
> Lysander, look how I do quake with fear:
> Methought a serpent ate my heart away,
> And you sat smiling at his cruel prey. (2.2.151–56)

Lysander is gone, and Hermia first assumes that he is dead:

> Lysander! What, removed? Lysander! Lord!
> What, out of hearing? Gone? No sound, no word?
> Alack, where are you? Speak, an if you hear;
> Speak, of all loves! I swoon almost with fear.
> No? Then I well perceive you all not nigh.
> Either death or you I'll find immediately. (2.2.157–62)

Hermia is then subjected to Lysander's cruel dismissal of her. "Why seek'st thou me? Could not this make thee know," he asks, "The hate I bear thee made me leave thee so?" (3.2.189–90). Hermia, distraught and disoriented, has literally lost herself: "Am I not Hermia? Are not you Lysander?" (3.2.273), she asks. Helena, convinced that Lysander, Demetrius, and Hermia are playing a cruel joke at her expense, suffers greatly while in the forest, too. Helena is so distraught by the changes that transpire in the forest, in fact, that she threatens to commit suicide (3.2.244).

The anarchic power that is unleashed in the forest as a result of Puck's careless actions is ultimately short lived. The play quickly begins to move toward a comic resolution: "Jack shall have Jill; / Naught shall go ill; / The man shall have his mare again, and all shall be well," Puck promises us (3.2.461–63). The cruelty of the forest, the text assures us, was only a bad dream. Oberon orders Puck to reverse the effects of the love-in-idleness potion: "When they next wake," he says, "all this derision / Shall seem a dream and fruitless vision" (3.2.370–71). Titania's affair with Bottom, too, will seem "the fierce vexation of a dream" (4.1.68). Act 4 begins with a series of awakenings from the lovers, Titania, and Bottom. They all express confusion: "Are you sure / That we are awake?," Demetrius asks, "It seems to me / That yet we sleep, we dream" (4.2.191–93). The waking world feels "small and undistinguishable" to them, and "everything seems double" (4.2.186, 189). Ultimately, however, the lovers and rude mechanicals are able to reenter Athenian society without much discomfort. The play ends with a triple royal wedding. The fairies bless the Athenians' marriage beds, and Puck asks for pardon from the audience in his final epilogue.

The primary difference between the play and the film, of course, is that the reentry into Welton Academy is not so simple for these boys. Their time in the forest changes them, and there are no fairies to convince them that it was all a dream. In some ways, Neil's suicide scene acknowledges the difference between the play and film, between comedy and tragedy. After his performance in *A Midsummer Night's Dream*, Neil's father forces him into his car and takes him to their family home. During the combative conversation with his father that follows, Neil clutches the crown of twigs and berries that he wore as Puck. After his parents have gone to sleep, Neil brings the crown into his bedroom. He runs his fingers slowly across it, lingering slightly over the smooth, red berries. He strips to the waist, opens the windows, and exposes his naked torso to the frigid night air. He places the crown on his head, and slowly lowers his chin toward his chest as if taking one final bow. When he leaves his bedroom to find his father's gun, he leaves Puck's crown behind. It is not a comedy that Neil lives in; it is not a dream. His waking reality proves too terrible for him to bear. He takes a revolver from a drawer in his father's desk, and chooses a tragic ending.

In addition to the ways in which *A Midsummer Night's Dream* seems to inform the structural and thematic elements of *Dead Poets Society*, the play also influences the development of certain characters in the film. Importantly, of all the play's characters, Neil plays the shape-shifting, disruptive, and often reckless Puck. The film goes to great lengths to establish a symmetry between Mr. Keating and Neil, at times condensing Mr. Keating, Neil, and Puck in very intentional and important ways. When we attend to this Mr. Keating/Neil/Puck compression, we begin to view Mr. Keating's pattern of disruption at Welton as an extension of the many and often reckless disruptions that Puck causes in the play.

Certainly, Mr. Keating shares more in common with the students at Welton than he does with his colleagues. As Mr. Nolan announces during the opening convocation, Keating is a graduate of Welton Academy, a fact that Mr. Keating himself reiterates during their first class session. Neil digs up an old school annual from Mr. Keating's senior year as visual proof that the teacher was once just like they were. Mr. Keating is younger than the other teachers, and closer in age to the boys. During one of their first classroom scenes together, Mr. Keating uses the word "excrement" to describe their textbook's introduction, which is the same word that the boys use to parody one of the four pillars of Welton Academy, Excellence. Throughout the film, Mr. Keating sides with the boys during run-ins with Welton authorities. For example, during an early scene in which Mr. Keating asks students to rip out the introductions to their poetry books, Latin teacher Mr. McAllister bursts into the room to control the chaos. Mr. Keating emerges from the anteroom and, much to their surprise, defends the students. The one time that Mr. Keating sides with the administration is after Charlie's prank; the boys feel somewhat betrayed by Mr. Keating's gentle correction.

There are significant parallels between Mr. Keating and Neil: both were editors of the student annual; both are leaders of the Dead Poets Society. Both are persistent in their attempts to cure Todd of his shyness. Weir reinforces the symbolic coupling of Neil and Mr. Keating in the spatial composition of an early outdoor scene set on the campus of Welton Academy. The boys, led by Neil, pursue Mr. Keating as he walks across the campus toward the lake. It is Neil who addresses Mr. Keating as "captain" for the first time in this scene, and inquires about the mysterious Dead Poets Society that is listed next to Mr. Keating's picture in the annual. As Keating peruses the annual, he turns away from the boys and squats down in the grass. The camera peers over his left shoulder as if to mimic Neil's gaze; Neil soon squats down in the same position as Mr. Keating. A close-up of Neil follows, and in a series of reaction shots between Neil and Mr. Keating, it seems as if the two are having a private conversation despite the fact that the group of boys surrounds them. Other boys slowly squat down and occupy the same spatial plane as Mr. Keating and Neil, but it is Neil who remains in a crouched position after the rest of the boys stand back up. Neil repeats the phrase "Dead Poets Society" in an awed, hushed voice. The camera dwells on Neil's face. School bells summon the other boys back to class, but when Neil rises, he assumes the role that Mr. Keating must have assumed nearly two decades earlier. Neil arranges the first meeting of the Dead Poets Society, and even makes special accommodations for Todd Anderson to participate despite his fear of public speaking.

Later that night, Neil returns to his dorm room to find that Keating has placed a weathered volume of poetry on his desk—the same volume that Keating himself used to lead meetings of the Dead Poets Society. The book is an invitation from Keating, a bond forged across space and time. A smile of recognition spreads across Neil's lips. The coupling of Mr. Keating and Neil progresses throughout the film and culminates in a scene after Neil's death has been announced. Mr. Keating, clearly upset by Neil's suicide, sinks down into Neil's desk and weeps. Keating's copy of the book of poetry is in Neil's desk. The teacher has become one with his student.

The coupling of teacher and student throughout the film allows us to view the spirit of Mr. Keating's disruption as essentially Puck-like. Like Puck in *A Midsummer Night's Dream*, Mr. Keating knowingly or unknowingly disrupts the boys' worlds in ways that cannot be entirely and easily resolved. Most disruptive is how Mr. Keating changes the boys' attitudes toward the passage of time. Before the boys meet Mr. Keating, time feels predictable and gradual. Like their parents, they will be "future doctors" and "future lawyers." The boys conduct "business as usual" by setting up study groups at designated times. On the first day of classes, Weir uses a montage of static and stultifying classroom scenes in which time is quantified by the teachers. Their chemistry teacher describes an assignment that will be due "every five weeks"; their first set of questions is due the next day. Throughout the film, authority figures give them warnings to stay within the confines of prescribed time: "You boys there, hurry up" and "All right gentlemen, five minutes."

That obedience to time will be an important part of transfer student Todd's initiation into the order and ritual of Welton Academy is established in a series of shots early in the film. In the first shot, Todd, having just arrived at the dorms, nervously sits and sets his alarm clock. He glances at his wristwatch as the sound of the academy's clock tower begins to chime. The camera moves outdoors and slowly pans upward toward the clock tower. The face of the clock reads five o'clock, and the next four shots show flocks of geese flying across fallow autumn fields and into the sky as Welton's clock tower continues to chime. It is as though the rhythms and seasonal movements of the natural world are regulated by Welton's clock, too.

Like the desk, clocks and watches are often visual symbols of authority throughout the film: Mr. Perry (Kurtwood Smith), for example, glances impatiently at his wristwatch while Neil performs onstage, and sleeps with one next to his bed. A grandfather clock hangs on the wall next to the stairs to Mr. Nolan's office, its pendulum rhythmically and predictably marking the passage of time. The clock tower chimes predictably throughout the film, and often looms over the boys like a stern parent.

The boys' initial encounter with Mr. Keating serves to fundamentally change the boys' relationship to and conception of time. During their first class session together, Mr. Keating leads the boys out of the classroom and into Welton's trophy room. The room is lined with photographs of former Welton students. Mr. Keating asks a student to recite Robert Herrick's seventeenth-century British poem, "To the Virgins, to Make Much of Time," a poem that characterizes time as fleeting and precious. The camera's point of view in this scene is largely from the perspective of the dead boys who look out from their photographs (Knox will later call the entire experience "spooky"). The boys in the photographs, Mr. Keating tells them, are now "food for worms." The boys are clearly uncomfortable with this new concept of time. Knox looks around nervously; Neil draws his book toward his chest and crosses his arms. As the boys lean in toward the glass cases, Mr. Keating walks behind them, Puck-like. The camera slowly pans across the faces of the living boys from the dead boys' perspectives and then makes a similar movement across the faces of the dead boys. The pictures and portraits of the past that had been comforting symbols of tradition and legacy are here used as memento mori.

Following their first meeting with Mr. Keating, the boys struggle to continue to see time as orderly and gradual. Time is no longer infinite; they must "seize the day." From this point in the film, Weir juxtaposes conflicting images of time in ways that represent the boys' internal struggles. For example, during an early dorm-room scene, Todd sits at his desk, flanked by a watch on his left and a desk clock on his right. The watch's rhythmic and persistent ticking is heard clearly. While flanked by these two timepieces, Todd opens his notebook and scribbles the words "CARPE DIEM" across a blank page. Weir's mise-en-scène in this shot emphasizes the fact that Todd is literally and metaphorically trapped between Welton's traditional conception of time and Mr. Keating's view of time as transitory. At this point in the film, Welton still holds more sway over Todd, and he ceremoniously tears out the page, crumples it up, and discards it.

In the end, Neil's suicide is motivated in part by Mr. Keating's disruptive notion of time. In his final confrontation with his father, Mr. Perry informs his son that he will be withdrawn from Welton the next morning. Neil will be enrolled in military school: "You're going to Harvard and you're gonna be a doctor," his father tells him. Neil, dismayed, protests, "But that's ten more years. Father, that's a lifetime!" Because Neil now views time with a sense of urgency, he is no longer willing to waste it in order to fulfill his father's dream for him.

Although the film applauds Mr. Keating's attempts to disrupt these boys' mundane and routine lives, the viewer is left to wonder whether or not Mr. Keating is too reckless in his efforts. Like Puck, Mr. Keating's anarchic and playful spirit inspires and confuses; like Puck, Mr. Keating transforms these boys in ways that they never could have imagined. In *A Midsummer Night's Dream*, however, Puck is able to quickly reverse the effects of his disruptions with a magic potion. In the world of Welton Academy, the consequences of Mr. Keating's Puck-like interventions are very real and very permanent. Viewing *Dead Poets Society* in concert with *A Midsummer Night's Dream* provides the viewer with a more complicated picture of the irreverent and deified Mr. Keating. Ultimately, Mr. Keating cannot "restore amends" or "mend" the offenses that he has committed.

NOTES

1. Jonathan Rayner, *The Films of Peter Weir*, 3rd ed. (New York: Continuum, 2003), 195.

2. All references to Shakespeare's *A Midsummer Night's Dream* are taken from *The Complete Works of Shakespeare*, 4th ed., ed. David Bevington (Boston: Addison-Wesley, 1997).

3. An earlier draft of Schulman's script (dated September 29, 1988) is available at http://www10.pair.com/crazydv/weir/dps/earlydraft.

4. Peter McLaren and Zeus Leonardo, "Deconstructing Surveillance Pedagogy: *Dead Poets Society*," *Studies in the Literary Imagination* 31, no. 1 (1998).

5. Peter Weir, "Close-Up," in *From Script to Screen: The Collaborative Art of Filmmaking*, ed. Linda Seger and Edward Jay Whetmore (New York: Henry Holt, 1994), 143.

6. Weir, "Close-Up," 143.

7. Weir, "Close-Up," 143.

Chapter Nine

"Whither Is Fled the Visionary Gleam?"

Wordsworth and Consumption in
Splendor in the Grass

Marlisa Santos

Elia Kazan's 1961 *Splendor in the Grass* featured the following tagline: "There is a miracle in being young . . . and a fear." This fairly restrained encapsulation—especially given what some critics have interpreted as the film's overwrought excesses—speaks to the confluence of opposites that permeates both the film and its titular poetic reference, a poem that is so integral to its central theme: William Wordsworth's "Ode: Intimations of Immortality." Wordsworth's 1805 ode muses upon the incongruities between the individual's perceptions and progresses from youth toward decay—the loss of the "miracle" of seeing the world through youthful eyes still glazed by divine light and the "fear" of never being able to recapture the glory of that idealism. Wordsworth's speaker laments, "The things which I have seen I now can see no more" (9).[1] The characters in *Splendor in the Grass* pass through these same stages of loss and lack of fulfillment. The sustenance longed for in Wordsworth's poem is long past in the film's world of late-1920s Kansas, and indeed, in the early-1960s world in which the film was released. Through his depictions of the spiraling decline of both the young and mature characters, Kazan weaves subtle metaphors of consumption and deprivation, of base and elevated need, ultimately revealing a starvation of meaning from which it is impossible to escape.

Wordsworth's ode vacillates between exuberant celebration of the innocent past and reluctant celebration of the mature present. This vacillation is woven through the entire text of Kazan's film, as even in scenes that glorify the prosperity (and prospect of an even more prosperous future), there is a shadow that hangs over the experiences of the characters—perhaps a historical acknowledgment of the imminent stock market crash, but more to the point, a sense of doom that such prosperity cannot go on forever. The Stamper oil fortune that has propelled the southeast Kansas town into sudden affluence is still observed with a certain watchfulness. For the Loomis family, this involves monitoring the stock, wondering when and if to sell to maximize their profit. In nearly every scene involving Mr. and Mrs. Loomis, there is some mention of either the stock price or the ramifications of selling or not selling at a particular time. They are holding out because the value of the stock is anticipated to grow, as if there is no limit to the height it might expand. They take advice from friends and social associates, like members of the Elks Club, or the newspaper pundits, to justify their day-to-day gamble, and there appears to be a calculated thrill to this, for the prospect of perhaps unlimited wealth. The viewer knows that the crash will occur, however, and as the young romance of Deanie Loomis (Natalie Wood) and Bud Stamper (Warren Beatty) plays out on the screen, the same dark cloud of imminent threat falls over their relationship as well, in all its youthful enthusiasm.

Similar to this zeal of monetary consumption, the desire between Deanie and Bud is almost hysterically intense. The film opens with their passionate embraces in Bud's car at the edge of the water plant, with the pounding waterfalls as backdrop, echoing Wordsworth's exclamation: "The cataracts blow their trumpets from the steep; / No more shall grief of mind the season wrong" (26–27). With similar abandon, Deanie and Bud hunger for each other, but a darkness looms that threatens to separate them, that of the restrictions of 1920s sexual mores, which dictate that "no nice girl" has those kinds of feelings for a man, as articulated by Deanie's mother, Mrs. Loomis (Audrey Christie). The dynamic of Deanie and Bud's relationship is an agonizing push-pull tension, fraught with ambivalence and the fear of desire's death. This ambivalence is at the core of Wordsworth's ode, the memory of the "freshness of a dream" (5) constantly being threatened by the "thought of grief" (22) brought on by the "philosophic mind" (187), the conceptions of the gravity of adult life. The desire that Deanie and Bud have for one another is continually whetted by imposed restraint. For instance, following this opening scene and Bud frustratingly telling Deanie that he'd better take her home, that she'd "had enough kissing for tonight," he then pulls her toward him and kisses her passionately, almost seeming to devour her. A breathless Deanie retreats inside her house, her bloom only to be shrunken by her mother's questioning. Deanie shows herself to be a sensual being, listening to the imaginary ocean in a conch shell, and writhing facedown on the couch and her bed, while her mother urges her to "drink her milk," as she eats a sandwich and prattles on about the rising price of the Stamper stock. However, Mrs. Loomis says, they won't sell the stock yet, because "everyone says the price will go up." The fantasy about future value based on current worth corresponds to Deanie and Bud's relationship; if Deanie will continue to be a "good" girl—that is, not capitalize on her current value, but wait for it to rise in Bud's esteem to the point that she can "sell" and become his wife—then she will reap maximum dividends. But if she fails to toe this delicate balance, she will be worthless, the other of the "two kinds" of girls that Bud's father describes.

The parallel scene at the Stamper household following Bud and Deanie's date also speaks to issues of value and consumption, as Bud arrives home and enters the kitchen to see his father, played by Pat Hingle, and his hired hands boisterously celebrating the success of a new well with venison and home-brewed beer. Here, the use of food and drink also ties directly to the promise of more financial success, though in a more extreme way than the modest sandwich and milk at the Loomis household. This celebration ushers in an important conversation between Bud and his father, in which the limping and drunk Mr. Stamper tells Bud in no uncertain terms that he has "pinned all [his] hopes" on Bud, and when his company merges with "one of those big Eastern companies," he is going to "put [Bud] in there," his way of "linin' up a future" for his son. Bud's father is inarticulate and earthy and ambitious; he and Bud have to punch each other first before they can talk, he robustly enjoys food, drink, and women (except his wife), and is like a bulldozer in pursuit of advancing his oil holdings. Ace Stamper says that he would erect a rig on his front lawn if he knew it would yield oil. Therefore, the prices he has paid for his ambitions and appetites—his damaged leg and the alienation of his wife and children, for instance—are acceptable casualties to achieve the greater aims of security and prosperity. His lack of consciousness exposes the potential empty and base nature of the accumulation of wealth; his refusal to accept Bud's viewpoint on his own future reveals how little the value of such wealth is when the cost is the viability of human relationships. Bud's pathetic attempt in a later scene to explain to his father his desire to forgo Yale and instead attend "a good agricultural college" and marry Deanie recalls the musings of Wordsworth's "Child among his new-born blisses" (86). Bud is metaphorically a "six years' Darling" (87) in his naïve imaginings that he will be free to pursue his dreams: "See, at his feet, some little plan or chart, / Some fragment from his dream of human life, / Shaped by himself with a newly-learned art" (91–93). Though "this hath now his heart, / And unto this he frames his song" (96–97), his father's rebuff propels him into the hollow value of Wordsworth's maturity. Bud will "fit his tongue / To dialogues of business, love, or strife" (98–99) as he acquiesces to his father's plan for him to attend Yale, marry Deanie later, and assume a position of responsibility in his father's business conglomeration.

Though Deanie's family is "poor" because Del Loomis is less "ambitious," according to Ace Stamper, than himself, they are both in the energy business, in a sense. Mr. Loomis owns a grocery store, and his vocation provides the town's citizens with foodstuffs that fulfill a basic need, though not as lucrative as the Stamper oil business, in which investors have supplied their money for a piece of the oil pie. Power is a higher-order need, but in the modern world perhaps almost as necessary as food, and both fathers have a stake in an elemental livelihood. Because Mr. Loomis "only" supplies food, he is "poor"—and if he is to ascend higher, he must invest in the Stamper stock, which means the potential for unimagined riches. The vacillation between yearning and fulfillment is illustrated as Deanie and Bud seek refuge for intimacy in the Loomis house; their passionate embraces outside the house lead them inside, where the walls border the Stamper store. Between their ardent kisses and embraces, the sounds of Mr. Loomis making change for the customers and retrieving a "ten-pound sack" of goods are clearly heard. These exchanges are juxtaposed with the romantic tyranny of Bud directing his "slave" Deanie to fall at his feet, and then his wonder at her wounded sensitivity in this acquiescence. She makes it clear that she belongs to him, regardless of the cost. But though he has pressed her to give in on other occasions, when she does lie on her back, moaning his name, he cannot act. What must be assumed is his father's voice in the back of his mind warning him about the risks to his future fortune. Though much is made of the film's apparent attention to sexuality, sexual desire and repression function more clearly as effective metaphors for broader concepts of consumption and destruction. According to Kenneth Hey, "The film discusses personal identity, healthy and unhealthy influences upon that identity, and how that identity affects behavior, only one part of which is sexuality. In a society which determines human worth through ownership, tradition, sexuality, and class, neither the victims like Deanie nor the potential benefactors like Bud ever realize their potential or experience joy from fulfillment. Memories supply identity and pleasure, and tradition subsumes knowledge and feelings."[2]

Despite their financial prosperity, life in the Stamper household shows no substantive gratification. The breakfast table scene at which all family members are seen interacting illustrates the emptiness and conflict that permeate their relationships. There is opulence on the table—no shortage of food and gleaming silver bowls heaping with fruit—but the roles of food (and therefore the significance of its metaphorical indicators of fulfillment) are either grotesque or meager. Ace Stamper shovels eggs, potatoes, and biscuits into his mouth, as he holds sway over the conversation; he bellows with his mouth full his intention to keep his free-spirited daughter Ginny (Barbara Loden) close to home so that she can no longer be the cause of any embarrassment. In recounting her many failures, he complains about the "cake eater" who wanted to marry Ginny for the money, and whom he had to send away. Contrasted with this ravenous display, of not only the literal eating of food, but also of the control Stamper exerts, is the demure nibbling of toast by the craven Mrs. Stamper (Joanna Roos), who seems forced to accept the crumbs of affection left behind by her husband. Meanwhile, the rebellious Ginny pours mere coffee as her only breakfast, a symbol of the stimulation she craves. Bud grabs some fruit on the run, as his mother futilely asks him how he wants his eggs, and his father calls after him that he "can't play a football game on a breakfast like that." The eggs signify his mother's impotent love at the same time that they signify a source of power, fuel to play the game of life that Ace Stamper encourages. Bud, for the moment, rejects both of these, preferring sweet Edenic fruit, a piece of which he tosses to Deanie when he picks her up for school. Mrs. Stamper tellingly laments, "Neither of my children gets any real nourishment." Not one member of the Stamper family is free from some form of Wordsworthian-like yearning and lack of fulfillment, and their interactions with food symbolize this: Ace Stamper voraciously consumes food and drink as fuel for his insatiable ambitions and to generate the power necessary to maintain firm control over his children; Mrs. Stamper takes the meager scraps of peace where she can find them, and ineffectually longs for harmony in the family; Bud's appetite is stifled by the outsized presence of his father's influence; and Ginny's hunger for freedom manifests itself in her own self-destruction.

Ginny's rebellious nature parallels her father's drive and inevitably clashes with it as well. While her father is away from home on a business trip, she is frustrated with the fact that no one "has the key" to the home liquor cabinet but Stamper, another "ingestion" symbol of his control. During the same family dinner, to which Ginny's muscular boyfriend, Glenn (Sean Garrison), and Deanie are invited, Bud doesn't "eat a thing" and Ginny is clearly frustrated with having to stay in the house without a drink. When her mother tries to entice her to stay by telling her that "there's a lovely dessert coming," Ginny retorts, "I don't want a lovely dessert." Food, though it is beautiful and abundant, cannot be a substitute for feeling, although throughout the film, its function appears to be just that—a symbol of hollow gratification. An intoxicated Ginny later calls Glenn, who works at a gas station, her "handsome filling station attendant," telling him, "Fill me up, please— I'm empty." For Ginny, alcohol and sex replace love and affection; what she takes into her body literally in this fashion does nothing to satisfy her desires in a larger sense, and only leads to her greater debasement. According to the town gossip, "Ginny Stamper is too low for the dogs to bite . . . she had one of those awful operations performed." Ginny's abortion further represents an increased deficit, an act of hollowing that arose ironically from an act designed to create fulfillment. Further complicating Ginny's conflict is the fact that at the same time that she wants to be free of her father's sway, and provokes conflict as a means to do so, she also desires his love and acceptance. This is no more clearly seen than at the New Year's Eve party ushering in the ill-fated 1929, at which Bud and Deanie's relationship meets its demise as well. The atmosphere is one of almost hysterical abandon, as if there were some urgency to the celebration that could see its own end. The mood is akin to Wordsworth's almost desperate recollection of past delight:

> And all the earth is gay;
> Land and Sea
> Give themselves up to jollity,
> And with the heart of May
> Doth every Beast keep holiday;—
> Thou Child of Joy,
> Shout round me, let me hear thy shouts, thou happy Shepherd-boy! (29–35)

Liquor flows abundantly at the party, from oil rig fountains and dished up by Ginny from a large bathtub, and the jubilation is nearly out of control. Ginny's making a spectacle of herself is not particularly out of place, but even in this ecstatic atmosphere, when Ginny shouts to her father to look at her and impulsively tries to kiss him, he rebuffs her, pushing her away and telling her to behave herself. This rejection sets a significant chain of events in motion, beginning with Ginny's drunk wanderings, including into the men's room, in the country club, leading to her inciting the attractions of multiple men on the porch, whose collective groping and kissing of her face and neck and arms, and culminating in an apparent gang rape in the parking lot, signify a kind of desperate devouring, an abandonment to the promise of any kind of feeling, even one that ultimately destroys. And it is Bud's attempt—and failure—to stop this consumption that makes him eschew any further affection from Deanie, as he is unable to reconcile his passions with the love that he feels for her. He seems to believe that as much as he desires the sex with her, the realization of it would taint the nature of their relationship, and he cannot bear the kind of debasement that he sees in Ginny to happen to Deanie. He is evidently not confident that he would have enough respect or restraint to stem the tide of passion that he sees manifested in the violence directed toward his sister.

Life in the Loomis household is no more fulfilling than life in the Stamper household. Food similarly functions there as the presence that fails to have any rewarding effect. At Christmas, their breakfast of french toast is punctuated by Mrs. Loomis wishing Bud had more "gumption" when she sees his gift to Deanie of a watch, rather than a ring. Deanie's happiness is thus undercut by Mrs. Loomis's disappointment. The nature of the gift is significant in that it symbolizes a measure of the passage of time—just the thing that Bud and Deanie do not appear to have—as opposed to the ring's symbolism of a closed circle, of eternity. And Mr. Loomis's contribution to the conversation is only to tell Deanie to "always drink plenty of milk." The continual encouragement of milk drinking has multiple significances. First, it reinforces Deanie's infantilization, also suggested by Mrs. Loomis's repeated references to her as "my baby" and the juvenile nature of her bedroom décor, in which the stuffed animals and frilly bedclothes contrast with the photos of Bud that inspire her very adult sexual feelings. Further, the milk is used as a panacea, or more accurately, an antidote to the conflicts and demands of adulthood—every time Deanie is told to drink her milk, there is something happening that involves Bud and sexuality, whether it is her arrival home after a date, the Christmas breakfast, or the dinner on the day that she begins to break down.[3] On that day, when asked by her English teacher, Miss Metcalf (Martine Bartlett), to explicate Wordsworth's meaning in his famous ode, Deanie is of course essentially relating her own predicament: How does one go on with life when a dream or ideal dies? Her inability to complete this explanation marks the first paralytic stage in her psychic deterioration. Once home, she seems almost shrunken in her thin robe, while she must face her parents' obliviousness to her troubles. Her mother gleefully proclaims that she has made "veal roast, mashed potatoes, and succotash for [her] girl" and a close-up shows her mother ladling gravy all over the plate, after which another close-up shows Deanie lifting the slices of sopping meat disgustedly with her fork. The choice of veal, a baby animal domesticated for human consumption, being served up as a main course, underscores the idea of Deanie being cut down at the cusp of adulthood. And the food that her mother intends as a balm for her troubles and what could function symbolically as a replacement for the intimacy she is not receiving from Bud is instead a source of repulsion for her. Her separation from Bud and her suspicion that he is being intimate with someone else cause her to reject food that otherwise would entice her, and moreover would sustain her physiologically. She says, "I can't eat, I can't study, I can't even face my friends. I want to die." Carole Zucker argues that Deanie "has been cast out of heaven without a word of explanation; there is no one who can understand, who might offer her comfort or solace."[4] Deanie's sense of being struck down from the kind of high pedestal that Miss Metcalf[5] spoke of when instructing about chivalric love, then a point at which Deanie's biggest concern was whether to sign her anticipated married name "Mrs. Bud Stamper" or "Deanie Stamper," parallels the sense of loss in Wordsworth's ode. The trees and fields that are triggers for Wordsworth are for Deanie, the experience of walking through the school halls and hearing the mention of Bud's new car: "both of them speak of something that is gone" (53).

Deanie's sense of loss and despair is further punctuated during the bathtub conversation with her mother. Mrs. Loomis famously asks Deanie whether Bud has "spoiled" her, and Deanie hysterically screams in response, "No, Mom! I'm not spoiled! I'm not spoiled, Mom! I'm just as fresh and virginal, like the day I was born!" She is displaying the "utter nakedness" (63) from which Wordsworth denies the human child suffers at birth; unlike Wordsworth's child, Deanie does not trail "clouds of glory" (64), but is at this point completely naked, exposed, and alone. And in this scene, Deanie has almost literally reached the boiling point, as a close-up shows her sitting in the tub with steam rising all around her; it is as if she is being cooked. Her mother comments earlier that "there's nothing like a good soak," and since the intent of the bath is to calm her and restore her normalcy, she is metaphorically being prepared as a well-adjusted dish to be consumed by her family and her friends. Bud has not "spoiled" her, has not defiled the quality of her flesh. But she is rotting on the inside, unable to resolve her torturous conflict, and her extreme reaction to this conflict at this moment is intended to provoke her puritan mother: her leaping out of the tub, exaggeratedly gesturing and screaming before running down the hallway.

This particular moment in the film, as well as others that show intensified reactions, is one of the primary reasons that, in Thomas H. Pauly's opinion, the film is marked by "a whole series of inadequately motivated breakdowns . . . deranged behavior seems to be the norm, and the viewer is overwhelmed with lurid scenes of hysteria and violence."[6] This kind of characterization parallels a number of reviews of *Splendor in the Grass* upon its release, reviews that often commented on the film's intense emotion and borderline overacting. For instance, Stanley Kauffmann's *New Republic* review claims that "a Martian who saw this film might infer that all adolescents deprived of sexual intercourse go crazy."[7] The review in the *New Yorker* calls the film "phony in a particularly disgusting way . . . a prolonged act of voyeurism."[8] In his *New York Times* review Bosley Crowther calls the film "embarrassingly intimate" and that sometimes Kazan "lays the purple on too thick," including his direction of Barbara Loden, whose performance Crowther calls "all fireworks and whirling razor blades."[9] But Crowther allows that where the film's sometime intense amplifications "might sound exaggerations and seem sensationalisms in other films, they are reasonable, plausible, convincing, and incisively significant here."[10] One may speculate that the reason for this allowance is an acknowledgment of Kazan's style manifested in *Splendor in the Grass*, his commitment to the spirit of the Method, sometimes manifesting itself in hyperbole. Zucker argues the following toward this point: "As in all of Kazan's work, there is a distinct heightening of emotion. It is important to remember that what Stanislavsky taught was not realism, but poetic realism. Kazan always believed that in order to achieve a fixed goal, the imagination lets different physical impulses create the required behavior, with the director's help."[11] Not only are the extremes of emotion portrayed in *Splendor* consistent with Kazan's poetic method of filmmaking, these extremes are also particularly significant when considering the overarching Wordsworthian theme of vacillation between the intensity of despair and exuberance.

Deanie's full-blown breakdown, precipitated ironically by her suicide attempt at the water plant where she and Bud had the film's initial passionate encounter, is placed in tandem to Bud's first disastrous year at Yale. They are both exiled from home for supposed learning experiences, to expunge their desire for one another, and their experiences are marked cinematically by depictions of apathy: Deanie sitting in a rocking chair, her back to the camera, facing a small window and rocking very slowly, and Bud mechanically drowning his sorrows at a New Haven pizza joint. It is here that he meets Angelina (Zohra Lampert), who acts as caregiver, telling him not to drink so much, and imploring him to have something to eat. She forces him to have pizza, which he's never eaten before, and moves him from the front part of the restaurant into the back, hearth area near the ovens, to feed him. The food that is unknown to him may be genuine affection; Angie is earthy and seemingly uncomplicated, and becomes a healing balm for Bud's afflictions. While a potentially positive force, she is something less than the aspirations he once had, and her charms very much match the characterization of the effect of nature on the young man:

> Earth fills her lap with pleasures of her own;
> Yearnings she hath in her own natural kind,
> And, even with something of a Mother's mind,
> And no unworthy aim,
> The homely Nurse doth all she can
> To make her Foster-child, her Inmate Man,
> Forget the glories he hath known,
> And that imperial palace whence he came. (78–85)

Angie represents sensuality and fertility, but nothing greater. Ace Stamper, on the eve before his suicide, tries to convince Bud that his future is an open book, telling him "the world is your oyster" and offering to "get" any girl he wants; but even before this financial collapse, Bud knows it is hopeless and Angie is his only outlet. Conversely, Deanie's sanitarium fiancé, John (Charles Robinson), is kind and restrained, but shows no passion; his defining characteristic, and apparent reason for being institutionalized, is an identity conflict arising from the fact that he rebelled against his father's wishes for his being a surgeon. He says, "I couldn't make that first cut into another man's flesh." Nina C. Leibman's Freudian reading of the film argues that the association of John's name "with the practice of prostitution suggests that Deanie must treat her sexuality as a salable commodity rather than an expression of her identity in order to accommodate herself to a 'healthy' marriage."[12] It is true that this union is most practical, given the fact that Deanie's marriage prospects, as she emerges from a mental institution in the early 1930s back into a small town, would not have been great. She therefore enters into it with the full knowledge that the "love" she feels for John is not the same as what she felt for Bud; there is a certain fatalism to her choice that parallels Bud's attitude toward Angie.

The poignancy of the film's final segment leads up to the reprise of the ode's "splendor in the grass" lines and indeed defines how the poem has spread itself over the text of the film. Upon her release from the sanitarium, Deanie is determined to see Bud, and not just to conquer the mystification of her memories about which the doctor cautions her; it is evident that she is hoping for some rekindling of the spark, "the glory and the dream" (57) that they once knew. Despite her mother's vigilance and her friends' reluctance, her father, whose input in her life always seemed more nurturing than her mother's, reveals his location. What Deanie does not know is that aside from the fact that he is living at his father's old farm outside of town, Bud is also married and has a child. Though the effect of this discovery is not as devastating as her initial breakdown concerning Bud, the realization is almost her earlier experience in miniature. Deanie's physical presence directly contrasts all elements of Bud's current life. The farm is dusty and dirty and sparse looking; when Bud learns that Deanie has come to see him, he immediately says that he does not want to see her being as dirty as he is. By contrast, Deanie is crisp, clean, and cool in a pristine white dress, hat, and gloves. Bud's reaction to Deanie and Deanie's reaction to Bud are similarly uncomfortable; she is embarrassed to be there, in the midst of his new and poor life, and he is embarrassed to have her there. They both display what Wordsworth describes as the "High instincts before which our mortal Nature / Did tremble like a guilty Thing surprised" (147–48). There is a sense of blame in their disquietude, a sense of something betrayed.

In the same way that food appeared in the earlier segments throughout the film to signify a lack of sustenance, the scenes at Bud's farm serve a similar function: though there are animals roaming about, the land has turned dust bowl—a stark contrast to the scenes of water and passion earlier in the film—and Bud's work has been hard, a consequence of the "inevitable yoke" (125) that Wordsworth describes as a consequence of adult life. Bud mentions twice in this brief visit that he and Angie are "eating regular now," as if even base survival has been a struggle. Their fortunes have somewhat reversed, since the Loomis family sold their stock just in time before the crash to pay for Deanie's institutionalization; Deanie's family now appears quite comfortable and she owns many new clothes, while the remaining Stampers are living in poverty, their old house turned into a funeral home. Angie seems very self-conscious about her own appearance and the appearance of the house, as she tries to pull her shabby housedress more tightly around her body and comments about how much of a mess the house is. Flies are buzzing around, and even Bud Jr. seems like a farm animal among the chickens on the kitchen floor; Bud refers to him as "the one without the feathers." Meanwhile, though Deanie gingerly picks up Bud Jr. and cuddles him, she seems reluctant to touch anything else in the house. And even in her apparent sense of half yearning that Bud Jr. might have been hers, it is clear that part of her recognizes that this is alien territory. Deanie even shaking hands good-bye with Angie, as she is frying a nondescript piece of meat in a pan for dinner, is awkward because one is dirty and the other clean. It is painfully obvious that Bud is like the Man in Wordsworth's ode who has seen the Light "die away / And fade into the light of common day" (76–77). Instead of the plenty that one would expect to see on a farm, and the hopes that Bud once imagined to find on this very property, the fruits of Bud's young life and labor seem meager indeed. Deanie and Bud muse about their relative happiness in the following way:

Deanie: You're happy, Bud?

Bud: I guess so. I don't ask myself that question very often, though. How about you?

Deanie: I'm getting married next month.

Bud: Are you, Deanie?

Deanie: (She nods.) A boy from Cincinnati. I think you might like him.

Bud: Gee—things work out awful funny sometimes, don't they, Deanie?

Deanie: Yes, they do.

Bud: I hope you're gonna be awful happy.

Deanie: Well, like you, Bud. I don't think too much about happiness either.

Bud: What's the point? You gotta take what comes.

In their mutual resignation, Bud and Deanie agree that the idea of happiness is not something on which to dwell because the world deals blows against which the mere human cannot hope to triumph. These are, perhaps, the "thoughts that do often lie too deep for tears" (204) that Wordsworth concludes at the end of the ode—the "food for thought" that one dares not consume. Bud's final words in the film are "When do we eat?" to the sad Angelina. Conversely, the reprisal of Wordsworth's lines in Deanie's voice-over at the end of the film seems a hollow finding of "strength in what remains behind."

It seems fitting that William Inge, who scripted *Splendor in the Grass*, plays the uncredited role of Reverend Whitman, the preacher who intones the following lines, paraphrased from Matthew 6:20–21: "Lay up for treasures for yourself in heaven. . . . For where your treasure is, there will your heart be also." As the reverend speaks these words, warning against pride in prosperity, the camera shows Deanie clutching Bud's arm imploringly and then cuts to the sleeping Mr. Stamper. This brief scene encapsulates the tragic starvation for meaning, the longing and loss, that hold the film's greatest meaning. The entirety of the film centers on the "spoiling" of human life, whether it be sexually, financially, or idealistically. The film's characters feed on hollow fruit, and even on each other, and wind up, even with struggle, to exist, rather than to live. The "visionary gleam" of which Wordsworth speaks is extinguished in the resolution of Bud's and Deanie's adult lives. Kazan said himself, in a 1966 interview about the film, that "one must never believe that things happen without one's having to pay for them. Even in victory there is a price to pay. You gain one thing, but you also lose another. In the film, both gain, in a sense, but the price has been frightful."[13] The "frightful" price that Bud and Deanie pay is the death of prosperity and idealism; these are managed, just as Deanie's fragile psyche, with bandages that seem all too insufficient and, like Wordsworth's conclusions, all too unsatisfying.

NOTES

1. William Wordsworth, "Ode: Intimations of Immortality from Recollections of Early Childhood," in *Romantic Poetry and Prose*, ed. Harold Bloom and Lionel Trilling (New York: Oxford University Press, 1973). All references are taken from this edition.

2. Kenneth Hey, "*Splendor in the Grass*: Another Look," *Film and History* 11, no.1 (February 1981): 9.

3. The equivalent to the milk drinking in Bud's world might be seen as the doctor's recommendation for "another shot of iron and a sunlamp treatment" when Bud tries to talk to him about his sexual frustration.

4. Carole Zucker, "Love Hurts: Performance in Elia Kazan's *Splendor in the Grass*," *Cineaste* 31, no. 4 (Fall 2006): 20.

5. The etymology of "Metcalf" lends further meaning to the film's subtext: "The name is of ancient Anglo-Saxon origin, deriving from two possible sources. Firstly, such Old English terms as *mete-corn*, meaning 'corn for food,' and *mete-cu*, meaning 'cow that is to furnish food,' make it conceivable that the name Metcalf is derived from an Old English word 'mete-calf,' meaning 'a calf being fattened up for slaughtering.'" http://www.houseofnames.com/metcalf-family-crest.

6. Thomas H. Pauly, *An American Odyssey: Eliza Kazan and American Culture Vision* (Philadelphia: Temple University Press, 1983), 233–34. Among the other "lurid" scenes that Pauly cites are the gang rape of Ginny, Deanie's aborted seductions of Bud and Toots at the dance, and the nightclub scene and subsequent suicide of Ace Stamper.

7. Stanley Kauffmann, review of *Splendor in the Grass*, *New Republic*, October 16, 1961, 21.

8. Brendan Gill, review of *Splendor in the Grass*, *New Yorker*, October 14, 1961, 177.

9. Bosley Crowther, "*Splendor in the Grass*: Review," *New York Times*, October 11, 1961, http://movies.nytimes.com/movie/re-view?res=EE05E7DF173DE170BC4952DFB667838A679EDE.

10. Crowther, "*Splendor in the Grass*: Review."

11. Zucker, "Love Hurts," 23.

12. Nina C. Leibman, "Sexual Misdemeanor/Psychoanalytic Felony," *Cineaste* 26, no. 2 (Winter 1987): 35.

13. Michael Delahaye, "Interview with Elia Kazan," in *Elia Kazan Interviews*, ed. William Baer (Jackson: University Press of Mississippi, 2000), 96.

Part III

Film as Poetry

Chapter Ten

"Qualcosa di concreto"

Mimetic Fiction and Spectrality in Pier Paolo Pasolini's Cinema of Poetry

Roberto Cavallini

There is no history, so to speak, there is substance as apparition.—Pier Paolo Pasolini[1]

In 1965, during the first edition of the Mostra Internazionale del Nuovo Cinema di Pesaro (Pesaro Film Festival), the Italian poet and director Pier Paolo Pasolini presented one of his most important theoretical interventions on film theory titled "Il cinema di poesia" ("The Cinema of Poetry").[2] In his text, Pasolini explored the possibility of the new cinema to create an aesthetic language analogous to the language of poetry through the technique of free indirect discourse. The latter is a mode of storytelling that molds the main narrative through the total adoption and identification of the character's psychology and language, a sort of filter that breaks the boundaries between fiction and reality in order to reconstitute and evoke a new relation with the world. Various scholars and critics engaged with Pasolini's seminal reflections (from Deleuze to Viano, from Metz to Ricciardi, just to mention a few). The first objective of this chapter is to rehearse the main arguments of Pasolini's text, exploring the potential conditions it can offer today on the recent debates about cinematic realism. More specifically, the break between fiction and reality, at the core of Pasolini's reflection, will be considered through the principle of *mimetic fiction* also in relation to Jacques Rancière's similar theoretical interest in what he defines as the labor of fiction. Subsequently, I will explore how a certain reflection on temporality is essential to understand Pasolini's cinema of poetry. For Pasolini, artistic expression is symbolized by the figure of Janus, the double-headed ancient Roman god of beginnings and transitions, who looks to the past and the future simultaneously. Finally, making use of Alessia Ricciardi's notion of spectro-poetics and Derrida's hauntology, I will explore Pasolini's poetic attempt at conveying a spectral vision of reality, focusing on a reading of his short film *La Terra vista dalla Luna* (*The Earth Seen from the Moon*, 1967). My overall objective is to show how the moment of invention and artistic creation in Pasolini is a place of resistance, a threshold posited at the junction between past and future. Reality is a nonobjective modality of the present time, which should be constantly rewritten by a politics of memory based on differential temporal trajectories of past, present, and future.

THE CINEMA OF POETRY AND MIMETIC FICTION

In the essay "The Cinema of Poetry," Pasolini investigates the potentiality of cinema for transforming and rendering reality as a poetic experience. At the beginning of the essay, Pasolini draws attention to a structural problem that affects both the making and the reception of the moving image—that is the lack of a dictionary of images from which the filmmaker could extract and select portions of reality ready to be used. The filmmaker, as Pasolini affirms, picks up images directly from chaos, which is essentially informed by the world of memory and of dreams. Both the world of memory and oneiric imagination are forms of visual reproduction that defy linear modes of storytelling because they are built around a sequence made of "im-signs" (or image-signs). The infinite possibilities that cinema has to write reality are based on a chaotic system of representation that is essentially irrational; it is "on the border of what is human."[3] Even though "im-signs" are premorphological and pregrammatical, Pasolini insists that they are caught in the double nature of cinema, which is both extremely subjective and extremely objective at once. On the one hand, cinema is extremely subjective and, as a consequence, lyrical, because it refers to archetypes that are chosen from our memory and dreams, or, as Pasolini puts it, "images of communication with ourselves,"[4] and the filmmaker *chooses* from an arbitrary vocabulary of im-signs. On the other hand, cinema is also concerned with objectivity because other archetypes are taken from signs that belong to visible reality, or as Pasolini puts it, "our communication with others" and with a series of images which shape the brief stylistic history of cinema.

Maurizio Viano, in his fundamental study on Pasolini's film theory and practice, aptly connects the idea of a cinema of poetry with the problem of "a certain realism"; it is indeed the double nature of the cinema of poetry that redefines the conditions of realism as a system of representation. As Viano notes, Gilles Deleuze is the first one who reads and understands Pasolini's intuitions constructively, exploring and defining the constitutive aspect of the cinema of poetry: the technique of the free indirect discourse.[5] Viano explains how Pasolini tries to overcome the traditional realist approaches (mimetic realism), which were based on a tendency toward "a normality of vision" (i.e., the Italian Neorealism's assumption that "reality is there, why change it?"), with the combination of the subjective/objective dichotomy that questions precisely the ways in which fact and fiction are interwoven together.[6] According to Pasolini, the works produced by the New Waves and in particular by Michelangelo Antonioni, Bernardo Bertolucci, and Jean-Luc Godard encapsulate the style of a cinema of poetry. Besides the specific characteristic that each director creates in his work, Pasolini points out three general notions that indicate how the cinema of poetry would perform "a certain realism": substitution (Antonioni), contamination (Bertolucci), and restoration (Godard) of reality. These three categories substantiate the technique of the free indirect discourse as that which formulates the author's sociological consciousness within different regimes of visuality, beyond mimetic realism.

In *Cinema 2: The Time-Image*, Deleuze reframes Pasolini's cinema of poetry in the context of the veracity of storytelling and the concept of the power of the false:

> In the cinema of poetry, the distinction between what the characters saw subjectively and what the camera saw objectively vanished, not in favour of one or the other, but because the camera assumed a subjective presence, acquired an internal vision, which entered into a relation of *simulation* ("mimesis") with the character's way of seeing. . . . A contamination of the two kinds of image was established, so that bizarre visions of the camera (alternation of different lenses, zoom, extraordinary angles, abnormal movements, halts . . .) expressed the singular visions of the character, and the latter were expressed in the former, but by bringing the whole to the power of the false. The story no longer refers to an ideal of the true which constitutes its veracity, but becomes a "pseudo-story," a poem, a story which simulates or rather a simulation of the story.[7]

Fact and fiction are shaped by a process of simulation that provokes a rupture in the ways in which a story is told; for Deleuze, it seems that when truth is defied by the fictional quality of the power of the false, the story loses its veracity in order to become a pseudostory—in other words, a poem. In the recent debate about realism in cinema, Jacques Rancière's notion of documentary cinema as a mode of fiction reopened a critical debate on the ways in which the relationship between fact and fiction can be reassessed in the context of aesthetic realism.[8] In an essay titled "The Paradoxes of Political Art," Rancière defends the need to reassess the potentiality of fiction performed by artistic and creative practices. For Rancière, "Fiction is a way of changing existing modes of sensory presentations and forms of enunciation; of varying frames, scales and rhythms; and of building new relationships between reality and appearance, the individual and the collective."[9] I would argue that Rancière's reflection could find an ideal reference in Pasolini's cinema of poetry. The moment of invention where novel relationships are configured also implies a notion of fiction, which could shed light on the relationship between fact and imagination, truth and narrative storytelling.

At the intersection between these various theoretical concerns, I would employ the principle of *mimetic fiction* in order to designate the relationship between reality and representation in the context of aesthetic realism. Mimetic fiction illustrates the moment in which reality is not mediated and constructed as a document but is, on the contrary, transfigured and put into motion again in order to make sense of the world. Mimetic fiction is an oxymoronic term, which allows me to understand the ambivalence of representation through Pasolini's categories of substitution, contamination, and restoration of reality. To make sense of reality would mean to configure a new thinking of cinematic realism, which combines subjective and objective points of view thus questioning simultaneously the relationship and intertextuality occurring between the character's, the director's, and also the spectator's points of view.[10] However, as Deleuze remarks, "The break is not between fiction and reality, but in the new mode of story that affects both of them,"[11] thus reinforcing Pasolini's insight about the stylistic condition of the cinema of poetry and its double nature. The new mode of story simulates a different order of symbolic signs in which reality and storytelling (fact and fiction) generate acts of exposure more than acts of representation. In other words, through substitution, contamination, and restoration, mimetic fiction configures an affirmation of the sense of the world more than its rational signification and explanation.

TEMPORALITY AND THE TRANSGRESSION OF REALITY

In the essay "Il Cinema Impopolare" ("The Unpopular Cinema"), while discussing the aesthetic dimension of World Cinema New Waves (Rocha, Godard, Straub, and American underground cinema among others), Pasolini formulates a reflection about cinema, realism, and transgression, employing a quite militant and poetic vocabulary:

> It is therefore necessary (in extremist terms or not) to compel oneself not to go too far forward, to break off the victorious rush towards martyrdom, and to go continuously backwards, to the firing line; only in the instant of combat (that is, of invention, enforcing one's freedom to die in the teeth of self-preservation), only in the instant when one is face to face with the rule to be broken and Mars is ancipital, under the shadow of Thanatos, can one touch the revelation

of truth, of the totality, or in short, of something concrete. Once the transgression has taken place—which is achieved through a new invention—that is, in a new constituted reality—the truth, or the totality, or that Something concrete, disappears because it cannot be lived or stabilized in any way. It is for this reason that Power, any Power, is evil, whether it preserves institutions or whether it founds new ones. If a Power which is "less worse" than others is conceivable, this could only be a Power that, in preserving or reconstituting the norm, took into account the appearances or possible reappearances of Reality.[12]

Pasolini's critical account on mimetic fiction emerges here in all its ambiguous yet lyrical distinction. The vital necessity to confront reality in the sphere of what he vaguely calls "general semiology" is an attempt also to emphasize once more the difference between expression and communication. Expression—expressing oneself in order to be understood, creative expression as such, that is poetry—remains always for Pasolini a precarious and critical achievement.[13] Pasolini here plays with different planes of significations in a very cryptic way. What is Pasolini trying to say here? All too quickly, one could probably understand this passage as an attempt to frame creative expression (in poetry or in cinema) as a practice essentially shaped by a certain notion of temporality, through the mythical figure of Janus. In ancient Roman religion and mythology, Janus was the god of beginnings, movement, and transitions, hence of the origin of time. Represented as a double-headed man (*Janus bifrons*), he was represented as time, one head looking at the past and the other looking at the future. He symbolized change and transitions and he was the god of gates and thresholds, worshipped at the beginning of harvests or during marriages or deaths. When Pasolini says, "Mars is ancipital, under the shadow of Thanatos," he is somehow creating a new mythological deity, which is a double-headed figure of Mars, the god of war under the influence of Thanatos, that is, Death.[14] The problem of temporality here is crucial, for Pasolini has often been erroneously criticized for his constant referral to a nostalgic past, an archaic origin lost forever.[15] The moment of entry into history by the subject is a fundamental topos in Pasolini. Through "*coscienza ed inconscienza*" (consciousness and unconsciousness), the subject struggles to position herself between, on the one hand, the contiguity and acknowledgment of the self's obliteration in bourgeois history and, on the other hand, the passionate light of mystical innocence without knowledge. In *Pasolini: Forms of Subjectivity*, Robert S. C. Gordon explains: "Only at the point of entry into consciousness and history, where the transitional, suspended status of being in time produces a dynamic of prospective transformation, is resistance possible."[16] This threshold, where the subject acquires an active role against the forces of history, is for Pasolini the place in which poetry (and art in general) finds its critical force to embrace "that something concrete" ("*qualcosa di concreto*"); and this threshold is the only possible place in which resistance can be put into motion. This paradoxical problem of the threshold, always present in Pasolini's work, is a problem of separation, but not of initiation. There is no beginning or new commencement after this threshold. As Gordon correctly points out, "The past, or prehistory, [in Pasolini] survives as a negative, immanent power that revitalises, but also dissolves the present." [17] The moment of combat of artistic expression, or on the "firing line" as Pasolini suggests, is a moment shaped by a spectral vision of temporality, like the figure of Janus at the junction between the past and the future. This ambivalence, this condition of *in-betweenness* is Pasolini's effective poetic statement about the potentiality of a certain realism to play with the appearances and, at the same time, the reappearances of reality.

In *The Passion of Pier Paolo Pasolini*, Sam Rohdie explains the significance and importance of "reality" in Pasolini's works: "Pasolinian reality has two dimensions: itself and its writing, reality and art, document and consciousness. Reality needed metaphor and art to transform it and thereby make it known. The need to artificialise signalled that the reality so altered—though often simply being cited—was anachronistic and no longer in existence." [18]

In Pasolini, reality (the present time) or "that something concrete" is never separated from its constant rewriting (past and future), and the fragmented actions at work in reality have the potential to be harmonized. Reality constantly appears and disappears, and it is through this process that a sense of dispossession emerges in all its full vigor. Rohdie specifies: "The image and the analogy were the record of a loss, and one not only recorded by analogy but formed by it." The world that Pasolini constructs is artificial, but it is not an attempt to escape reality. On the contrary, Pasolini uses analogy and the construction of an artificial and ideal reality in order to install a radical and endless questioning at the heart of representation itself. Rohdie explains: "What had disappeared in reality became present in memory and language. Consciousness was a consciousness of the impossibility of all that he [Pasolini] desired (the past, reality) and of the need to keep the desire alive and himself alive: the desire was the desire to write all that remained of the lost reality." [19]

Throughout his life, Pasolini contested and disputed the dissolution of our present condition (the lost reality) in all its contemporary forms, as for example the irreversible anthropological transformation caused by the consumer society. [20] Pasolini confronts the desacralization of reality because it seriously affects a certain question of memory, of living memory—an absolute desire of society that infects the way we interpret and read history, the conflict between generations, the substantial alienation that does not precede memory but nullifies the restlessness of memory. The language of cinema for Pasolini, as we have seen at the beginning of this chapter, is essentially informed by the world of memory and of dreams (past and future). Reality, as seen through the eyes of the double-headed Janus, is shaped by a spectral vision whereby presence and absence give form to our present condition.

SPECTRALITY AND MEMORY

Pasolini's fascination with the mystery of reality is an attempt to understand a notion of presence, of living present, as affected also by absence. In this sense, his reflection resonates an analogous preoccupation that runs through twentieth-century philosophy of time, which probably finds a remarkable example in the work of Jacques Derrida and his attempt at challenging precisely the aporetic conjunction of past, present, and future.[21] Alessia Ricciardi has brilliantly introduced the notion of "spectro-poetics," in light of Derrida's *Specters of Marx*, to consider Pasolini's "elaboration throughout his career of a political imaginary, a political attitude that is immanent in its anthropological, religious, and phantasmatic components and that finds in cinema its most original phenomenological manifestation. . . . We might say that for Pasolini, even melancholia is a form of hospitality to a fundamental Otherness at the core of modernity."[22] If we turn our attention directly to *Specters of Marx*, here Derrida summarizes the central aspects of his reflection. He begins with an affirmative utterance or "strange watchword," as he describes: "I would like to learn to live finally."[23] For Derrida, "to learn to live" is ethics itself, and an experience constantly tied to life and death: my life and death and the life and the death of the other. At this point of conjunction, Derrida takes one step further: the temporal dimension of this middle ground, this "in-between" in which the expression "to learn to live" is situated, refers to "a time without tutelary present."[24] "To learn to live"—or perhaps experience itself—dwells in a temporal dimension connotated by the nonpresence of ghosts. To learn to live means to learn to live together with ghosts, in their company. This condition of "being with" ghosts and with specters "would also be, not only but also, a *politics* of memory, of inheritance, of generations."[25]

In order to develop further the relationship between spectrality and reality, I would like to make a short diversion, turning my attention to Pasolini's short film *La Terra vista dalla Luna*.[26] The film tells the story of two men, a father, Ciancicato Miao (Totò), and his son Baciù Miao (Ninetto Davoli). While they are crying over the grave of their wife and mother, Crisantema, recently dead, Ciancicato Miao agrees with his son to look together for another wife. After one year of wandering, they meet Assurdina Gaì (Silvana Mangano), a deaf-mute woman. Ciancicato immediately marries her and they go to their house, a rustic hut on the periphery of Rome, in the middle of nowhere. In the second part of the film, Ciancicato attempts to improve the economic status of his family and he tries to buy a proper house. Of course, his attempt is not without an expedient: in order to come across some money quickly, he convinces Assurdina to go to the top of the Colosseum and act out a pathetic suicide attempt, while claiming the need of some money in order to feed his sons. However, while crying desperately, Assurdina falls down and dies. Ciancicato and Baciù are then shown in the cemetery, crying over the grave of Assurdina. They return to their little hut and as soon as they open the door, they find Assurdina, with her white wedding dress. She is a ghostly appearance in flesh and bones. The film ends with an explicit moral that reads: "To be dead or to be alive is the same thing."

As Viano correctly affirms, *La Terra vista dalla Luna*, as much as *Che cosa sono le nuvole?* are film essays in the form of comedy sketches that explore the potentiality of cinema in relation to a explicit discourse about death. In a short essay entitled "Observations on the Long Take" (1967) written at the same time of shooting *La Terra vista dalla Luna*, Pasolini briefly elaborates on this theoretical position.[27] Montage, for Pasolini, operates simultaneously as fragmentation and recomposition because it deconstructs the language of reality. In the context of cinema, montage is that procedure that allows the director to reconcile the disordered flux of the represented subjects. It follows, for Pasolini, that in the context of reality or life, death is that which frames the action's consequences, reconstructing the sense of reality and its contradictions. Two years later the talk on "The Cinema of Poetry," in another essay titled "The Fear of Naturalism," Pasolini insists in this thinking of cinema as a practice in which reality is symbolically transfigured into a sensual and poetic system of signs. Our memory is that which transforms reality into something that is unreal while cinema is defined as follows: "[Cinema is not] unreal, like reality which is founded on an illusion: that is on the passing of something that is not there, that is time. Cinema is founded, on the contrary, on the abolition of time as continuity, hence on its transformation in a significant and moral reality, always. . . . Cinema, practically, is like a life after death."[28] Cinema's spectral condition gives birth to a new sense of reality, which is substantially poetic. The relation between cinema and reality provokes a contradictory affirmation: on the one hand, reality is founded on an illusion because it is defined by the nonexistence of time; on the other, cinema is (the written language of) reality. Cinema abolishes time because it operates at the thresholds of the work of memory and dreams, on differential temporal planes, which are contaminated by presence and absence at the same time.

In *La Terra vista dalla Luna*, the dead one returns. In the last scene, Pasolini seems to play with a sort of ironic detachment. The dead mother returns to stay, to continue everyday life as if nothing happened. Here, there is no separation between life and death; there is no invention of death as the limit of life. Rather, what returns in the form of the ghost is what defines our relation to the past and to the future. In other words, employing a Derridean expression: *hauntology of existence.*[29] The desire to achieve a better condition of living—for Pasolini the neo-capitalist drive toward destruction—leads to the negation of life. Yet Pasolini is not interested in a passive or active nihilistic approach to ethics and politics. Rather, he is concerned with the ironic delimitation of the tragic sense of our everyday life, with the possibility of instating a *beyond* within the real. The point is not a transgression of reality, but rather a transgression within the limits of the code. The "firing line," the moment of rupture, is the instant of death in which the limit of transgression is self-assured; the threshold becomes a place of resistance, with "Mars ancipital, under the shadow of Thanatos."

CONCLUSION

The return of Assurdina's ghost is the moment of full exposure to the firing line. The dead mother returns and she is not even the biological mother. Furthermore, this return is a nonevent because she literally never left. The return of the dead mother remains an unreadable appearance. The viewer bears witness to this return that erases the immediacy of the present—a return that reveals the "hauntological" condition of this full exposure. One should note that there is a fundamental difference between Pasolini's expression "To be dead or to be alive is the same thing" and Derrida's theoretical observation that ghosts never leave. Pasolini's statement implies that one cannot escape finitude. By contrast, Derrida's "hauntology" implies that one cannot live or articulate oneself without taking into consideration the presence or absence of ghosts. Yet, this discrepancy between Pasolini's admission and Derrida's resolution is directed toward an analogous objective: to learn to live finally (together with ghosts). Hauntology thus remains within the field of erased writings and configures an empty space that announces a break into the immediacy of the present. This empty space is perhaps Pasolini's "firing line." One should remain there, at this conceptual threshold, in the moment of betrayal that always verges on becoming institutionalized, and, finally, in the moment of invention. The return of the dead mother does not present the transgression of reality or a condition of living *beyond* reality.

In Pasolini there is never the attempt to supersede the current reality that could be framed within the language of a cinema of poetry. In order to build new relationships between reality and its appearances, no action produces disobedient or provocative gestures *beyond* reality. For Pasolini, the *beyond*, in a contradictory way, always comes as an *in-between*: a threshold between reality and its questioning, between innocence and consciousness and between revolution and the past. It is in this perspective of a differential temporality that a cinema of poetry could reframe reality as a reflective condition of fiction. Mimetic fiction could therefore never be reconciled totally with

the real as such, but rather is affirmed and configured as a poetic reappropria-
tion of reality.

NOTES

1. Pier Paolo Pasolini, *Bestemmia, Tutte le Poesie*, vol. 2 (Turin: Garzanti, 1993), 1903. Original Italian text: "La storia non c'è, diciamo, c'è la sostanza; che è apparizione."
2. The "cinema of poetry" speech was delivered at the first International Festival of New Cinema in Pesaro in 1965, and published for the first time under the title "Le cinema de poesie" in *Cahiers du cinéma* (1965, 171), and later in *Uccellacci e Uccellini* (Milan: Garzanti, 1966), and in the journal *Marcatrè*, nos. 19–22 (April 1966). In this chapter I use the version published in Pier Paolo Pasolini, *Heretical Empiricism*, ed. Louise K. Barnett, trans. Ben Lawton and Louise K. Barnett (Bloomington: Indiana University Press, 1988).
3. Pier Paolo Pasolini, "The Cinema of Poetry," in *Heretical Empiricism*, ed. Louise K. Barnett, trans. Ben Lawton and Louise K. Barnett (Bloomington: Indiana University Press, 1988), 169.
4. Pasolini, "Cinema of Poetry," 173.
5. Maurizio Viano, *A Certain Realism: Making Use of Pasolini's Film Theory and Practice* (Berkeley: University of California Press, 1993), 93–95.
6. Already in *Cinema 1: The Movement-Image*, Deleuze summarizes his argument as follows: "It is a case of going beyond the subjective and the objective towards a pure Form which sets itself up as an autonomous vision of the content. We are no longer faced with subjective *or* objective images; we are caught in a correlation between a perception-image and a camera-consciousness which transforms it." See Gilles Deleuze, *Cinema 1: The Movement-Image* (London: Athlone Press, 1992), 74.
7. Gilles Deleuze, *Cinema 2: The Time-Image* (London: Athlone Press, 2000), 149.
8. See Jacques Rancière, *Film Fables* (Oxford: Berg, 2006), 158. For a thorough examination of Rancière's views on documentary cinema also in relation to previous debates in film theory (Bazin, Kracauer), please see Nico Baumbach, "Jacques Rancière and the Fictional Capacity of Documentary, *New Review of Film and Television Studies* 8, no.1 (March 2010): 57–72.
9. Jacques Rancière, "The Paradoxes of Political Art," in *Dissensus: On Politics and Aesthetics* (London: Continuum, 2010), 141.
10. See Viano, *A Certain Realism*, 55–67. Viano brilliantly illustrates the problem of realism in the context of Italian and European film culture and Pasolini's attempt at restoring a new perspective on realism as mode of reading.
11. Deleuze, *Cinema 2: The Time-Image*, 150.
12. Pier Paolo Pasolini, "The Unpopular Cinema," in *Heretical Empiricism*, ed. Louise K. Barnett, trans. Ben Lawton and Louise K. Barnett (Bloomington: Indiana University Press, 1988), 274–75.
13. Pasolini's distinction, in his late writings, about expressive language as opposed to communicative language, is telling in this sense. Communicative language is the language of capitalism and technocracy; expressive language, that is, poetry, dialects, and jargons, are instead in the process of disappearing. Please see Pier Paolo Pasolini, *Saggi sulla politica e sulla società* (Milan: Mondadori, 1999), 271–73, 322, 512–13. On the influence of the Italian philosopher Benedetto Croce on this specific distinction and a reflection on Pasolini's thoughts about cinema, please refer to Robert Samuel Clive Gordon, *Pasolini: Forms of Subjectivity* (Oxford: Clarendon Press, 1996), 51.
14. In ancient Roman mythology, there are indications that Janus and Mars, together with Jupiter, were considered as a triad and that Janus was logically worshipped in wartime when his gates were opened to hold sacrifices. See C. Scott Littleton, *The New Comparative Mythology* (Berkeley: University of California Press, 1966), 1973.
15. Silvana Mariniello explores this issue and rereads Pasolini's political position as an intellectual, arguing that he expresses a nonlinear conceptualization of time in which the over-

lapping between past, present, and future opens up the way of critically engaging with these modalities of time. See Silvana Mariniello, "Temporality and the Culture of Intervention," *Boundary 2* 22, no. 3 (Autumn 1995), 111–39.

16. Gordon, *Pasolin*, 127.

17. Gordon, *Pasolini: Forms of Subjectivity*, 127.

18. Sam Rohdie, *The Passion of Pier Paolo Pasolini* (London: BFI, 1995), 129.

19. Rohdie, *Passion of Pier Paolo Pasolini*, 129.

20. It is worth recalling here Pasolini's famous expression "anthropological genocide." With this term, Pasolini meant how the postwar Fascistic technocracy and the hedonistic consumerism of "late capitalism" inevitably entails an anthropological genocide. See Pasolini, *Saggi sulla politica e sulla società*, 599–603. See also Lorenzo Chiesa, "Pasolini and the Ugliness of Bodies: Salò, Petrolio, Lettere luterane," in *In Corpore: (Im)material Bodies in Italy, from the Middle Ages to the Present Day*, ed. L. Polezzi and C. Ross (Madison, N.J.: Fairleigh Dickinson University Press, 2007), 208–27.

21. It is necessary to observe that this reformulation of temporality also affects the linear metaphysical concept of history. In *Of Grammatology*, Derrida writes, "The word history has no doubt always been associated with a linear scheme of the unfolding of presence." See Jacques Derrida, *Of Grammatology*, trans. Gayatri Chakravorty Spivak (Baltimore: Johns Hopkins University Press, 1974), 85. See also Jacques Derrida, *Positions*, trans. Alan Bass (Chicago: University of Chicago Press, 1981), 56–60. The proliferation of books on the question of time in Derrida has been quite significant in recent years. See, for example, John D. Caputo, *Deconstruction in a Nutshell: A Conversation with Jacques Derrida* (New York: Fordham University Press, 1997); Joanna Hodge, *Derrida on Time* (London: Routledge, 2007); David Farrell Krell, *The Purest of Bastards: Works of Mourning, Art, and Affirmation in the Thought of Jacques Derrida* (University Park: Pennsylvania State University Press, 2000); Paul Patton and John Protevi, *Between Deleuze and Derrida* (London: Continuum, 2003); David Wood, *The Deconstruction of Time* (Evanston, Ill.: Northwestern University Press, 2001).

22. Alessia Ricciardi, *The Ends of Mourning: Psychoanalysis, Literature, Film* (Stanford, Calif.: Stanford University Press, 2003), 126.

23. Jacques Derrida, *Specters of Marx: The State of the Debt, the Work of Mourning, and the New International*, trans. Peggy Kamuf (New York: Routledge, 1994), xvi.

24. Derrida, *Specters of Marx*, xvi.

25. Derrida, *Specters of Marx*, xviii.

26. *La Terra vista dalla Luna* (*The Earth Seen from the Moon*, 1966) is a short film that was included in the film *Le Streghe* (*The Witches*, 1967), along with episodes by Luchino Visconti, Franco Rossi, Vittorio De Sica, and Mauro Bolognini. It was also supposed to be part of a series of short films by Pasolini, titled *Che Cos'è il Cinema?* (What Is Cinema?), which was unfortunately never realized and in which *Che Cosa Sono le Nuvole?* was also to be included. *La Terra vista dalla Luna* and *Che Cosa Sono le Nuvole?* are thus the only two episodes completed.

27. See Pier Paolo Pasolini, "Observations on the Long Take," *October* 13 (1967; Summer 1980). Original Italian title: "Osservazioni sul Piano-Sequenza."

28. Pier Paolo Pasolini, "La paura del naturalismo," in *Empirismo eretico* (Milan: Garzanti, 1972), 253.

29. Derrida introduces the category of hauntology for the first time in *Specters of Marx*. As Colin Davis explains, hauntology "supplants its near-homonym ontology, replacing the priority of being and presence with the figure of the ghost as that which is neither present nor absent, neither dead or alive." Colin Davis, "État Présent: Hauntology, Spectres and Phantoms," *French Studies* 59, no. 3 (July 2005): 373–79.

Chapter Eleven

Terrence Malick's Intimations of Immortality

The Tree of Life *as Cinematic Ode*

Suzanne Ferriss

As Hannah Patterson has noted, the term "poetic" has been used often to describe Terrence Malick's films "usually in admiration, sometimes in derision, often in bafflement."[1] This unquestionably applies to critical response to Malick's recent film *The Tree of Life* (2011). References to "poetry" or "poetic" abound in reviews of the Oscar-nominated film. Peter Simek claims that Malick is "a philosopher, the lyric poet of filmmakers, . . . the American transcendentalist movie maker."[2] *The Tree of Life*, according to *Denver Post* critic Lisa Kennedy, "is an intimate and willfully cosmic rendering of one family that unfolds as a requiem, a tone poem, as anything but a traditional narrative feature."[3] Writing for the *New York Times*, A. O. Scott singled out a specific poetic text for comparison, declaring, "It is like Wordsworth's 'Intimations of Immortality' transported into the world of 'Leave It to Beaver.'"[4] Malick's film is, in fact, a cinematic version of William Wordsworth's great ode. The two texts—literary and cinematic—meditate on the relationship between natural and divine existence, in particular on the place of human perception in the interchange between the two realms. The film's episodic structure, shaped by reverie and memory, further allies it with Wordsworth's epic *The Prelude*.

The Tree of Life is certainly not the first of Malick's films to qualify as cinematic poetry. Patterson and the other contributors to *The Cinema of Terrence Malick: Poetic Visions of America* have sought to refine the term's definition as applied to cinema and specifically to Malick's films, contending that his emphasis on landscape, preoccupations with identity and subjectivity, combined with a paucity of dialogue are the distinguishing features of his poetic vision. Other scholars have noted Malick's training as a philosopher, defining him as "modern American cinema's great poet-philosopher."[5] Given his recurrent focus on American history—from the murderous spree of Charles Starkweather and Caril Fugate in *Badlands* (1973) to the initial encounters of American colonists with indigenous inhabitants in *The New World* (2005)—Malick's vision has been classed as emphatically American.[6] While the subject matter of his films, including Texas-based *The Tree of Life*, is unquestionably American, his poetic vision is not so geographically circumscribed.

His previous filmic and philosophic works share Continental roots. As Lloyd Michaels notes, the director has frequently been described "as an essentially European filmmaker, with a narrative pace, visual style, and thematic opaqueness more akin to the continental art cinema than the New Hollywood."[7] Patterson has argued his films could easily be aligned with those of Michelangelo Antonioni.[8] As a translator of Martin Heidegger, Malick is further aligned with Continental philosophy.[9] Marc Furstenau and Leslie MacAvoy have analyzed his films in relation to Heideggerian metaphysics, arguing that they demonstrate "cinema's unique presencing of Being."[10] Malick's poetic cinema could, however, be seen as a hybrid of another sort, applying Continental aesthetics and philosophy to American landscapes and history. This would ally Malick's art with the poetry of the American transcendentalists, who in the 1830s transported the subjective idealism of German philosophers and poetic imaginings of the British Romantics to New England. It may be possible, then, to link Malick as a "stubbornly romantic artist" to Emerson, Whitman, and Dickinson, as Michaels has.[11] But I would argue that Malick's cinematic romanticism in *The Tree of Life* can be traced more directly to the Romantics themselves, particularly Wordsworth.

A CINEMATIC INTIMATIONS ODE

The full title of Wordsworth's ode—"Ode: Intimations of Immortality from Recollections of Early Childhood"—captures the narrative essence of Malick's film. An adult protagonist, Jack O'Brien (Sean Penn), reflects on his *Leave It To Beaver*–era childhood in Texas, seeking to resolve a spiritual crisis brought on by loss of his younger brother R. L. (Laramie Eppler), who died at nineteen, a wound that lingers after several decades. The first words of the film are spoken in whispered voice-over as a flame-shaped light flickers on the screen: "Brother. Mother. It was they who led me to your door." This evocative, ambiguous opening tantalizes viewers in its complexity, as poetry does: the flame is not representative of a candle flame, nor does it replicate conventional images of heavenly light. Instead, it appears as an amalgam of the natural and ethereal, with a warm, red-hued glow and shimmering motion reminiscent of a candle flame but of amorphous shape and origin, suggestive of an otherworldly source.

The flame's celestial dimensions are intimated by the film's epigraph:

> Where were you when I laid the foundations of the earth? . . .
> When the morning stars sang together, and all the sons of God shouted for joy?
> —Job 38:4,7

God's words, directed toward Job, introduce a central preoccupation of the film: human knowledge of divine creation. The form of address—God speaking in the first person to Job ("you")—appears the inverse of the voice-over's final line: "It was they who led me to your door." Jack appears to address God, stating that his brother and mother led him to God's door. His initials— J. O. B.—further enforce the connection.

However, this interpretation is further complicated, as is God's address to Job. God's use of "you" refers as well to the reader of his words in the Bible, and encompasses not simply one human being, Job, but all humans. Similarly, Jack's references to "they" and "your door" shift in the moments of the film that follow the flame's appearance: a young girl stands looking through the open half of a barn door onto a rural landscape. In voice-over, his mother (Jessica Chastain) says, "The lambs taught us there were two ways through life: the way of nature and the way of grace. You have to choose which one you'll follow." Is the door, then, God's door, the door to heaven, to grace, or the door to the barn or to the home that figures so frequently in later scenes, the doors of the natural, human world? The flame, flickering ambiguously between the epigraph and this scene, links these competing interpretations, which contend over the course of the film.

Jack's opening voice-over further implies that the conundrum—grace or nature—plays itself out in his head. The film alternates between images of the universe, including—confoundingly to many—the big bang, the evolution of life, and prehistoric dinosaurs, and flashes of Jack's existence—in both the present (his life as an architect in Dallas) and in the past, unfurled in recollections of his childhood in Waco in the 1950s. These childhood scenes dominate the film and provide the most direct link to Wordsworth's poem.

Wordsworth's ode similarly considers the interpenetration of the immortal and mortal realms, with the human mind as the hinge between the two. In both texts—cinematic and poetic—the perceptions of an adult, wracked by grief, shape the whole. In Malick's film, loss of human life—his brother's— prompts the protagonist's quest for insight, but not directly. Jack's brother died at nineteen, long before the contemporary setting of the film. This remembered loss, however, sparks a contemporary crisis. Jack despairs,

"World's going to the dogs. People are greedy, keep getting worse. I try to get into their heads." He has not only lost his brother but his way, his sense that human existence in the world has purpose, value, or connection. The adult speaker of Wordsworth's poem describes a similar loss. The poem opens:

> There was a time when meadow, grove, and stream,
> The earth, and every common sight,
> To me did seem
> Apparell'd in celestial light,
> The glory and the freshness of a dream. (1–5)[12]

He once could perceive the natural world pervaded with "celestial light," but mourns the passing of "a glory from the earth" (18). Once, recalling God's words to Job that "all the sons of God shouted for joy" at the moment of creation, the speaker did feel the joy pervading the creatures around him:

> Ye blessèd creatures, I have heard the call
> Ye to each other make; I see
> The heavens laugh with you in your jubilee;
> My heart is at your festival,
> My head hath its coronal,
> The fulness of your bliss, I feel—I feel it all. (37–42)

But now the feeling does not last. The peak of the speaker's despair coincides with his sole reference to a tree:

> ... there's a tree, of many, one,
> A single field which I have look'd upon,
> Both of them speak of something that is gone:
> The pansy at my feet
> Doth the same tale repeat:
> Whither is fled the visionary gleam?
> Where is it now, the glory and the dream? (52–58)

The speaker envisions the natural landscape that had once inspired vision now mocking him in his impotence.

While the poem originally ended there, Wordsworth later appended an affirmation of the imagination, finding consolation in memories of childhood.[13] His speaker reasons that if we once possessed imaginative vision, vestiges of this originary gift must remain in the adult:

> ... in our embers
> Is something that doth live,
> That nature yet remembers
> What was so fugitive!
> The thought of our past years in me doth breed
> Perpetual benediction. (134–39)

The adult speaker realizes that "those first affections, / Those shadowy recollections" (153–54) present in the child remain "the fountain-light of all our day, . . . a master-light of all our seeing" (156–57).

Wordsworth's "fountain-light" or "master-light" is registered cinematically as the image of the flaming light that punctuates Malick's film. Its reoccurring appearance divides the film into movements, as in a poetic or musical composition, parallels reinforced by the film's haunting score.[14] The first movement initiates Jack's childhood recollections. His brother leads the way: "Find me," he beckons from an empty seashore, and Jack complies by recalling an image of his brother in his mother's arms. As in his opening words, his brother and mother are intertwined in his mind. Jack recalls the moment of his brother's death not from his own vantage point but hers: the scene shifts to Jack's mother reading a telegram and collapsing in grief. A brief shot reveals the adult Jack looking on, as he asks, in voice-over, "How did she bear it? Mother." Since he was not present at the time, the sequence that follows, of his mother and father (Brad Pitt) reacting to news of their son's death, can only be his imagined re-creation.

Jack's imagined re-creation is structured by the two ways through life announced earlier: the way of nature and the way of grace. His father and mother are each associated, in their reactions to his brother's death, with one way. The mother, in her grief, seeking consolation in church and from the Christian homilies of neighbors and family, is associated with grace, which "accepts insults and injuries." She is pictured outside, on the lawn or in the street, as an unidentified woman, in voice-over, comments, "He was in God's hands the whole time." By contrast, the father—who receives the news by telephone, at work, where engine noises from a nearby plane drown out his words—is associated with nature, or at least the world: "Nature only wants to please itself and get others to please it, too. Likes to lord it over them. To have its own way." The father, also grieving, laments, "I had no chance to tell him how sorry I was." He criticizes himself for causing his son shame by criticizing and judging him. The contrast between the two ways is not as stark or stable as it first appears, however. As Jack later says, "Father . . . Mother . . . Always you wrestle inside me. Always you will." The two realms—grace and nature—intertwine.

A voice-over tells us that nature "finds reasons to be unhappy when all the world is shining around it and love is shining through all things." This is the dilemma of Wordsworth's speaker who castigates himself for being "sullen / While Earth herself is adorning" (43–44). The way of nature is the way of all humans. The parable of Job teaches, in part, the same, as a preacher recites in a later scene in Malick's film: "Misfortune befalls the good as well. We can't protect ourselves against it. We can't protect our children. . . . We run before the wind. We think that it will carry us forever. It will not. We vanish as a cloud. We wither as the autumn grass and like a tree are rooted up. Is there some fraud in the scheme of the universe? Is there nothing which is deathless? . . . We cannot stay where we are." Our choice is not between grace and nature but our perception of the world and the relation between the two. How are we, to borrow Wordsworth's words, to find "intimations of immortality," particularly when faced with mortality?

The second movement opens with the ethereal flame, now tinged with blue, fading into diffused, trailing lights of a city and vehicle traffic as Jack asks, in voice-over, "How did you come to me? In what shape? What disguise?" Again, the referent is ambiguous: "you" could refer to his mother and brother, to the shadowy "they" or the "you" of "your door." The latter interpretation gains traction for, as Jack speaks, we see a wooden door, ajar, opening onto bright light, then a cut to an isolated door frame against a desert expanse with an adult Jack standing in the foreground. Another cut takes us to Jack in bed, awakening, as if emphasizing that the images we have just seen come from his mind, in this case perhaps even his dreams. Dressed formally, Jack and his wife congregate in their modern kitchen. He lights a candle in a blue glass, igniting, as it were, a flashback to childhood: "I see the childhood that was. I see my brother. True. Kind." The next few moments of the film cut between images of Jack at his workplace, a glass office building, and incidents from his remembered childhood, such as boys playing. The quick interchange between the present and past implies the interpenetration of the two—on the screen and in Jack's mind.

But another set of images occupies a third dimension, disconnected from the present or past. Surveying his office building, Jack muses in voice-over: "How did I lose you? Wandered. Forgot you." As we hear his words, flashes of discontinuous images appear on-screen. Some feature the adult Jack in the frame: standing on a shore, reflected in a pool of water, wandering through desert canyons. Others feature objects or the landscape alone: a shot of a pier or clouds. These images recur in the film's epiphanic closing moments, but appear here as glimmers of Jack's later insight. But first his brother appears, hiding behind a sheer curtain, just before he beckons to Jack: "Find me." The remaining images in the second movement fuse Jack's loss and his mother's. As Jack imagines her distress, her questions become his: as he surveys a scene of bats gathering over the city at sunset, she asks, in voice-over, "Was I false to you?"

The flame appears again, signaling the third shift in the film, the red light tinged with even more blue. The intertwining colors are symbolic of the fusion between past and present, the mother and Jack. The remembered scenes from childhood in the film are shot in warm, sepia tones, while Jack's present existence is shot with a blue filter. The urban landscape he occupies is starkly modern, composed of open glass structures with windows that reflect the light and sky. He looks up at the natural world as it appears reflected on the skyscraper's mirrored windows, while his mother looks directly at the sky or filtered through the leaves of trees. Simultaneously, they search for lost grace, the fountain-light.

Their questions overlaid in voice-over—"Why? Where were you?" "Did you know?" "Who are we to you?"—highlight the uncertain relationship between humankind and the divine, between divine creation and human creation—both reproductive and imaginative. The answer provided by Malick's film is Wordsworth's:

> Our birth is but a sleep and a forgetting:
> The Soul that rises with us, our life's Star,
> Hath had elsewhere its setting,
> And cometh from afar. (59–62)

Our "life's Star" is coincident with the "master-light" of our being and seeing. As Wordsworth describes it, we come "trailing clouds of glory" (65). Malick's film offers this same insight cinematically, in an exalted sequence tracing the origin of the universe (the "astrophysical realm"), set to Zbigniew Preisner's score *Requiem for My Friend* (Part 2, Life-Apocalypse-Lacrimosa–Day of Tears).

The sequence begins as the flame that opens the third movement dissolves into successive images of more vibrant light—first, the Northern Lights, and then celestial fires, the big-bang explosion that set the universe in motion. Stars and planets appear, their surfaces convulsed by successive explosions, volcanic eruptions spewing fiery ash. The earth's elements— clouds, water, canyons, geysers, and thermal pools—appear. A shot of cells dividing and a burst of lightning announce the origins of life (the "microbial realm"). The musical score shifts to Tavener's *Lamentations and Praises* (the final piece, "Resurrection in Hades") as the camera descends into the ocean, providing lingering shots of sea plants and creatures, including hammerhead sharks circling at the surface and a menacing ray floating by. A cut takes us to a close-up of blood pumping through arteries to a beating heart then an amphibian eye. Another cut takes us to a dinosaur isolated in a primeval forest. A group of the creatures appears in a river. The sequence cuts to an asteroid floating in space, before it crashes into the earth. Bells tolling on the sound track comment on the extinction of the species, echoing the bells tolling for Jack's lost brother earlier in the film.

As these images of creation unfurl on the screen and in Jack's mind, his mother's questions are heard at various moments in voice-over:

> "Answer me."
> "We cried to you. My soul. My son."
> "Hear us."
> "Light of my life, I search for you. My hope."
> "My child."

As the bells toll, Jack says, "You spoke to me through her. You spoke with me from the sky, the trees, before I knew I loved you, believed in you." He fuses memories of his mother with those of nature, suggesting that the way of grace *is* the way of nature. Like Wordsworth, Malick imagines the natural world as imbued with divine energy. The speaker of the poem explains:

> Earth fills her lap with pleasures of her own;
> Yearnings she hath in her own natural kind,
> And, even with something of a mother's mind,
> And no unworthy aim,
> The homely nurse doth all she can
> To make her foster-child, her Inmate Man,
> Forget the glories he hath known,
> And that imperial palace when he came. (78–85)

Earth is maternal, providing parallel, natural wonders. In Malick's film, this maternal comfort is expressed in the fusion of Jack's mother and the natural setting of their home. As he recalls, the divine "spoke with me from the sky, the trees."

The film registers his birth in the same dreamlike flashes that accompany Jack's initial appearance. Flashes of his father and mother during her pregnancy transition to a shot of a tiny book, then to another of wind blowing through sheer curtains, riffling the pages of a full-size book. A sudden cut takes the viewer to an underwater scene: a child, in a house turned on its side, floats to the surface, through an open door. Another, parallel shot shows Jack's mother ascending through water to the surface, then quickly cuts to her in labor, in a hospital. This sequence enacts a set of complex fusions. The undersea images connect to the preceding images of emerging life: the origins of human life and that of primal creatures, such as the dinosaurs, are the same. The sequence further intertwines dreamlike and naturalistic images: the shots of the figures ascending through water are bookended by naturalistic shots of book pages and the scene in the hospital. The juxtaposition implies the coexistence of the imaginative or dreamlike and the real.

These fusions of past and present, natural and supernatural are sustained in a complex sequence centered on the infant Jack. Wordsworth singled out the infant in his poem as possessing unfiltered access to the "fountain-light" of our being: "he beholds the light, and when it flows, / He sees it in his joy" (70–71). For this reason, Wordsworth calls the child a "Mighty prophet! Seer blest!" (115) for he remains haunted by "the eternal mind" (114). His imaginative perceptions retain vestiges of "the visionary gleam," "the glory and the dream." Malick's film alternates between objective and subjective point of view to represent the infant's imaginative vision. For instance, we see a shot of infant Jack climbing up the stairs, followed by a chair appearing to move back from the dining table of its own accord. The first shot, captured from an objective point of view, registers his size: it comments on, but does not show, the enormity of his surroundings in relation to his small size. The second shot represents the child's vision of the chair: an adult hand—unseen in the frame—undoubtedly pulls the chair back, but in the child's subjective point of view it moves of its own accord. The viewer sees as the child does: we see a butterfly float through the sky, land on his mother's hand and then watch her pet it in the grass, before another shot offers a third-person point of view of Jack shaking a rattle and learning the names of animals.

If, however, such images all appear as Jack's recollections then Malick's film dramatizes our ability, as adults, to recover "the visionary gleam" through memory. This is the same consolation Wordsworth supplies in his ode, namely, that we can revive childhood ways of seeing, that they endure and provide solace. Our "shadowy recollections":

> Uphold us, cherish, and have power to make
> Our noisy years seem moments in the being
> Of the eternal Silence: truths that wake,
> To perish never:
> Which neither listlessness, nor mad endeavor,
> Nor Man nor Boy,
> Nor all that is at enmity with joy,
> Can utterly abolish or destroy! (158–64)

The infant's early access to "the glory and the dream" endures in the man and in the boy, ready to be revived by memory. Malick's film stages the process in a scene when the young Jack (Hunter McCracken) asks, in voice-over: "Make some stories . . . in words. . ." His father tells him the story of his birth. As he does so, the film represents the boy's point of view: he reviews a sequence of lights—the light over the dining table as seen through his bedroom door, a night light, light streaming through a window in the attic. These images of light suggest his access to Wordsworth's "fountain-light" or "master-light." The first images of light reveal it as present in the everyday, in concrete shape in the house itself. The final image, however, recalls an earlier image of the infant's: the light streaming from outside through the attic window along the floor. The young Jack appears to recall the infant Jack's perception. But both—the young boy's sights and the infant's—are recalled by the adult Jack. The lights—all white—connect perceptions of the infant, the boy, and the man.

TERRENCE MALICK'S "SPOTS OF TIME"

While Wordsworth's ode describes the child's imagination, it does not dramatize the process. That occurs not in his great ode, but in *The Prelude*. Wordsworth's poetic technique in his epic more closely resembles Malick's cinematic vision: the director employs film images in place of language to display the workings of memory and the transforming powers of dream and imagination.[15] Subtitled *Growth of a Poet's Mind*, the poem traces the origin of adult imaginative vision to infancy. In its opening book, Wordsworth argues,

> . . . even then I felt
> Gleams like the flashing of a shield: the earth
> And common face of Nature spake to me
> Rememberable things (I.614–16)

He employs the same vocabulary—"gleams"—as in his ode to describe insight as light. They appear as reflected flashes, a term that easily applies to the quick successions of partial images that appear frequently in *The Tree of Life*.

These "rememberable things" endured, the poet explains, "Until maturer seasons call'd them forth / To impregnate and to elevate the mind" (I.624–25). Then they appear as "spots of time":

> There are in our existence spots of time,
> Which with distinct preeminence retain
> A renovating Virtue, whence, depress'd
> By false opinion and contentious thought,
> Or aught of heavier or more deadly weight
> In trivial occupations, and the round
> Of ordinary intercourse, our minds
> Are nourish'd, and invisibly repair'd,
> A virtue by which pleasure is enhanced
> That penetrates, enables us to mount
> When high, more high, and lifts us up when fallen. (11.258–68)

These "spots of time," remembered, revive and restore the mind, lifting us from depression to recovered joy. They are "scatter'd every where" (11.275) throughout our lives but "most conspicuous" in childhood (11.275–77). In his epic, Wordsworth recalls several: stealing a boat, ice-skating, witnessing a drowned man. Jack's recollections of childhood similarly appear as "spots of time," episodes on which the film lingers: seeing a drowned boy at the swimming pool, throwing rocks at windows, stealing a female neighbor's slip.

The climax in Wordsworth's poem occurs when, describing his ascent of Mount Snowdon, he experienced

> The perfect image of a mighty Mind
> Of one that feeds upon infinity,
> That is exalted by an underpresence,
> The sense of God, or whatsoe'er is dim
> Or vast in its own being (13.69–73)

He perceives his own mind in perfect harmony with the creative force of nature. The power animating the world before him has its "genuine Counterpart" (13.88) within him in "the glorious faculty / Which higher minds bear with them as their own" (13.89–90). His imagination can create just as the creator of the universe can. Minds such as these "are truly from the Deity; / For they are Powers; and hence the highest bliss / That can be known is theirs" (13.106–108).

In Malick's film, the young Jack seeks to match his vision to God's, asking him, in a bedside prayer, "Are you watching me? I want to know what you are. I want to see what you see." Images shot from above, as when Jack looks down on his brother as if from among or above tree branches, may suggest this omniscient view. "What was it that you showed me?" Jack asks. But as before, the referent is uncertain: is he addressing God or his brother, the center of his vision? The ambiguity intermingles the divine and human, further linked by the framing natural setting. Jack also prays to his mother: "Mother. Make me good. Brave." He speaks these words in voice-over between two peaks of imaginative vision. Asked by her sons to "Tell us a story from before we can remember," Jack's mother tells of a plane ride. Yet we see the flight from his imagined view, offering an aerial perspective of a passenger. The elevated vision of fields gives way to an otherworldly image of his mother suspended in air, back arched, as though dancing above the ground. In Jack's imagination, the mother's flight becomes the mother *in* flight. He can achieve a perspective akin to that of a transcendent deity but also create a vision of his own that, godlike, defies natural law. In his mind, he has the power to transform and manipulate the world.

For Malick as for Wordsworth, imaginative power, itself akin to the creative power that set the universe in motion, further enables its possessor to perceive the world as "divine and true" (13.143) and to feel love, from which "all grandeur comes, / All truth and beauty" (13.150–51). Wordsworth distinguishes this all-pervading love from ordinary, human affection:

> . . . there is higher love
> Than this, a love that comes into the heart
> With awe and diffusive sentiment;
> Thy love is human merely; this proceeds
> More from the brooding Soul, and is divine.
> This love more intellectual cannot be
> Without Imagination, which in truth
> Is but a another name for absolute strength
> And clearest insight, amplitude of mind,
> And reason in her most exalted mood. (13.161–70)

This "higher" love, love "more intellectual," depends on the imagination. Those who possess it can achieve "The feeling of life endless, the one thought / By which we live, Infinity and God" (13.183–84).

Malick's film ends with a similarly transcendent—and ascendant—vision. Jack's recollections of childhood come to a close as the family prepares to move, after his father loses his job. Over images of the family's departure, Jack's mother says, in voice-over: "The only way to be happy is to love. Unless you love, your life will flash by." She issues imperatives: "Do good to them. Wonder. Hope." A cut to the blue flame returns us to Jack in the present, in the office building, ascending in a glass elevator. The film then cuts to an epiphanic vision with motivic elements of Jack's earlier dreamlike state: he walks, following a woman, through an arid desert, approaching the same empty doorway from the opening moments of the film. This time, he walks through the door. Scenes of a planet floating before a red disk suggest a complementary internal, imaginative transition to "the end of time" (as the voice-over implies), where Jack encounters his younger self, experiencing the "feeling of life endless" Wordsworth describes, as present coexists with the past. Eventually, as though guided there by his young self, Jack stands on a seashore, surrounded by others, many recognizable as the people populating his childhood memories: a boy scarred by fire, his youngest brother, his mother, and his father.

The parallels to Wordsworth's poetic vision are startling. In his ode, Wordsworth writes,

> Though inland far we be,
> Our souls have sight of that immortal sea
> Which brought us hither,
> Can in a moment travel thither,
> And see the children sport upon the shore,
> And hear the mighty waters rolling evermore. (166–72)

The human imagination allows us to transport ourselves to an immortal world, untouched by death. Jack sees "the children sport upon the shore," comforting himself with the vision of his brother—and others he has lost. Just as Wordsworth's vision fuses the divine and the natural, so does Malick's. The music accompanying Jack's vision—Berlioz's *Requiem*, Opus 5 (*Grande Messe des Mort*)—and the repetition of "Amen" suggest a biblical interpretation of the scene, while its emphatically natural setting on the seashore emphasizes the natural (and recalls the scenes of primordial life's watery origins). In Jack's imagination, as in Wordsworth's, the way of grace fuses with the way of nature. Malick underscores the point with a cut to a field of sunflowers before we see Jack, returned to the elevator, descending.

Closing images of Jack on the street before the building convey his transformation of mood, his attainment of the "exalted mood" described in *The Prelude*. Returned to the present and the street, Jack appears disoriented, looking around as though seeing his common surroundings anew. He smiles, recognizing the immortal presence of nature, in the sky reflected in the glass buildings, a bridge suspended over a watery expanse. His grief appears transmuted to joy, as though he has, through memory and imagination, experienced the "primal sympathy" Wordsworth describes in his ode:

> In the primal sympathy
> Which having been must ever be;
> In the soothing thoughts that spring
> Out of human suffering;
> In the faith that looks through death,
> In years that bring the philosophic mind. (186–91)

By the poem's conclusion, Wordsworth's speaker no longer despairs that age has dimmed "the visionary gleam," "the glory and the dream," but boasts that it refines the childish imagination into the "philosophic mind," capable of transcendent insights into immortality. In an earlier poem, "Lines Written a Few Miles above Tintern Abbey" (1798), he had described it in similarly expansive language, as a mood:

> . . . that blessed mood,
> In which the burthen of the mystery,
> In which the heavy and the weary weight
> Of all this unintelligible world,
> Is lightened:—that serene and blessed mood,
> In which the affections gently lead us on,—
> Until, the breath of this corporeal frame
> And even the motion of our human blood
> Almost suspended, we are laid asleep
> In body, and become a living soul:
> While with an eye made quiet by the power
> Of harmony, and the deep power of joy,
> We see into the life of things. (36–48)[16]

This intense visionary capacity emerges out of the act of "recollection in tranquility," allowing us to see not simply into ourselves but into the origins of existence. The final shot of Malick's film suggests that Jack—and by extension the viewer who has experienced the whole from his perspective—has attained the power to "see into the life of things." A final image of the celestial flame flickers as gulls cry in the distance: nature and grace entwined.

The light that opens and closes *The Tree of Life* further reminds us that we are watching the flickering lights of film. Jack's imaginative vision is, in fact, Malick's creation (with the assistance, of course, of cinematographer Emmanuel Lubezki, special-effects supervisor Douglas Trumball, and composer Alexandre Desplat). The director is the cinematic equivalent of the poet. As Marc Furstenau and Leslie MacAvoy have argued, Malick, in his films, is

> performing the function of the artist, of the poet during what Heidegger called "destitute times," when the world is voided of mystery and depth, as language, thought and representation themselves are put to merely instrumental ends.

Heidegger accorded to poetry and art an important and specifically restorative function. The poet's task, as Heidegger insists in *What Are Poets For?* is to reveal what metaphysics has obscured: the presencing of Being through the use of evocative, poetic language.[17]

To put this more simply, perhaps: Malick's cinema rejects commercial Hollywood conventions and attains the ideal of art, as Heidegger defines it, by fusing visual image and language to illuminate the condition of being in the world. If, as Furstenau and MacAvoy contend, "Malick has assumed the role of the poet-philosopher, putting the cinema to poetic and philosophical ends," then in *The Tree of Life* we witness the fruits of the "philosophic mind" Wordsworth described in his ode. And, as Wordsworth did in *The Prelude*, Malick crafted his art out of his own "spots of time," his own childhood in Waco, Texas. Like his protagonist, Malick also lost a brother, who committed suicide at nineteen while studying guitar in Spain.[18] Yet his film, like Wordsworth's poetry, is not limited to the story of one life. In the tranquil space created by the cinematic experience, Malick's film unfurls in the minds of its viewers who see, through it, into the very "life of things."

NOTES

1. Hannah Patterson, "Introduction: Poetic Visions of America," in *The Cinema of Terrence Malick: Poetic Visions of America*, ed. Hannah Patterson, 2nd ed. (London: Wallflower, 2007), 2.

2. Peter Simek, "*The Tree of Life*: Is Terrence Malick's Film Brilliant Cinematic Poetry or Pretentious with a Capital 'P'?" *D Magazine*, June 3, 2011, http://frontrow.dmagazine.com/2011/06/the-tree-of-life-is-terrance-malicks-film-brilliant-cinematic-poetry-or-pretentious-with-a-capital-p/.

3. Lisa Kennedy, "Terrence Malick's Family Portrait *The Tree of Life* Unfolds Like Carefully Crafted Verse," *Denver Post*, June 10, 2011, http://www.denverpost.com/movies/ci_18233462.

4. A. O. Scott, "Heaven, Texas and the Cosmic Whodunit," *New York Times*, May 26, 2011, http://movies.nytimes.com/2011/05/27/movies/the-tree-of-life-from-terrence-malick-review.html.

5. Geoff Andrew, *The Director's Vision: A Concise Guide to the Art of 250 Great Filmmakers* (Chicago: A Cappella Books, 1999), 140. For a brief overview of Malick's biography, see Lloyd Michaels, *Terrence Malick* (Urbana: University of Illinois Press, 2009), 14–20.

6. John Orr considers Malick's films in the "American Reveries" chapter of *Contemporary Cinema* (Edinburgh: Edinburgh University Press, 1998), 173–80. James Morrison and Thomas Schur describe *Days of Heaven* as an amalgam of classic American literary sources: it "weds Whitman's poetic idea of the democratic vista to the interior landscapes of Henry James, with a plot that evokes *The Wings of the Dove*," while also evoking Mark Twain, Willa Cather, Rebecca Harding Davis, and Stephen Crane. See *The Films of Terrence Malick* (Westport, Conn.: Praeger, 2003), 23–24, 33.

7. Michaels, *Terrence Malick*, 2.

8. Patterson, "Introduction," 2. Malick's limited use of dialogue and preference for voice-over have been discussed by Morrison and Schur, *Films of Terrence Malick*, 26–27. Owing to their paucity of dialogue, the films have also been linked to the aesthetics of silent cinema (Michaels, *Terrence Malick*, 3).

9. Morrison and Schur, *Films of Terrence Malick*, 1.

10. Marc Furstenau and Leslie MacAvoy, "Terrence Malick's Heideggerian Cinema: War and the Question of Being in *The Thin Red Line*," in *The Cinema of Terrence Malick: Poetic Visions of America*, ed. Hannah Patterson, 2nd ed. (London: Wallflower, 2007), 182.

11. Michaels, *Terrence Malick*, 4–5.

12. William Wordsworth, "Ode: Intimations of Immortality from Recollections of Early Childhood," *The Oxford Book of English Verse*, ed. Arthur Quiller-Couch (Oxford: Clarendon, 1919), http://www.bartleby.com/101/536.html.

13. In draft form, the poem originally ended there, and when Wordsworth shared it with his friend and collaborator Samuel Taylor Coleridge, it prompted Coleridge to pen his own ode in reply: "Dejection: An Ode." In it, Coleridge's speaker similarly expresses his grief at losing his "genial spirits" (39), "the passion and the life, whose fountains are within" (46). Coleridge's speaker claimed that he once possessed the "shaping spirit of imagination" (86) given to him at birth by "nature" (85)—and by nature itself revived within him. Inspired by his natural surroundings, he experienced "the spirit and the power, / Which wedding Nature to us gives in dower / A new Earth and new Heaven" (67–69). The speaker's imagination, inspired by nature, re-created it anew in the mind—and in his poetry. He describes it as "This light, this glory, this fair luminous mist, / This beautiful and beauty-making power" (62–63). But, burdened by "viper thoughts" (94), "Reality's dark dream" (95), he no longer feels the power or the joy it once gave him. After reading Coleridge's poem, Wordsworth appended an affirmation of the "beautiful and beauty-making power" of the imagination. For an overview of the relationship between the two poets and their poems, see Thomas MacFarland, *Romanticism and the Forms of Ruin: Wordsworth, Coleridge, and Modalities of Fragmentation* (Princeton, N.J.: Princeton University Press, 1981). For more detail, consult Gene W. Ruoff, *Wordsworth and Coleridge: The Making of the Lyrics, 1802 – 1804* (New Brunswick, N.J.: Rutgers University Press, 1989).

14. This further connects Malick's work to Wordsworth's: in *The Prelude*, he writes, "The mind of man is framed even like the breath / And harmony of music. There is dark / Invisible workmanship that reconciles / Discordant elements" (1.152–55). William Wordsworth, *The Complete Poetical Works* (London: Macmillan, 1888), http://www.bartleby.com/145/ww287.html.

15. Michaels notes that *The Thin Red Line* closes by "virtually quoting" *The Prelude*, so Malick is clearly familiar with the text. See Michaels, *Terrence Malick*, 73.

16. William Wordsworth, "Lines Written a Few Miles above Tintern Abbey, on Revisiting the Banks of the Wye during a Tour, July 13, 1798," *Lyrical Ballads* (London: J. & A. Arch, 1798), www.rc.umd.edu/reader/tabbey.html.

17. Furstenau and MacAvoy, "Terrence Malick's Heideggerian Cinema," 182.

18. Michaels, *Terrence Malick*, 16.

Chapter Twelve

A Step Away from the Cinema

Hollywood and the Poetry of Frank O'Hara

Walter Metz

At the 2007 Literature/Film Association Annual Conference, Tom Leitch observed that, despite poetry's aesthetic importance to the cinema, the Internet Movie Database lists some one hundred films based on poems, compared with over one thousand entries for films based on toys![1] In his presentation, "Filming Poetry," Leitch added that adaptation scholars, with their narrow focus on the novel, have been of little help, citing Brian McFarland's observation that poetry is not of interest for adaptation studies. Indeed, the best academic article published on the relationship between poetry and cinema is to be found in Robert Richardson's seminal book, *Literature and Film* (1969).[2] Over forty years later, our interest in adaptation can finally turn toward a wider range of sources than the traditional novel or the commercially obvious (toys and comic books). The intervening rise of intertextual studies provides an opportunity for assessing the relationship between poetry and cinema in nonreductive ways. In this chapter, I will argue for analogical relationships between the linguistic poetics of Frank O'Hara and the visual aesthetics of Otto Preminger's *Anatomy of a Murder* (1959). Although vastly different artists, engaging diversely with American culture, O'Hara's and Preminger's works share an interest in the political rhythms of everyday human interaction.

Frank O'Hara was an important member of the New York School, a group of post–World War II poets and painters. O'Hara contributed to the centering of American art in late-1950s New York City by applying the techniques of French symbolism (for example, Arthur Rimbaud's sensual linguistic explorations) to the postwar American locale. O'Hara's poems build informal stories of his autobiographical experiences walking around the city. Having worked at the front desk of the Museum of American Art (MOMA), his poems expressed his escape into a world of ideas, often while wandering around the city. Included in *The Collected Poems of Frank O'Hara*, "A Step Away from Them" and "Steps" emphasize the ephemeral nature of cognition, moving from one observation to another in a string of references that map both the physical space and cultural diversity of New York City.[3] His poems also dialectically link high art (jazz, abstract expressionist painting, modernist literature) with popular commercial artifacts (popular music, movies, and, a favorite of his, the trademarked name Coca-Cola).

The poems emphasize the communal joys of the city, found not in its landmarks like MOMA, but instead in the everyday experiences of people doing mundane things like eating. "A Step Away from Them" begins with the line, "It's my lunch hour, so I go / for a walk, among the hum-colored cabs."[4] One of O'Hara's beautiful love sonnets is titled "Having a Coke with You," a stunning expression of how the emotional impact of everyday life transcends high art:

> I never think of the *Nude Descending a Staircase* or
> at a rehearsal a single drawing of Leonardo or Michelangelo that used to wow me
> and what good does all the research of the Impressionists do them
> when they never got the right person to stand near the tree when the sun sank[5]

Indeed, in ways beyond his reflections on art history, O'Hara's poetry finds buoyancy from the intertextual, the focus of my analysis in this chapter: he loved both classical and popular music, a medium that finds its way into many of his poems, most famously, "The Day Lady Died," in which O'Hara learns of the death of blues singer Billie Holiday while wandering around New York City on his lunch hour. My O'Hara-driven reading of *Anatomy of a Murder* will focus on the eating of eggs at a downtown lunch stand in the middle of Preminger's film.

By drawing together such disparate texts, I am trying to resist the banal connections between poetry and cinema that are characteristic of adaptation studies' interest in novels and films. In the world of Beat poetry, this would lead to analyses of films such as *Pull My Daisy* (Robert Frank and Alfred Leslie, 1959), written by Jack Kerouac and starring Allen Ginsberg. A beautifully shot black-and-white short, the film ends in typical Beat narcissism, as the men hit the road, abandoning the women whom the film has associated with repression and a Catholic bishop who has come to visit them in their Greenwich Village apartment. While a remarkable confluence of a major visual artist (the photographer Frank) with linguistic masters (the Beats Ginsberg and Kerouac), the one-to-one correspondence between film and poetry implied in this analysis leads toward seeking only the prior defined Beat culture in the cinematic artifact, rather than engaging my quest to define cinema's more general poetic nature.

On the other end of the spectrum, literary scholars forward abstract theoretical linkages between cinema and poetry. This is the approach taken by Robert Richardson's early work, arguing:

> Montage . . . is the most characteristic feature of film form [and] the aspect of film that has had the greatest impact on literature. The excesses into which this technique can lead are most evident in the work of Robbe-Grillet and the numerous writers who see as he does a mandate for chaos in the film's technique of juxtaposition, while the greatest constructive uses of montage in literature are to be found in modern poetry.[6]

Richardson offers an historical tour from Vachel Lindsay (a poet who also wrote a foundational history of cinema) to Edwin Arlington Robinson, a poet tragically too early for the cinema with which he would likely have been fascinated, and then Wallace Stevens and T. S. Eliot, the heroes who fulfill a "logic of imagery," a form of visual wordplay predicted but not fulfilled by Walt Whitman in the nineteenth century.

Recent work on the relationship between poetry and cinema has taken up in more sophisticated terms this imagist linkage. In his highly instructive article, "T. S. Eliot and Cinema," David Trotter engages in thoroughly researched literary biography to establish Eliot's engagement with the cinema, something that others have tried to defend Eliot from, seeing him as "the mandarin high modernist who remained, in this one respect at least, a mandarin high modernist."[7] Trotter then effectively traces the ways that Eliot's life and poems represent a complex engagement with the cinema.

This is all well and good—it tells us about the cinematic nature of Eliot's poetry—but tells us little about the poetic nature of the cinema. To accomplish this latter goal, I am interested in establishing midlevel intertextual connections (not too precise, yet not too abstract) between great works of poetry and great works of cinema, not abiding subordinating one form to the other. One might argue, for example, that Alfred Hitchcock is a poet of the cinema. To do so, we would have to engage in analogical argumentation, suggesting that the function of the "To be or not to be" soliloquy in William Shakespeare's *Hamlet* (1601), interrupting the plot, but deploying linguistic virtuosity, is replicated in Hitchcock's *Notorious* (1946). An interior crane shot introduces us to the party scene, beginning in extreme long shot but coming to rest on an extreme close-up of Alicia's hand holding a stolen key, which she must pass to her American agent lover without her Nazi husband finding out. The showy effect of this shot is less about narrative development, and more about poetically celebrating the cinema's ability to deploy, and indeed to distort, space. The crane shot is Hitchcock's visual bravura, the analogue to the verbosity of the Shakespearean soliloquy.[8]

"IT'S MY LUNCH HOUR": O'HARA, PREMINGER, AND THE INTERRUPTED WORKDAY

Clearly, just as William Shakespeare is not the only poet of the English theatrical tradition, nor can Hitchcock be the only poet of the cinema. Otto Preminger's *Anatomy of a Murder* (1959) is an adaptation of a popular novel by John Voelker (a.k.a. Robert Traver), a judge on the 1950s Michigan State Supreme Court. Unless all films are poetic by nature of their aesthetic and linguistic style, there is nothing at first glance peculiarly poetic about *Anatomy of a Murder*. It does feature a taut script, fine acting, particularly by Jimmy Stewart and George C. Scott, and an excellent jazz score by Duke Ellington, but what I am interested in is just one minor scene, in which two characters go downtown to eat lunch.[9]

An alcoholic lawyer, Paul Biegler (James Stewart), is offered a strange case to defend a ne'er-do-well army soldier, Lt. Frederick Manion (Ben Gazzara). Paul refuses to take the case until at an impromptu lunch meeting his drunken assistant Parnell McCarthy (Arthur O'Connell) convinces him that they need the money. Just as it seems the case has brought them both back to life—Paul wins a tough legal battle against assistant state attorney general Claude Dancer (George C. Scott)—Manion and his sultry wife, Laura (Lee Remick) skip town without paying their legal fees.

In the scene that concerns me, the two men, Paul and Parnell, go to lunch at an outdoor diner, the "Waterfront Lunch Stand" near the shipping docks in Marquette, a city on the southern shore of Lake Superior in Upper Peninsula Michigan, the setting of Traver's novel, and the actual location of Preminger's filming. The men are discussing whether or not Paul should take the case. The first shot in the sequence begins with a two-shot of a bald man wearing a tie, working behind the counter at the diner, and a customer sitting at the front of the counter. The customer is sitting with his back to the camera, and is wearing a black hat. In the background of the image, we can see Paul in between these two men in the foreground. He is wearing a gray hat with a black brim, and is bending over his plate, peeling an egg. Directly behind Paul lies a vast area of open water, Lake Superior. The top of the image frames the overhang of the diner, a black structure that obscures our view of the sky over Paul's head. In the upper right-hand corner of the image, a crane on the docks moves to the left. The man working at the diner hands the first customer his change, picks up an empty beer bottle and a dirty plate, and walks offscreen left of the image. The customer gets up from his stool at the counter and walks offscreen right.

As the two men in the foreground leave the image, Paul and Parnell are reframed in an eye-level two-shot. They are sitting on the other side of the counter, and both have boiled eggs on their plates. A beer bottle sits to the left of Parnell's right hand. A saltshaker sits to the right of Paul's left arm.

The camera tracks in at the two men slowly, over the top of the front counter, where the first customer previously sat. A train traverses the rear of the image, from left to right, disappearing quickly. The train dominates most of the image, as it is directly behind where Paul and Parnell sit. As the middle car is passing the center of the image, Paul grabs the saltshaker, placing it on the counter between himself and Parnell. Then, Parnell picks up the saltshaker and begins to season his egg. The crane previously seen in the upper right now travels down and to the right of the image, behind the train. The camera comes to a rest as soon as the last part of the train leaves the right-hand side of the image, resulting in a slightly low-angle medium shot of the two men. The camera lies directly in between the two men, and thus we are made to peer straight at them.

Behind Paul and Parnell, a large bridge made of iron trusses dominates the image. The bridge takes up nearly a quarter of the image, despite being dozens of yards behind them. A smokestack, on top of the bridge, in the upper right-hand corner of the image spews a large amount of soot. The crane rises over Parnell's right shoulder, and is controlled by a rectangular structure mounted to the bottom of the bridge's trusses, presumably housing the human operator of this gargantuan machinery. The crane moves upward and to the right, passing directly behind Parnell's head, and then passes behind Paul.

Parnell, talking to Paul, gestures with his hand, in which he is holding the saltshaker. He gestures for Paul to take some salt, but Paul shakes his head in refusal. After fifteen seconds, the crane travels downward and to the left, passing from behind Paul's head to behind Parnell's left shoulder. Parnell has put the saltshaker down on the counter offscreen to the left, and now holds a beer bottle in his hand, gesturing with it as he talks. The crane again rises over Parnell's right shoulder and resumes its travel back toward the right-hand side of the image. Parnell puts the beer bottle down on the counter offscreen to the left. Parnell now grabs the saltshaker and puts it down in the middle of the counter, directly between himself and Paul. The shot concludes as Paul grabs the saltshaker and seasons his egg. As he does so, the crane behind him travels from right to left, disappearing once again behind Parnell.

The mise-en-scène described above informs an analysis of Preminger's treatment of the two characters, and their relationship with each other, particularly as that relationship is informed by their environmental surroundings. The key to understanding the expressivity of the shot lies in the many layers of depth therein present. These layers are inhabited by (from closest to the camera to farthest away): the first customer, the man who serves the food, the two lawyers, the train, the crane and the bridge, and Lake Superior in the far background. Preminger's choice to first show the worker at the diner and another customer in front of the main characters suggests a less focused relationship between Preminger and his characters than would ordinarily be present in classical Hollywood narration, which generally only shows what is necessary to forward the plot. The large number of distractions provided by Preminger's process shot affirms his interest not so much in what the characters are saying, but in the two characters' relationship to their lived environment. The smallness of the two men in comparison with the huge train and shipping equipment that dominates the image shows the small influence that men have on both the physical world (the bridge trusses) as well as the moral world (the law as articulated by the flawed judicial system). The mechanics that subtend the men are much more powerful than the influence either one of them can possibly exert.

The characters' relationship to each other is also a concern of the mise-en-scène. Paul and Parnell are filmed at the same plane of depth, but Paul takes up more of the image because he is taller (because Stewart is taller than O'Connell). Paul's presence dominates the image; his importance in the world is visually displayed through his height. This difference, however, is ultimately miniscule in comparison with the variance in size between the men and the scale of the physical world behind them.

The relationship between the characters and the other objects in the shot is what renders the images so poetic. First, Parnell is associated with the beer bottle, while Paul is seen with a beer bottle only for one brief moment. The influence of alcohol as an "irresistible impulse" becomes a large part of Preminger's presentation of Parnell's character. Paul is also seen with beer, suggesting that he is not immune to alcohol or what it represents for Parnell. However, Paul is visually shown to be able to deny temptation. The images determine our understanding of this difference via the variable amount of time that beer is associated with each character.

The saltshaker also serves as such a visual icon of morality. Only one character at a time is associated with the saltshaker. At the beginning of the shot, the condiment is next to Paul. Then for most of the duration of the shot, Paul holds it in his hand. Only at the very end of the shot does Paul actually season his egg with this object. Never in the shot do the two men touch it at the same time. As the men discuss the morality of defending Lt. Marion, the saltshaker is passed back and forth between them, as if an integral part of their deliberations. The saltshaker comes to be associated with Paul as he enters the scene, his mind filled with thoughts of defending the guilty man so that he can earn much-needed income. The saltshaker is associated with Parnell during the bulk of the shot as he actively convinces Paul to confront what he calls his "purity" and go ahead and take the case. At one moment, Parnell gestures to give the saltshaker back to Paul, thinking that he has convinced his boss to take the case. However, he is premature in this assumption, as Paul shakes his head negatively, and refuses to take the saltshaker, because, as he says, he is "not ready yet," either to accept the salt or to take the case. As the shot comes to a close, Paul has been convinced to take the case, and at last takes the saltshaker in his hand, picking it up off the counter. The fact that the men never touch the shaker at the same time shows Preminger's refusal to link Paul and Parnell on equal terms in their unholy alliance of moral corruption.

The movement of the crane functions similarly to the back-and-forth of the saltshaker. The crane travels between the two men in rhythm during the conversation about the morality of taking the case. The crane begins on Paul's side of the image, but then quickly moves to Parnell. As Parnell suggests that Paul turn his back on his purity and defend the lieutenant, the crane moves back toward Paul. It stays down behind Paul for a good deal of the time that Parnell is talking. As Paul explains to Parnell that he is not the right lawyer for the job, the crane then moves back toward Parnell. Now, the crane moves back toward Paul quickly, as Parnell suggests that Paul is afraid of being beaten in the courtroom, taunting his boss's masculinity. The shot ends as Paul finally agrees to take the case. As this happens, the crane begins to move from Paul back to Parnell again, but the shot ends before it can make its way all the way across the image one last time.

In this way, *Anatomy of a Murder* suggests that both Paul and Parnell are caught up in the moral corruption that their decision was wrought. The movement of the crane indicates a way in which they are visually separated from one another. When they finally come to the agreement to take the case, the crane is directly in between the men, as the dissolve into the next shot begins, connecting them in a visual logic of moral ambiguity.

The bizarre setting of this scene suggests the incongruous visual poetry of Preminger's images. Why are these lawyers eating, not at some upscale downtown eatery, but instead at a working-class lunch stand? Since the diner is outside, we see the location—the docks of a shipping area, complete with iron bridges and cargo trains—in a striking way. Also, it is clear that the men are eating as if they are working-class laborers, consuming beer and boiled eggs for lunch. The visuals here accentuate the fact that these two lawyers are struggling to survive, and the ethics of their decision to take the case must be processed through that materialist framework.

The relationship between the characters and the frame itself contributes to this ethical analysis. As the shot begins, the frame is in one sense closed, as the roof of the diner is present atop the image. Also, the rectilinear movement of the train confines and delimits the space inhabited by Paul and Parnell. However, as a result of the camera movement, the framing opens up, as there is in fact no roof where the men are sitting; what we believed to be the roof was merely the lunch stand's metallic awning. Later in the shot, we can see the sky behind Paul, as well as the large amount of machinery that dominates the background of the image. The men are fully integrated into the outside world, the heavy equipment of which subtends their decision to engage once again in the machinations of the legal system. Preminger shows the dichotomy between the men as isolated beings and them as players in a spectacle, outside and in full view of the public.

The spirit of this scene oddly dovetails with a 1950s poem by the New York School poet Frank O'Hara. In his poem, "A Step Away from Them," O'Hara describes in completely informal language leaving his job as a curator at the Museum of Modern Art to wander on his lunch hour around the city. O'Hara begins his poem:

> It's my lunch hour, so I go
> For a walk among the hum-colored
> cabs. First, down the sidewalk
> where laborers feed their dirty
> glistening torsos sandwiches [10]

The poem thus begins with a throwaway informality. The narrator tells us that, on his lunch hour, he strolls in the city, first noticing laborers. This narrator gazes sexually at these workers, the initial notice of their "glistening torsos" falling into place with "if / I ever get to be a construction worker / I'd like to have a silver hat please" from a different O'Hara work, "Personal Poem." [11] There is no such overt queering of the downtown space in *Anatomy of a Murder*. However, Paul and Parnell's choice to eat with the construction workers is indeed the most remarkable thing about an already pretty remarkable movie. Throughout the scene, a huge crane glides back and forth between Paul and Parnell, an iron analogue to the debate between the characters. In O'Hara's terms, these two, as out of place as they appear, find their resolve amid the construction life of the city. While Paul and Parnell do not appear to embrace gay desire, they do find themselves at home in the same space as does O'Hara's narrator, the vast differences between Marquette and New York City notwithstanding.

The mise-en-scène of the scene offers us the film's visual poetry. Paul carefully cradles his beer bottle while Parnell flings it around as he gestures to speak. Paul holds his arms close to his body as he meticulously peels his egg before consuming it. Parnell wolfs down his egg. Finally, and most importantly, Paul refuses to take the salt from Parnell's hands, even after he has agreed to take the case because they need the fee, refusing to fall completely into Parnell's corrupted state. This visual attention to detail resonates with O'Hara's interest in the small objects of the city: Coca-Cola, queered construction hats, and old posters advertising a bullfight.

There are other scenes in *Anatomy of a Murder* that resonate with "A Step Away from Them." However, in these other cases, the film explores the thematic material without O'Hara's informality. For example, both the film and the poem resist the 1950s urge to negate the presence of African Americans. O'Hara observes:

[A] Negro stands in a doorway with a
toothpick, languorously agitating.
A blonde chorus girl clicks: he
Smiles and rubs his chin. [12]

Anatomy of a Murder establishes Laura's scandalous behavior via these tropes of black and white desire. While her husband is in jail, Laura goes to an African American club where Pie Eye (Duke Ellington) plays jazz. Paul follows her there, attempting to get clues, but ends up policing Laura's behavior, in a very different way than O'Hara's narrator, who observes but does not judge.

More importantly, though, the one scene in *Anatomy of a Murder* devoted to the subaltern life of African Americans serves the film's rigid narrative structure: all is inexorably moving toward the film's climax, the betrayal of Paul by the Manions, sending him back to the drunken cesspool from which he came. Conversely, O'Hara never returns us to his job at MOMA during "A Step Away from Them." The poem is radically committed to the ineffable, chaotic flow of the city. Indeed, the line that immediately follows the image of the African American man looking at the blonde chorus girl is the poem's signature line that parodies such filmic narrative precision: "Everything / suddenly honks: it is 12:40 of / a Thursday." [13] That is, O'Hara defines precisely the time and location, but this mechanism is completely belied by his wandering on his lunch hour. This is the one time of the day that the narrator is not defeated by the city's temporal logic of clocks and punch cards. The scene at Pie Eye's club in *Anatomy of a Murder* does not foreground this alternative life for white America. Only the scene at the lunch counter embraces the informal visions of Frank O'Hara.

CONCLUSION

What I have attempted via this collision of the work of Otto Preminger and Frank O'Hara, is not a monolithic theory of the relationship between poetry and cinema. Indeed, I do not hold out any promise for such a project. Instead, I believe the most fecund relationship will be found in ineffable, midlevel intertextual linkages between poems and films. That is, good attentive criticism, of both poetry and cinema, will lead the way.

Indeed, looked at rationally, *Anatomy of a Murder* and "A Step Away from Them" are very different pieces of culture. O'Hara's range of referencing is on a higher cultural level than Preminger's. O'Hara's narrator lives in the world of abstract expressionism ("First / Bunny died, then John Latouche, / then Jackson Pollock. But is the / earth as full as life was full, of them?"). [14] He loves poetry itself: "My heart is in my / pocket, it is Poems by Pierry Reverdy" (257). [15] Yet, differently but no less importantly, *Anatomy of a Murder* engages with the everyday details of American political life: the trial judge is played by Joseph N. Welch, the army attorney who stood up to Joseph McCarthy during the Army-McCarthy hearings. Thus, I offer this exploration of a relationship between poetry and cinema as an engagement with the beauty and substance that both art forms offer to our quest for a better humanity.

Methodologically, this essay also reimports the method of close textual analysis still necessary in poetry studies back into film studies. While formalism was, in the 1970s, a major part of our discipline, it has since fallen theoretically out of favor. While Bordwell and Thompson, both via their textbook, *Film Art,* and through a more general defense of neo-formalist analysis, have kept the torch alive, it is largely the case that formalist analysis in film studies is only deployed nowadays to support larger theoretical arguments.[16]

This chapter points to the missed opportunities produced by this turn away from formalism, both biographically and theoretically. My return to an essay I wrote as an undergraduate is for me a way of reflecting back upon how I have developed as a film critic over the past twenty-five years. Would I have noticed when I read Frank O'Hara's poem a few years ago its relationship to the lunchtime digression of *Anatomy of a Murder* without having pored over the videotape images for countless hours in 1988? It seems unlikely.

However, this is not merely a nostalgic gesture in film criticism's methodological history. The deployment of poetry studies—the careful line-by-line analysis of O'Hara—demands in my intertextual method a similar attention to the shot-by-shot analysis of *Anatomy of a Murder.* There must be a place in contemporary film studies for such "line-by-line" analysis of the visual image, one that results in a greater appreciation for the poetry of words and images through which not only O'Hara and readers, but also Preminger and spectators, wander.

NOTES

My thanks to Robert Bennett for introducing me to the astonishing poetry of Frank O'Hara in our "Introduction to American Studies" course at Montana State University, which we first cotaught with Robert Rydell in fall 2007. My analysis of *Anatomy of a Murder* was thoroughly reimagined by Prof. Bennett's sparkling reading of "A Step Away from Them" in a lecture he gave in Bozeman, Montana, on October 4, 2007.

1. Thomas Leitch, "Filming Poetry" (paper presented at the Annual Meeting of the Literature/Film Association, Lawrence, Kans., October 11–14, 2007).

2. Robert Richardson, "The Question of Order and Coherence in Poetry and Film," in *Literature and Film* (Bloomington: Indiana University Press, 1969), 91–103.

3. Frank O'Hara, *The Collected Poems of Frank O'Hara,* ed. Donald Allen (Berkeley: University of California Press, 1995).

4. O'Hara, *Collected Poems,* 257.

5. O'Hara, *Collected Poems*, 260.

6. Richardson, "Question of Order," 91.

7. David Trotter, "T. S. Eliot and Cinema," *Modernism/Modernity* 13, no. 2 (2006): 237.

8. This reading of *Notorious* derives from a famous lecture Thomas Schatz has been delivering in his course, "Narrative Strategies," at the University of Texas at Austin for well over twenty years.

9. This scene has haunted me since I first saw it as an undergraduate film student. This section of my essay is an adaptation of a paper I wrote in William Paul's film analysis course in 1988 at the Massachusetts Institute of Technology. I am grateful to Prof. Paul for both introducing me to *Anatomy of a Murder*, as well as to careful formal analysis of the cinema, a sadly dying art.

10. O'Hara, *Collected Poems*, 257.

11. O'Hara, *Collected Poems*, 335.

12. O'Hara, *Collected Poems*, 257.

13. O'Hara, *Collected Poems*, 257.

14. O'Hara, *Collected Poems*, 257.

15. O'Hara, *Collected Poems*, 257.

16. David Bordwell and Kristin Thompson, *Film Art: An Introduction*, 7th ed. (New York: McGraw-Hill, 2003).

Chapter Thirteen

Poetic Dialogue

*Lyrical Speech in the Work of Hal Hartley
and Jim Jarmusch*

Jennifer O'Meara

*You have a certain innate sense of the musicality of language, a good ear
maybe, but you do nothing significant with it.—Henry Fool* (Hal Hartley,
1997)

I open with a line of criticism offered by a book publisher (Chuck Montgomery) to Simon (James Urbaniak), *Henry Fool*'s protagonist who accidentally writes a manuscript in iambic pentameter. The comment can also be read as a self-aware comment on Hal Hartley's part, acknowledging a criticism his work could potentially receive. This chapter deals with the poetic qualities of Hartley's dialogue, as well as that of Jim Jarmusch, another independent writer-director. I contend that their use of rhythm, repetition, and other lyrical forms is in keeping with Siegfried Kracauer's request that the content of film dialogue be made secondary to its material, sound properties.[1] I focus on Hartley's work between his debut feature *The Unbelievable Truth* (1989) and *Henry Fool*, after which his stylistic experimentation became more visually oriented. Jarmusch's dialogue style has proved consistently experimental, and he openly praises lyrical language, explaining that "I admire poets more than any other artists," since "you can't [fully] translate their work."[2] As a result, I discuss a selection of his films spanning two decades, from *Stranger Than Paradise* (1984) to *Broken Flowers* (2005). Although both bodies of work include overt references to poetry, I suggest their dialogue *generally* reflects a strong interest in language's rhythmic properties. However, unlike the opening declaration from *Henry Fool*, I would argue that Hartley and

Jarmusch do something significant with language's musicality, by poetically blurring the boundaries between dialogue, music, and sound effects.

While considerable writing on speech emerged at the beginning of the sound era, this was predominantly negative and distanced subsequent film scholars from analyzing dialogue's creative and narrative functions.[3] And, despite the prominence of dialogue on the sound track, dialogue has not received commensurate attention in sound theory literature. Although discussed from a technical perspective, unlike music, it is rarely discussed aesthetically. However, this is slowly starting to change, particularly since the publication of Sarah Kozloff's monograph, *Overhearing Film Dialogue*.[4] In terms of dialogue's functions within cinema, Kozloff identifies two broad categories: the first deals with the way speech is used to communicate narrative detail through anchorage, causality, character revelation, adherence to conversational realism, and as a means by which emotional meaning can be transferred to the spectator. The second deals with the ways in which dialogue can go beyond narrative communication and be used for aesthetic effect, thematic or authorial messages, and as an opportunity for actor "star-turns."[5] In considering the work of Hartley and Jarmusch, I will argue that while the dialogue has dramatic functions, it is strongly oriented around aesthetics. Although Kozloff's book follows a genre-focused model, auteurist studies of dialogue are beginning to emerge. For instance, Todd Berliner has analyzed the dialogue of John Cassavetes,[6] and Paul Coughlin that of Joel and Ethan Coen.[7]

While the dialogue of both Hartley and Jarmusch has been singled out as distinctive, little in-depth analysis has been carried out. However, Mark L. Berrettini does point out how Hartley's style of dialogue highlights "the sometimes amusing problematic of communication." He also explains how Hartley attempts to disorient the viewer and "stimulate an active, even cerebral sort of spectatorship."[8] Jarmusch is generally more subtle in this regard, but he too conceives of the audience as cocreator of meaning and I will provide evidence that, for both, poetic dialogue encourages active audience engagement. I begin by outlining how Hartley and Jarmusch incorporate non-English language and accents. As well as drawing attention to the aural properties, I suggest this is part of a broader aim of advancing the theme of miscommunication in their work. Next, I discuss the listing of vaguely related words as a technique that foregrounds sound components, before considering how definitions are incorporated to encourage audiences to hear familiar words anew. I then look at their use of verbal repetition, arguing that it aligns with Bruce F. Kawin's assertion that repetition of sound is "the glue of poetry."[9] A notable feature of Hartley's and Jarmusch's dialogue, I detail how both use repeated words and lines as a source of humor and an aesthetic effect. Finally, I consider how speech is harmonized with other effects on the sound track.

LOST IN TRANSLATION

In *Sound Design*, David Sonnenschein draws attention to speech's "pure acoustical characteristics," and suggests non-English accents, nonsense sounds, and technical jargon can be used to focus the mind on the sound of the voice rather than the content it transfers.[10] When Hartley and Jarmusch include foreign languages (French, Hungarian, and Japanese, to name but a few) the viewer is encouraged to listen to a variety of aural qualities without focusing on their meaning, particularly when subtitles are omitted. Another character generally translates or pieces fragments of meaning together; however, this too provides opportunities for the dialogue to convey a deeper message, while adding novelty by using less familiar sounds.

Emanuel Levy emphasizes how characters in independent cinema are often marked out as socially different,[11] but the insertion of characters that are different linguistically can disturb this balance; verbal outsiders who have trouble making themselves understood force characters to reassess their marginal status, since it is often based on ideological differences rather than basic misunderstanding. Consider the following exchange from *Simple Men* (Hartley, 1992) when Dennis (Bill Sage) brings a motorbike to the garage where Mike (Mark Bailey) works:

Mike: Bonjour, monsieur.

Dennis: What?

Mike: It's French.

Dennis: Oh.

Mike: (*Of bike*) Outta gas?

Dennis: No. It's busted.

Mike: Qu'est-ce qui ne va pas?

Dennis: You mean, what's wrong with it?

Mike: You parlez-vous français?

Dennis: Un peu.

Mike: Excuse me?

Dennis: Just a little.

Hartley uses French here to exaggerate inconsistencies in their communication, in keeping with his view that what he finds interesting about speech is "that it can be equally compelling by virtue of its success or its failure."[12] Since Dennis understands Mike's second and third French comments, he should understand the first, which is more basic. While even a viewer with no knowledge of French can understand that, by the end of the exchange, the characters have neatly reversed roles; Mike now has the poorer grasp of French.

Miscommunication based on foreign dialogue is also a feature of Jarmusch's work. Juan Suárez notes that Roberto Benigni's poor grasp of English is a key source of humour in *Down by Law* (Jarmusch, 1986), particularly when his character, also named Roberto, distorts common expressions (for instance, "I yam a good hegg") after mishearing their pronunciation.[13] In interviews Jarmusch stresses the interpretative possibilities opened up by foreign language. He fondly recalls when, as a student, he asked another American living in Paris to translate poetry from French to English: "The poetry that he wrote was really beautiful, he interpreted things all wrong. . . . There's something very powerful about translating something you don't understand." [14] When Jarmusch incorporates another language into his film he therefore recreates this type of interpretative situation for the viewer. For instance, in *Coffee and Cigarettes* (1986; 2003) Benigni plays another character named Roberto with limited English, and he starts or ends nearly every line with "yes" or "yeah," even if this conflicts with the rest of his line (as when he responds, "Very good! I don't understand nothing! Yes"). This gives the impression that basic English forces him to rely on tone rather than content. As a result, he responds positively to Steven's (Steven Wright) absurd ideas, such as caffeine Popsicles for children, since there is nothing unusual about the *way* the words are delivered. Roberto's accent also allows Steven opportunities to misunderstand, despite being American:

Roberto: Do you, when do you leave?

Steven: United States.

Roberto: No, here.

Steven: Oh, I've to leave soon.

As with "I yam a good hegg," the dialogue takes advantage of speech's sound properties since, depending on the pronunciation, "where do you live" and "when do you leave" sound similar. In cinema, the vocal embodiment of words can therefore be used to create effects not possible in a purely literary format, something Hartley also draws on; in *The Unbelievable Truth* (1989), Audry (Adrienne Shelly) tells Emmet (Gary Sauer), "Don't be maudlin," and he mirrors the rhythm of "maudlin" several lines later by compressing the syllables of the word "modeling." Non-English dialogue and accents also allow them to acknowledge the strong support of non-U.S. audiences, along with the influence of *Nouvelle Vague* auteurs on their work; Jean-Luc Godard explained that a foreign character speaking French gave "to ordinary words a certain freshness and value that they normally have lost."[15]

LISTING AND DEFINITIONS

Lists are another technique used to partially disconnect speech from its meaning, when characters disrupt exchanges with collections of vaguely related words. In *Stranger Than Paradise*, Eddie (Richard Edson) reads Willie (John Lurie) two lists of racing horses in quick succession. Neither serves any narrative purpose, although the first one ("Indian River, Face the Music, Inside Dope, Off the Wall, Cat Fight, Late Spring, Passing Fancy, and uh, Tokyo Story"), gives Jarmusch an opportunity to reference the work of Yasujiro Ozu.

Streams of loosely connected words are an ideal form of poetic dialogue, since they require the audience to bridge the gaps between often unrelated expressions. *Simple Men* incorporates several, as when the sheriff (Damian Young) confuses two relative strangers when he launches into an oblique and unmotivated monologue: "Guarantee. Promises. Expectation. Consideration. Sincerity. Selflessness. Intimacy. Attraction. Gentleness. Understanding. An understanding without words. Dependence without resentment. Affection. To belong. Possession. Loss." The sheriff's aggressive tone indicates a cynicism, while his voice lowers and slows from "Dependence without resentment," hinting at a personal pain that is confirmed when he gets to "Loss." This stream-of-consciousness style can also allow for the inclusion of words that are aurally interesting but would not ordinarily be grouped together. This is the case when Martin (Martin Donovan) ends a debate about Madonna, to which he failed to contribute, by reading out a selection of creatively named musical artists, with many of the names abbreviated or altered: "Hendrix. Clapton. Allman Brothers. Zeppelin. Tull. BTO. Stones. Grand Funk Railroad. James Gang. T. Rex. MC5. Skynyrd. Lesley West. Blackmore. The Who. The old Who. Ten Years After. Santana. Thin Lizzy. Aerosmith. Hot fucking Tuna." By closing the scene in this way, Hartley mocks lines that provide clear finality to a scene. If this is an answer, then the audience is left to determine the unasked question. With lists, it is virtually impossible to predict what words will come next, let alone how other characters will respond, if at all. This marks them out from more formulaic mainstream dialogue and allows a character to drag a conversation away from an apparent narrative function. It can also be traced back to the French New Wave, with an overt example found in *Jules and Jim* (Francois Truffaut, 1962) when Catherine (Jeanne Moureau) speedily recalls over twenty wine regions. When no one responds verbally to her digression, it reinforces the idea that the list's real function is to draw attention to the names themselves and the contrived nature of scripted speech.

HEARING WORDS ANEW

It would be wrong to suggest that Hartley and Jarmusch are trying to depart from the dialogue's meaning altogether. This becomes clear whenever characters struggle to reach a consensus on the meaning of words, often providing, refining, or repeating definitions. Dialogue that details the meaning of words sounds dull in theory, but both weave it in with considerable humor. In *Trust* (1990), Maria's (Adrienne Shelly) repeated pronunciation of "naïve" as "*nave*" allows Hartley to comment on her ironically. Since Matthew (Martin Donovan) can only correct her when she shows him the word written down, this also draws attention to ambiguity in how words are written versus spoken. More generally, the film showcases a push-pull conflict between the same words reappearing throughout and Maria gradually learning new ones:

Matthew: Move away from the TV. The news is on and I want to hear about the earthquake victims.

Maria: Why? What are you going to do for them?

Matthew: Commiserate.

Maria: What's "commiserate"?

Matthew: To express sympathy. Now move aside.

Maria: Is that like compassion?

Matthew: No. Compassion means to suffer *with*. Which is different than just feeling pity. You need a thesaurus.

Maria: A what?

Given their bonding over words, it is fitting that Matthew does eventually buy Maria a thesaurus in a gesture of commitment. In his discussion of *Amateur* (Hartley, 1994), Steven Rawle uses a circular conversation about the term "floppy disks" as evidence that the failure of language is one of the film's important themes; "Floppy Disks are neither floppy nor disks, but this particular designation seems to have been applied arbitrarily to the object."[16]

Jarmusch also hints at the absurdity of common expressions, combining this with the Hungarian Eva's (Eszter Balint) unfamiliarity with English in *Stranger Than Paradise*; Willie tries to convince her that when you vacuum it is described as "choking the alligator." Like Maria and Matthew in *Trust*, definitions and recurring words are used to trace how Eva learns language from Willie. This is a rich source of humor in both films, as when Willie tells his friend Eddie that Eva "bugs" him; she later says that a dress Willie gave her "bugs" her. This is one of several kinds of verbal repetition in Hartley's and Jarmusch's work, and I will now consider its broader functions.

REPETITION AND POETIC VARIATION

In "The Musicality of the Filmscript," John Fawell explains how "the most memorable lines in the film are simple ones that are repeated, as a line of poetry might be, or a phrase in a musical score, and which through this repetition achieve a dramatic resonance that is central to the meaning of the film."[17] So although David Bordwell uses the term "dialogue hook" to describe how a question posed at one scene's close is answered (visually or verbally) at the start of the next,[18] musical hooks or poetic refrains can be equally relevant to film speech, when the same words take on new meaning. Even if the technique is borrowed from other lyrical forms, Jarmusch and Hartley use it for narrative purposes. When a certain line or word is repeated throughout, its narrative significance is a function of the change in context that occurs with each use. If there is little to no change—for example if the same character keeps repeating the same phrase in new but similar situations (common in mainstream comedies)—then its repetition can be tedious. But one person's repetition can be more subtle and ironic, as is the case when Eva remembers Willie's insult and uses it later to insult him.

In *Trust*, Matthew becomes associated with the words "fix" and "fixed," and this gives way to a moment crucial for revealing his depth of feelings. While his father (Christopher Cooke) describes how "he can fix anything," Matthew's view is that "some things shouldn't be fixed." This includes TVs, and he refuses a job when his terms ("I'll do radios. Phone answering machines. Calculators") are not met ("But TVs is what we fix"). In a later scene, Matthew is in the waiting room at an abortion clinic, when a stranger uses the term with respect to Maria's situation: "You come in here the first time—your whole life's a mess. All this tension and stuff. Then she goes in there and when she comes out everything's fixed." At this point, Matthew grabs the man and throws him to the floor because, as he said earlier, "some things shouldn't be fixed." Since he wanted Maria to keep the baby this, presumably, is one of them. So, while the timing of his aggressive reaction seems unexpected, it is the repetition of ordinary words in a variety of contexts that reveals a hidden motivation.

In *Flirt* (1993), Hartley reworks the same basic script in three different countries, and Tom Gunning praises the experiment for the surprise generated "as a repeated line finds a new inflection in an altered context."[19] Juan Suárez similarly praises Jarmusch's repetition for "uncover[ing] difference at the heart of the same."[20] But Hartley does this intratextually as well as intertextually, as when the expression "drop dead" reappears throughout his work. Characteristic of Hartley's blunt phrasing, it initially appears in *The Unbelievable Truth* when Audry uses it to dismiss Josh (Robert John Burke). In *Trust*, Maria says it just minutes after learning about her own father's sudden death, while it carries similar irony in *The Unbelievable Truth* since Josh was accused of murdering someone who fell down the stairs. When the words appear again in *Henry Fool*, the context is more bizarre still: a publishing house sends Simon back his manuscript, saying, "Drop dead. Keep your day job. Sincerely, The Editors." Indeed, it seems likely that Hartley included the line as a reference for loyal fans to pick up on, again encouraging audiences to engage with the verbal material on a deeper level.

Jarmusch's repetition also extends beyond one diegetic world, as in *Coffee and Cigarettes*, where characters in different shorts discuss the same things, sometimes almost verbatim.[21] In *Broken Flowers*, words spill out from Don's (Bill Murray) television to his life. The film opens with him watching *The Private Life of Don Juan* (Alexander Korda, 1934), with its dialogue about Juan's womanizing continued when Don's girlfriend Sherry (Julie Delpy) enters, announces she is leaving, and describes him as an "over-the-hill Don Juan." Sherry departs, but the disillusioned women on-screen continue to speak for her: "Don Juan said I was the girl whose kiss he'd been seeking on a thousand women's lips." This sentiment is then recalled each time he introduces himself to new characters as Don *Johnson*, since he repeatedly corrects those who mishear his last name as *Juan*.

As Bruce F. Kawin notes in *Telling It Again and Again*, repetition of sound binds poetry, with refrain, rhyme, and alliteration each increasing a sense of unity.[22] In *Henry Fool*, alliteration contributes to the title character's dramatic self-aggrandizing, when he describes his notebooks as: "My life's work. My memoirs. My confession. It's a philosophy. A poetics. A politics if you will. A literature of protest. . . . A pornographic magazine of truly comic book proportions." Although Henry's (Thomas Jay Anderson) description becomes progressively ridiculous, the repetition of "my" and then "p" sounds lends his riff an aurally pleasing coherence. Conversely, in Jarmusch's *Down by Law*, the central characters bond over rhyme in their prison cell, chanting, "I scream, you scream, we all scream for ice cream," with various intonations and at various volumes for approximately two minutes.[23]

Hartley also uses looped dialogue to indicate the hypnotizing quality of repetition, as when Audry asks Josh how the car part he is holding works. As he begins to explain, the shot moves into a close-up of the part, and each line of his complicated explanation is looped a second time, at the same volume, distorting its meaning and giving the impression Audry is too entranced by him to concentrate on the words themselves. In fact, even the looped words include repeated terms, making it even more difficult to follow them semantically.[24] In another sequence, Hartley loops the nagging dialogue of Audry's parents to convey her sense of claustrophobia, as well as comparing them, literally, to a broken record. In both cases, echoed dialogue cleverly provides a glimpse of interiority which, unlike in literature, is difficult to achieve in cinema.[25]

Returning to Kawin, he makes a crucial distinction between repetitive and repetitious. While both repeat something multiple times, the latter recurs with less impact or to no particular end, while the former repeats with an equal or greater impact.[26] I would argue that Jarmusch's and Hartley's use of repetition is generally in keeping with Kawin's description of "repetition for poetic value" as depending on "artful variations."[27] However, at other times, characters get stuck in what Berrettini describes in relation to Hartley as "dialogue loops and circular conversations."[28] When the same words are repeated at high frequency and speed, the temptation is to class it as "repetitious." In a paper on Hartley's use of repetition, Steven Rawle argues that it is perhaps Hartley's most distinctive feature and he considers the influence of the "Theatre of the Absurd," particularly its emphasis on repetition's destructive effect.[29] While Rawle's analysis is illuminating, I think Hartley's repetition need not be considered "destructive" or "repetitious," since both he and Jarmusch have another overarching motive for such dialogue; it parodies how quickly patterns of speech take hold in everyday life.

In her analysis of the "poetics of talk," linguist Deborah Tannen uses transcripts from reality to illustrate how "repetition is pervasive, functional, and often automatic" in conversation.[30] When Hartley's and Jarmusch's characters come close to repeating the same line back to the person who initially said it, they exaggerate speech's natural momentum for aesthetic effect. Consider the following short sequence in *The Unbelievable Truth*:

Maria: No, I mean why do you carry it around with you all the time?

Matthew: Just in case.

Maria: Just in case what?

Matthew: Just in case.

Although Matthew repeats the same words, his delivery becomes both softer and slower, as though communicating through a changed rhythm that his answer is final. This is in keeping with Tannen's explanation that repetition can be used to stall a conversation by filling "the response slot without giving a substantive response."[31] Maria's addition of "what?" to Matthew's line is in keeping with Tannen's description of repetition as a device that can urge a staller to expand since, when their statement is made into a question, it becomes "a scaffold" for further talk.[32] So while, as Rawle notes, Hartley partly uses repetition to disrupt narrative practices of realism and emphasize how uncommunicative his characters are,[33] verbal repetition *is* grounded in the reality of everyday speech, and Hartley makes this a feature of his speech style.

This is also the case with Jarmusch who indicates that, when it comes to dialogue, the repetition is inspired by everyday life: "I love listening to the way people talk, the way they *elide* things, and the way people are *inarticulate.*"[34] In *Stranger Than Paradise*'s opening scenes, Willie tells Eva that she cannot travel to Cleveland tomorrow, since their aunt is in hospital, and so she will stay with him for "ten days." Surprised and aware that she may have misheard, Eva repeats "ten days" back in a questioning tone, and once more before the scene ends; the final time with a flat delivery that conveys resignation, but also reinforces that this is still on her mind. In *Coffee and Cigarettes*, that circularity is an intended feature is also clear from the mise-en-scène and movement. In addition to Roberto and Steven constantly returning to the same conversation points and words, they literally move in circles around the table where they sit; Steven suggests they switch seats and he walks counterclockwise to Roberto's original position, before deciding he preferred where he was and walks clockwise back. Aerial shots of their table also capture the circular shape of their coffee cups. When taken to an extreme, the viewer is aware of the repetition and so it can be considered an antirealist technique,[35] but given that repetitive speech is also a feature of reality, Hartley and Jarmusch highlight the artifice of mainstream dialogue; because its function is largely to provide expositional information, it is less prepatterned and better articulated. Indeed, in mainstream films the advancement of the plot is usually such a priority that characters do not have time to respond to what has been said, let alone directly repeat the same words back.

SPEECH AS SOUND EFFECT

Robynn Stilwell refers to the process of crossing from diegetic to nondiegetic sound (or vice versa) as "the fantastical gap," and suggests "the geography of the soundscape" is more complex than currently understood.[36] I am also concerned with such border regions, particularly Hartley's and Jarmusch's blurring of dialogue with effects and music, which is in keeping with a verbal style that highlights language's aural properties. Both filmmakers occasionally require a character to speak a sound effect, as when Ray (Henry Varga) in *Ghost Dog: The Way of the Samurai* (Jarmusch, 1999) lists some imagined names for "Indians" ("Red Cloud, Crazy Horse, Running Bear, Black Elk") before delivering an extended mooing sound. In *The Unbelievable Truth*, Audry is haunted by the sound of bombs and, at one point she pushes her lips out in time with the explosion. The sound of a hand grenade plays an important role in *Trust* (since Matthew keeps one with him at all times) and Maria asks him to explain how it works. Like Audry in another scene in *The Unbelievable Truth*, she dramatically verbalizes this as "boom." Comic books are mentioned in several Hartley films and Berrettini notes that his rapid jumble of action shots can give this impression.[37] Yet here the dialogue suggests the influence, while in his screenplays sounds are often written in a speech-bubble style, such as "SLAM!" or "KABOOM!"[38] Dialogue also becomes a sound effect when speech is intentionally muffled. At times this is due to their distance from the camera (Jarmusch aims to maintain accurate sound-to-image scale),[39] or when dialogue is mumbled due to a character holding a cigarette in his or her mouth. In *Stranger Than Paradise*, Willie also provides a catalog of vocal sound effects. Some, like sighs, are a reasonably common addition to sound tracks, but John Lurie reveals his jazz musician persona when his mouth becomes an instrument that randomly whistles, clicks, and blows. Jarmusch therefore follows Kracauer's advice that "the spoken word is most cinematic if the messages it conveys elude our grasp."[40]

Hartley also uses sound effects to highlight the mechanical quality of his flat, repetitive speech. His protagonists often work in factories filled with industrial sounds, and where machine rhythms serve as repetitive music. In *Henry Fool* sound effects give a tempo to the mechanical bin trucks Simon operates. While this type of "mickey-mousing" is used elsewhere to give machines a positive, anthropomorphic quality—such as Danny Elfman's scores to Tim Burton's animated films—here the rhythm emphasizes a painful monotony, as though Simon's robotic voice is a side effect of spending hours alone with this equipment. Similarly, Ned's (Jeffrey Howard) declaration in *Simple Men* (that "there's nothing like a machine to make a man feel insignificant") is what comes to mind when he repeats, "There's nothing but trouble and desire," eight times. When Hartley's characters repeat words in this way it emphasizes how contrived their speech is, by giving the impression they too have been programmed to repeat a limited number of things. By combining dialogue with similarly mechanical sound effects grounded in visual action, Hartley gives his words more of a physical weight. Indeed, in many ways, *Henry Fool* is a playful exploration of the physical impact of words; Simon's notebooks are locked out of reach in the kitchen as though a dangerous medicine or weapon, and his mother commits suicide after reading his poetry.

LYRICAL OR LOGICAL LANGUAGE?

Discussing music, Michel Chion writes, "In a way, the cinema gives us the ability to rediscover what we call music, what we have heard thousands of times, in conditions that approximate the first time by virtue of creating its own new context."[41] I would argue that the same can be said for language; when characters argue over pronunciation or provide each other with definitions, they capture the sense of what it's like to hear or understand a word for the first time. In *The Unbelievable Truth* and *Stranger Than Paradise*, Hartley and Jarmusch take advantage of creative misunderstanding by including characters with limited English. The incorporation of definitions and scenes in which foreign language is translated also points to awareness of the two levels at which their dialogue is working. While he does not relate it to speech in cinema, Jean Mitry's comparison of lyrical language with "the language of logic" is relevant here; with the latter, "each phrase has one single meaning, not several . . . [so] it becomes possible to agree totally as to their meanings."[42] Lyrical language, on the other hand, is "intimately related to and uniquely dependent on their rhythm."[43] When words cannot simply be substituted with others of the same meaning then they are lyrically creative. This tension between logical and lyrical language can also be related to that of dialogue used for narrative or aesthetic purposes. Just as "the 'secondary' (or lyrical) meaning of a word exists and can only exist as the consequence of the logical meaning which determines and guarantees the word,"[44] dialogue is generally used for aesthetic effect only when it *also* serves some narrative function—even if this is only to convey boredom or, as discussed, the theme of miscommunication.

In this chapter, I have shown that dialogue in Hartley's and Jarmusch's work poetically incorporates the rhythmic and musical qualities of language. Highly stylized speech draws attention to the artificial nature of scripted speech, while the meaning of repeated dialogue, in particular, is dependent on the viewer's ability to consider the new context as a function of the old. Passive consumption of the dialogue is therefore discouraged. Furthermore, by creating synergies between dialogue, music, and effects, Hartley and Jarmusch take advantage of cinema's mixed media, which makes it ideal for capturing film speech's creative but generally latent aural properties.

NOTES

1. Siegfried Kracauer, "Dialogue and Sound," in *Theory of Film* (Princeton, N.J.: Princeton University Press, 1997), 102–32.

2. Peter Von Bagh and Mika Kaurismaki, "In Between Things," in *Jim Jarmusch: Interviews*, ed. Ludvig Hertzberg, trans. Ludvig Hertzberg (Jackson: University Press of Mississippi, 2001), 78.

3. Voice-over narration is the clear exception, since it has a well-developed body of literature. Its association with particular genres or subgenres (film noir, horror, adaptation) has encouraged discussion of its stylistic and narrative functions. Voice-over also receives considerable attention since it challenges the primacy of the image, since its words can mobilize images or scenes.

4. Sarah Kozloff, *Overhearing Film Dialogue* (Berkeley: University of California Press, 2000).

5. Kozloff, *Overhearing Film Dialogue*, 33–34.

6. Todd Berliner, "Hollywood Movie Dialogue and the 'Real Realism' of John Cassavetes," *Film Quarterly* 52 (1999): 2–16 .

7. Paul Coughlin, " Language Aesthetics in Three Films by Joel and Ethan Coen, " *Film Journal*, no. 12, accessed December 10, 2012, http://www.thefilmjournal.com/issue12/coens.html .

8. Mark L. Berrettini, *Hal Hartley*, Contemporary Film Directors Series (Champaign: University of Illinois Press, 2011), 2.

9. Bruce F. Kawin, *Telling It Again and Again: Repetition in Literature and Film* (Ithaca, N.Y.: Cornell University Press, 1972), 45–46.

10. David Sonnenschein, *Sound Design: The Expressive Power of Music, Voice, and Sound Effects in Cinema* (Studio City, Calif.: Michael Wiese Productions, 2001), 137–38. Jeff Jaeckle has analyzed verbal style in the films of Preston Sturges and Wes Anderson, and the use of dialects and languages other than English is one of four "verbal embroideries" he identifies in their work. Combined with a discussion of wordplay, metalanguage, and explicitly scripted language (indicated by printed texts or voice-over), Jaeckle's analysis offers strong evidence that verbal aesthetics in cinema is a rich and unexplored area. See Jeff Jaeckle, "The Shared Verbal Stylistics of Preston Sturges and Wes Anderson," *New Review of Film and Television Studies*, 2012, 1–17, accessed December 12, 2012, doi:10.1080/17400309.2012.728917.

11. This is one of the underlying premises of his book. See Emanuel Levy, *Cinema of Outsiders: The Rise of American Independent Film* (New York: NYU Press, 2009).

12. Hal Hartley, introduction to *Flirt* (London: Faber & Faber, 1996), xviii.

13. For a more detailed discussion of Roberto Benigni's dialogue in *Down by Law*, see Juan A. Suárez, *Jim Jarmusch*, Contemporary Film Directors Series (Champaign: University of Illinois Press, 2007), 54.

14. Von Bagh and Kaurismaki, "In Between Things," 78.

15. Richard Roud, *Jean-Luc Godard* (Bloomington: Indiana University Press, 1970), 11.

16. Steven Rawle, "Hal Hartley and the Re-Presentation of Repetition," *Film Criticism* 34, no. 1 (2009): 62–63.

17. John Fawell, "The Musicality of the Filmscript," *Literature/Film Quarterly* 17, no. 1 (1989): 24.

18. David Bordwell, "The Hook: Scene Transitions in Classical Cinema," David Bordwell's Website on Cinema, January 2008, accessed December 10, 2012, http://www.davidbordwell.net/essays/hook.php.

19. Tom Gunning, preface to *Flirt* (London: Faber & Faber, 1996) , viii.

20. Suárez, *Jim Jarmusch*, 63–64.

21. Twice someone explains how Nikola Tesla, the early twentieth-century inventor, considered the earth "a conductor of acoustical resonance.'" As Suárez notes, perhaps this is Jarmusch's explanation for why bits of conversation echo throughout. See Suárez, *Jim Jarmusch*, 87.

22. Kawin, *Telling It Again,* 45–46.

23. Jeff Jaeckle identifies the recurring use of rhyming effects in Wes Anderson's films, extending to character names such as the twins Ronny and Donny Blume in *Rushmore* (1998), and Ari and Uzi Tenenbaum in *The Royal Tenenbaums* (2001). As Jaeckle explains, "Alliteration and its related techniques of assonance and consonance—the bases of all rhyme—are perhaps the easiest means of making language strange, for they draw an audience's ears and eyes to the fact that poetic sound patterns can and do underwrite conversational language." Jaeckle, "Shared Verbal Stylistics," 4–5.

24. The following excerpt from the looped dialogue shows the repeated use of certain words (gear, sun, planet, attached to): "This is what you call the 'sun' gear in the middle. The 'ring' gear around the circumference. And the 'planet' gears here in between. The sun gear is attached to the input shaft while the output shaft is attached to the planet gears. . . ."

25. See Richard Dyer, *Stars* (London: BFI, 1979), 100–20.

26. Dyer, *Stars*, 4.

27. Dyer, *Stars*, 37–38.

28. Berrettini, *Hal Hartley*, 4.

29. Rawle, "Hal Hartley," 58, 66–69.

30. Deborah Tannen, *Talking Voices: Repetition, Dialogue, and Imagery in Conversational Discourse* (New York: Cambridge University Press, 1989), 54.

31. Tannen, *Talking Voices*, 72–73.

32. Tannen, *Talking Voices*, 73.

33. Rawle, "Hal Hartley," 65, 73.

34. Emphasis in original. Ludvig Hertzberg, introduction to *Jim Jarmusch: Interviews* (Jackson: University Press of Mississippi, 2001), ix.

35. Steven Rawle describes Hartley's repetition as "a key alienating device employed to remind the viewer of both the constructed basis of the film text and behavioral aspects of compulsions to repeat." Rawle, "Hal Hartley," 59.

36. Robynn J. Stilwell, "The Fantastical Gap between Diegetic and Nondiegetic," in *Beyond the Soundtrack*, ed. Daniel Goldmark, Lawrence Kramer, and Richard Leppert (Berkeley: University of California Press, 2007): 186–87.

37. Berrettini, *Hal Hartley*, 54.

38. Hal Hartley, *Simple Men and Trust* (Winchester, Mass.: Faber & Faber, 1993), 172, 176.

39. Von Bagh and Kaurismaki, "In Between Things," 77.

40. Kracauer, "Dialogue and Sound," 107.

41. Michel Chion, "Mute Music: Polanski's *The Pianist* and Campion's *The Piano*," in *Beyond the Soundtrack: Representing Music in Cinema*, ed. Daniel Goldmark, Lawrence Kramer, and Richard Leppert (Berkeley: University of California Press, 2007), 94–95.

42. Jean Mitry, *The Aesthetics and Psychology of the Cinema* (Bloomington: Indiana University Press, 1997), 22.

43. Mitry, *Aesthetics and Psychology*, 22–24.

44. Mitry, *Aesthetics and Psychology*, 23.

Chapter Fourteen

The Written Verse in Cinematic Verse

Eliseo Subiela's El lado oscuro del corazón
as a Metapoetic Text

Juan G. Ramos

Eliseo Subiela's film begins with its protagonist, Oliverio Fernández, rendering a declamation of Oliverio Girondo's "Espantapájaros 1" [Scarecrow 1] after the protagonist has finished having sex with a nameless woman.

> No me importa un pito que las mujeres tengan los senos como magnolias o como pasas de higo; un cutis de durazno o de papel de lija. Le doy una importancia igual a cero, al hecho de que amanezcan con un aliento afrodisíaco o con aliento insecticida. Soy perfectamente capaz de soportarles una nariz que sacaría el primer premio en una exposición de zanahorias; ¡Pero eso sí!—y en esto soy irreductible—no les perdono , bajo ningún pretexto, que no sepan volar. [Si no saben volar, pierden el tiempo conmigo.] [1]

> [I could care less if women have breasts like magnolias or like dried-up figs; a complexion like a peach or like sandpaper. It makes no difference to me if they were to wake up with an aphrodisiacal breath or with an insecticide breath. I am perfectly capable of withstanding a nose that would win the first prize in an exhibition of carrots; Oh, yes!—and in this I am unyielding—I don't forgive, under any pretext, their inability to fly. If they don't know how to fly, they are wasting their time with me.] [2]

For viewers unfamiliar with Girondo's avant-garde poetics, the verses Oliverio recites are as shocking as the way the protagonist gets rid of his sex partner, since he merely has to press a button and the women that accompany him fall into an abyss. After all, Oliverio, who is also a poet, is endlessly searching for a woman who "knows how to fly" [que sepa volar]. This initial poem and this particular verse reappear throughout the film and become the connecting poetic and visual thread. It is this perpetual search for this elusive and gravity-defying woman that leads Oliverio from Buenos Aires to Montevideo, where he falls in love with Ana, who proudly embraces her profession as a prostitute. The film's director, Eliseo Subiela, has acknowledged in an interview the function of this particular poem from Girondo as one that enabled a poetic structure for the rest of the film: "From the main idea of 'a man who was looking for the woman who could fly,' I created a dramatic structure capable of bearing other poems, as if they were the songs in a musical comedy. . . ."[3] Through these particular verses by Girondo, the film creates an entire narrative, which generates the space and narrative structure through which Oliverio recites other poems by Girondo. In addition, Oliverio also recites several of Mario Benedetti's and Juan Gelman's love poems as though they were his own.

As an approach to reading this film, I propose to go beyond the binary tension between word and image, particularly since this film actively contests the separation between poetry and film as distinctive art media and genres. If as spectators we are "genre-driven," as Thomas Beebee has suggested, I contend that *El lado oscuro del corazón* (1992) forces us to ask questions about the delimitations of genres and works of art.[4] While it can be argued that Subiela draws his inspiration from poetry to create a screenplay and a visual narrative, it can also be argued that poetry takes on a more prevalent visual and aural dimension as it transgresses the boundaries of the page to permeate the screen, generates the dialogue among its characters, and drives the film's story. Moreover, the incorporation of Girondo's, Benedetti's, and Gelman's poetry is not merely a matter of adaptation in the conventional sense, but it becomes a way to have poetic texts reappear in a film that questions the place and function of poetry in everyday life.[5] As such, I argue that *El lado oscuro del corazón* is a metapoetic text given its self-awareness about poetic praxis (Oliverio as a poet), its concern with poetic language (the recitation of avant-garde and contemporary poetry from Argentina and Uruguay), while also positing practical and metaphysical questions about poetry's role in contemporary times.

To return to a discussion of how Girondo's, Benedetti's, and Gelman's poems make their way into this film, we should keep in mind the rather unconventional way in which the recitation of poetry becomes an integral part of the film's dialogue. After the opening credits, and under four minutes into the film, it would appear that the recitation of a second poem is yet another of Oliverio's poetic fabrications. Instead, a second poet's work appears at this early point in the film. If in the opening scene, before the credits, Oliverio recites Girondo's poem as a way to extricate himself from any relationship, responsibility, or proximity to women with whom he cannot connect on an emotional, spiritual, and erotic level (the implications of the search for the woman who knows how to fly), in the second scene of the film, Oliverio recites Juan Gelman's "Poco se sabe."[6] In this scene, Oliverio is aboard a ship and we are unaware of its destination, though soon we come to find out that he is crossing from Buenos Aires to Montevideo. The recitation of the poem comes by way of an internal monologue in which he simultaneously invokes the woman he wants and dreams of, while lamenting the impossibility of finding her.

Within the first ten minutes of the film, the narrative makes yet another reference to Gelman by placing us inside a cabaret called "Sefiní" (like Gelman's homonymous poem). It is at this site where Oliverio first meets Ana. Instead of establishing a normal conversation, Oliverio recites to her Girondo's poem about the woman who knows how to fly. This enunciation can be interpreted as Oliverio's unwillingness to waste time in embarking upon empty conversations, as well as searching for and dealing with women who cannot stimulate his intellectual curiosity and poetic sensibility. Ana surprises Oliverio by responding in a witty manner in which she announces the prices of her services if he wants to spend any time with her or learn how to fly. As we come to find out, Ana knows some of the same poems Oliverio recites at various points in the film, including Mario Benedetti's "Táctica y estrategia," which she is able to complete for him during this sequence of scenes.[7] It is because of this initial exchange, along with the erotic and sexual pleasures Oliverio can only experience while he is with Ana, that he keeps going back to her from Buenos Aires to Montevideo.

At a first glance, one might be inclined to assume that Subiela has incorporated poems by Girondo, Benedetti, and Gelman in a mere gesture of adaptation. In a move that aims to rehabilitate the status of adaptations, Linda Hutcheon has argued for the need to treat adaptations as adaptations and not as secondary texts evaluated in reference to an original.[8] Moreover, Hutcheon suggests three ways of looking at adaptations. First, an adaptation should be seen as a *"formal entity or product . . .* [which is] an announced and extensive transposition of a particular work or works."[9] In its most basic sense, Hutcheon suggests that the genre or medium of adaptation might change. In the case of *El lado oscuro*, for instance, Benedetti's poems become part of a poetic film, which is to say that they shift from a written medium onto a primarily visual medium. In doing so, then, the reference to these poems remains intact, but the means through which they are presented is what transforms the written verse into a cinematic verse. Taking someone's words, inserting them into a dialogue, creating a story with and around them, and assigning a common poetic voice to all of them that seems to collapse poetic differences among Girondo, Benedetti, and Gelman is what Hutcheon calls adaptation as a process of creation.[10] This aspect of adaptation is more closely related to the practices and mechanisms of "(re-)interpretation and then (re-)creation," which also have elements of "appropriation and salvaging."[11] In taking avant-garde poetry, as well as contemporary poetry, Eliseo Subiela engages in a reinterpretive act, which is to say that he interprets or assigns meaning to these poems. In doing so, Subiela reinterprets and recreates their meaning so that they coincide with the mood of the story and its protagonists. Third, Hutcheon echoes Gerard Genette by assigning a palimpsestuous quality to the "process of reception," given its intertextual dimension.[12] When viewers receive a film adaptation, for instance, they are aware of resonances, echoes, references, and affinities with other cultural artifacts, which may include other films, music, and literature, among other cultural texts. It is perhaps this notion of the adaptation as a palimpsestuous text that enables audiences to make their own connections to other texts, to seek meaning within and outside the text, and thus gives audiences the agency to become active participants in the process of adaptation through its consumption.

In the case of Subiela's film, it becomes clear that not all viewers are aware of the exact poems the director incorporates in the film's story line, even if these poets receive an acknowledgment in the opening credits. These viewers, then, consume the film without necessarily making connections with the written verses by Girondo, Benedetti, and Gelman, though they are free to look for the poems after the film-viewing experience. On the other hand, for those viewers who are aware of the specific references, they can actively engage in making connections between the visual metaphors present throughout the film (e.g., Oliverio's heart served on a platter for Ana to accept, death dressed as a woman, writing and reciting poetry as a way to ward off death, Oliverio and Ana flying as their sexual encounters become more intimate and emotional, roller-coaster rides replacing the graphic depiction of some sexual encounters, etc.) and the moments in the film in which the poems appear, which are rather intentional. In both viewership cases, a second film viewing might affect the adaptation on the level of reception, but also as a product. At the same time, a second view of the film enables the viewer's awareness of how poetry becomes reinterpreted and appropriated in the film, without turning the poetic film into a text secondary to the "originals." In fact, the presence of poetry in the film and the ways in which Oliverio and Ana are able to recite them, as though they are part of their everyday speech and sensibility, enable us to look at the film as metapoetic text.

A metapoetic text is preoccupied with its own relation to poetic praxis, exploring how language works, shedding light on the function of the poetic voice or enunciator, positing metaphysical questions on poetry's role and function in society, or delimiting the genre in which a metapoetic text can be located.[13] As we observe in *El lado oscuro del corazón*, despite society's seeming dismay for Oliverio's craft, the poet's constant preoccupation with earning a living through poetry appears as a mechanism that points to the film's self-awareness about poetic praxis. This same concern about poetry lends itself to question the poet's role and place in our contemporary world. On a different level, the film makes no apologies for the way poetry seemingly becomes common currency in everyday speech and quotidian sensibility, as exhibited through Oliverio's and Ana's actions, how they express their feelings, and how they communicate through verse. It is precisely the audience's suspension of disbelief, and the ways in which a viewer must accept and embrace the recitation of avant-garde and contemporary poetry as though they are part of our everyday world, that allow for the film to become preoccupied with questioning what is the difference between poetic expression and everyday speech. Rather than thinking about the transference of printed poetry onto the screen, which continues to accentuate the divide between word and image, Francesco Casetti has suggested that we shift our attention to the reappearance of the discourses. As Casetti states, "What we are dealing with is the *reappearance, in another discursive field, of an element (a plot, a theme, a character, etc.) that has previously appeared elsewhere.*"[14] While this concept of reappearance aims to move away from the idea of merely rereading, rewriting, and recontextualizing a text from its "original" medium onto a different one, the implications of this conceptual shift are rather unproblematic for more conventional adaptation processes in which novels, plays, or even other films become the main source of inspiration for a film. One might wonder: What does it mean for a poem to reappear elsewhere, in a different medium, as Casetti might suggest?

Part of the answer to this question comes precisely from an early exchange between Oliverio and Ana, after they have had their first sexual encounter. Since Oliverio has paid for Ana's services, they agree to go back to her apartment. As part of their level of intimacy that goes beyond a pure sexual transaction, Ana shows Oliverio how she used to disassemble poetry books and keep their separate parts in different parts of her house. Ana's reason for fragmenting a poetry book is that it is an old habit she kept from the days of the dictatorship in Uruguay during the late 1970s and into the mid-1980s. Oliverio takes a deep interest in this enigmatic woman and confronts her with the question of why she likes poetry. To this, Ana responds by saying, "Es parte de mi trabajo. Me permite conocer gente culta como vos." [It's part of my job. It allows me to meet learned people like you.][15] This metaphor of fragmenting poetry collections, reassembling them at will, and providing poetry a function in real life is key to understanding how poetry reappears from its original discursive medium onto a new one.

Contrary to the way readers remember novels, for instance, readers tend to remember isolated poems from dispersed collections. It is precisely this gesture of seemingly taking random poems from different points of Girondo's, Benedetti's, and Gelman's poetic trajectories that is symbolically represented through this act of dismembering a poetry collection only to later reassemble it, as Ana does. While the way poetry is fragmented in the film might be construed as a postmodern gesture, in fact, said fragmentation presents us with a more nuanced perspective on how poetry occupies a central place in the protagonists' lives.[16] For Oliverio, poetry functions as a lens through which he sees and experiences the world. It allows him to ward off death (represented in the film in the image of a woman) in literal and metaphorical ways. Poetry allows him to connect on a deeper level with Ana who is from a different country and has a seemingly incompatible profession. Furthermore, poetry has the quality of collapsing social barriers in the sense that Oliverio has found his muse and his intellectual match much in the same way that a poet during the Renaissance might have had with a courtesan. For Ana, instead, poetry functions as a means to engage in deeper conversations with her clientele. It also allows her to escape her humdrum everyday reality. Poetry, for Ana, not only functions as a way to find solace from her solitude but also enables her to find respite from the feelings she does not allow herself to have once she discovers that she is falling in love with Oliverio. More importantly, poetry acts as the means through which both characters are able to express themselves in ways that the average person around them cannot.

At a later point in the film, after Oliverio and Ana have had a small fight and he has returned to Montevideo to make up, Ana tells Oliverio at the Sefini cabaret that he should go to her apartment after she gets off from work at four a.m. Upon arrival, and much to his surprise, Oliverio overhears Ana's moans, as though she is having sex with a client. In fact, the viewer sees that Ana is faking the whole scene as a way to prevent herself from feeling any type of love or allowing Oliverio to come any closer to her. Oliverio rushes off from Ana's apartment building and heads back to Buenos Aires. It is at this point in the film that Oliverio recites Benedetti's "Rostro de vos" to a random bank teller. With Oliverio's voice-over, the camera also shows Ana standing in line waiting to buy her groceries and feeling an overwhelming solitude and despair, and how both Oliverio and Ana gradually return to their respective routines. After this sequence, the camera uses medium shots and quick cuts to show how Oliverio and Ana are looking toward the sea that separates them, and are taking turns to recite two of Benedetti's poems, namely, "Me sirve y no me sirve" and "Canje." Ana seems to be talking to Oliverio as she claims that she cannot remember him anymore and Oliverio responds with the first verse from "Canje": "Es importante hacerlo / quiero que me relates / tu último optimismo / yo te ofrezco mi última / confianza." [It is important to do so / I want you to narrate / your very last optimism / I offer you my last / assurance.][17] Ana replies with the first verse of "Me sirve y no me sirve": "La esperanza tan dulce / tan pulida tan triste / la promesa tan leve / no me sirve." [A Hope so sweet / so polished so sad / so slight a promise / is of no use to me.][18] The exchange of verses continues for another round and Ana's concluding words are "no me quieras" [don't love me].[19] Of course, this is yet another of Subiela's subtle metaphors and usage of the camera to suggest how these poems connect kindred spirits, and bridge the distance that separates them at these particular moments since Ana is still in Montevideo and Oliverio is facing the sea from Buenos Aires. Through this exchange in which Oliverio and Ana are seemingly communicating through two different poems, the films suggests that, in fact, poetry has replaced other forms of oral communication and that it can convey a multiplicity of emotions and meanings in the economy and subtlety of the poems' language.

Subiela's choice of poets who are known for using simple language is quite conscious and suggests the director's own take on how these poets' works match and reflect his own visual poetry. In the case of Benedetti and Gelman, their early style of poetry has been linked to a conversational style of poetry that closely resembles everyday speech. Yet, the film presents us with a loaded question: What is it about poetry that seemingly turns people away from it? This preoccupation is present in the film at several points. For instance, when Oliverio prints his own collection of poetry, and, upon finding that no one is buying it, he decides to buy all copies for himself. Through this action, Oliverio acknowledges that he cannot earn a living by selling collections of poems. In other instances, poetry is used as a means of currency, as when Oliverio trades poems for food with a guy who owns a food truck. The poems are so successful that the man who gives Oliverio and his friends food becomes engaged and married. This man's success in making his girlfriend want to marry him is his ability to pass off Oliverio's poems as his own. At an earlier point in the film, Oliverio works in the streets of Buenos Aires, at traffic lights, like many homeless adults and children. Instead of cleaning windshields or selling knick-knacks, Oliverio recites isolated verses to those drivers stopped at traffic lights who are willing to hear him. In exchange, Oliverio receives any banknote or coins that might come his way. At another point in the film, Oliverio asks a woman working at a coffee shop if she knows Benedetti. To this question, the woman inquires "¿él trabaja acá?" [does he work here?]. Oliverio retorts: "No se preocupe que las putas van a llegar primero al cielo" [Don't worry because whores will it make it to heaven first].[20] This particular exchange appears in the film as a possible critique of how poetry has lost its place with the common reader or that even the most accessible and "popular" poets, such as Benedetti, are not as readily known as one might initially believe. On a different level, the subtlety of this exchange appears as a question directed to the film viewer, almost as a way to ask if said viewer knows who Benedetti might be and if he or she can recognize the poems recited in the film.

While the film might initially appear simply as a love story between Oliverio and Ana, in fact, one can argue that it presents a number of challenges to the role and status of poetry in our world by repurposing poetry to make a film that is at once poetic and critical. To discern what makes a poetic film, it might help us to delineate the ways in which a director adapts poetry for his purposes, or how a director appropriates a poem at the levels of interpretation and transformation, or even how the reappearance of a poem in a film underscores the specificity of each media's respective discursive contexts and functions. So, what are the implications of making and consuming a poetic film? In making a distinction between the language genre films employ and how poetry makes its way into films, Barry Keith Grant has been clear in his assertion that "a poetic soundtrack does not necessarily constitute a poetic use of the film medium as such."[21] By this Grant means that a simple usage of a poem, by way of recitation or through other means of diegetic sound, does not necessarily constitute the creation of a poetic film. Instead, Grant suggests that films can be poetic on two essential premises: films rely on the "visual iconography" pertinent to the genre "to communicate" meaning and also because films rely heavily on "audience engagement."[22] If we situate *El lado oscuro del corazón* within the romantic film genre, for instance, Subiela certainly makes use of several techniques that mirror Oliverio's and Ana's actions as though they are complementary souls longing and searching for each other.[23] From scenes in which Oliverio and Ana are respectively shopping alone in Buenos Aires and Montevideo to scenes in which they are at home consumed by their routines, the camera employs close-ups, medium shots, and establishing shots with rapid cuts to suggest the parallel universes of two lovers who will inevitably find each other. The film certainly relies on the conventions of a romantic film (visual iconography), while also meeting the expectations of film audiences (audience engagement). Yet Subiela goes beyond using mere conventions to create a poetic film. As suggested earlier, the film is a metapoetic text in that it incorporates and appropriates poetry by Girondo, Benedetti, and Gelman, but it also creates its own poetic language. In other words, it is a film that concerns itself with the poets' craft, but also engages with the poetic craft of filmmakers. When an interviewer asked Subiela about the role that poetry plays in his craft, and whether or not his choice of poems are as random as they might initially seem, Subiela responds with the following: "I think film is essentially a poetic language. Poetry is, in a sense, a different way of dealing with reality, a different, superior way of understanding reality. It appeals to me."[24] Subiela's conception of film as having a close correlation with poetry and poetic language suggests that his choice of poets is quite conscious, particularly as he is making a metapoetic film that is both romantic and about poetry. In fact, one can argue that the moments in which Girondo's, Benedetti's, and Gelman's poems appear in the film complement Subiela's own efforts to create poetry with the camera. The choice of love poems and Subiela's treatment of what appears to be a trite love formula of two lovers seemingly destined to be alone is what makes this film innovative, poetic, and even metapoetic. The film's own consciousness about poetic praxis, and its place in a society that does not seem to have space for it, is what moves us beyond a mere formula of equivalence or transference in the traditional adaptation model. Instead, the creation of a film that feeds on and builds upon the written verse to create a cinematic verse is what constitutes *El lado oscuro del corazón* as a metapoetic text.

The very structure of the film, and the ways in which poems are incorporated, attest to this metapoetic textuality. Toward the end of the film, after Oliverio and Ana allow themselves to break down their respective walls that have prevented them from loving each other fully, as part of their sexual experience they physically and metaphorically begin to fly around the places they have frequented in Buenos Aires and Montevideo. Since Oliverio has found the woman who can fly, which was the initial challenge of the film, at this point, Oliverio recites the last two verses of Girondo's "Espantapájaros 1," though with some modifications:

> Después de conocer a una mujer etérea, ¿puede brindarnos algún tipo de atractivo una mujer terrestre? ¿Qué diferencia hay entre vivir con una vaca o con una mujer que tenga las nalgas a setenta y ocho centímetros del suelo? Ya no me es posible concebir, ni tan siquiera imaginar, que pueda hacerse el amor mas que volando. Te quiero.[25]

> [After meeting an ethereal woman, can an earthly woman offer us any sort of attraction? What difference is there between living with a cow or with a woman who has her gluteus seventy-eight centimeters from the floor? I cannot conceive, not even imagine, that one can make love in any other way than flying. I love you.]

To this poetic statement, Ana replies: "Yo también, pero puedo quererte sin tenerte. Hemos volado juntos. ¿Qué más hace falta?" [Me too, but I can love you without having you. We have flown together. What else is necessary?][26] At this moment, Ana presses a button and Oliverio drops into an abyss, as many of his lovers had done. With this inversion of the initial sequence of the film, and the completion of Girondo's poem, the metapoetic and circular structure of the film seemingly comes to an end, though we know that a wounded and bandaged Oliverio will continue searching for a new love, while Ana is on her way to Barcelona to meet with her daughter.

While the film has taken six poems from Girondo, seven poems from Benedetti, and four poems from Gelman, their incorporation into the dialogue of the characters and their convergence with Subiela's own visual metaphors enable us to move beyond making a binary distinction between poem and film, or between original text and adaptation. If at times the poems appear in their complete and original form as part of dialogues, recitations, and voice-overs, at other times Subiela reinterprets and appropriates them so that they reappear in a different context and in a different medium. For those familiar with Girondo's, Benedetti's, or Gelman's poems, their reappearance in the film enhances the ways in which poetry and film work as both separate and complementary art forms. At the same time, their reappearance also points to the fact that we are not dealing with the exact same poetic texts, but rather that their transference has turned them into independent texts within a cinematic text that should not be evaluated as secondary to the "original" poems, but rather as a complex and multilayered metapoetic film. In this sense, the film's ultimate preoccupations with poetry have been its own consciousness about what it means to be a poet, to write poetry, to read poetry, and to communicate by way of poetry in a world where poetry has seemingly lost its place. By foregrounding poetry that "speaks" to viewers, and coupling it with visual and aural metaphors, *El lado oscuro del corazón* forces us to also reflect on these pressing questions and not just focus on the love story that appears on the surface level of the film.

NOTES

1. Oliverio Girondo, "Espantapájaros 1," in *Obra Completa*, ed. Raúl Antelo (Mexico: Fondo de Cultural Económica, 1999), 78. The bracketed verse was modified in the film from the original version: "Si no saben volar! Pierden el tiempo las que pretenden seducirme!" This subtle change subdues the weight placed on women to seduce the poetic male voice, which is present in Girondo's version.
2. Unless otherwise noted, all translations of the poems are my own.
3. Cathleen Rountree and Nancy Membrez, "The Poet of Argentine Cinema: An Interview with Eliseo Subiela," *Jung Journal: Culture and Psyche* 1, no. 3 (2007): 96.
4. Thomas O. Beebee, "Introduction: Why Genre?," in *The Ideology of Genre: A Comparative Study of Generic Instability* (University Park: Pennsylvania State University Press, 1994), 7.
5. Francesco Casetti, "Adaptation and Mis-adaptations: Film, Literature, and Social Discourse," in *A Companion to Film and Literature*, ed. Robert Stam and Alessandra Raengo (Malden, Mass.: Blackwell, 2004), 82.
6. Juan Gelman, *De Palabra* (Madrid: Visor, 1994).
7. Mario Benedetti, *Inventario uno* (Buenos Aires: Editorial Sudamericana, 2006).
8. Linda Hutcheon, *A Theory of Adaptation* (New York: Routledge, 2006), 6.
9. Hutcheon, *Theory of Adaptation*, 7 (italics in original).
10. Hutcheon, *Theory of Adaptation*, 7.
11. Hutcheon, *Theory of Adaptation*, 8.
12. Hutcheon, *Theory of Adaptation*, 8.
13. Beebee, "Introduction: Why Genre?," 1–29; Arturo Casas, "About Metapoetry and Performativity," *CLCWeb: Comparative Literature and Culture* 13, no. 5. (2011): 2–9, accessed December 1, 2012, http://docs.lib.purdue.edu/clcweb/vol13/iss5/6.
14. Casetti, "Adaptation and Mis-adaptations," 82 (italics in original).
15. *El lado oscuro del corazón*, directed by Eliseo Subiela, perf. Darío Grandinetti and Sandra Ballesteros (CQ3, Max Films, Zafra Video, 1992), DVD, 12:29.
16. For a postmodern reading of the film, see Joanna Page, "Postmodernism, History and Social Critique in Post-dictatorial Argentine Cinema: A Reading of Eliseo Subiela's *El lado oscuro del corazón*," *Modern Language Review* 96, no. 2 (2001): 385–96.
17. Mario Benedetti, "Canje," in *Inventario uno*, 505.
18. Mario Benedetti, "Me sirve y no me sirve," in *Inventario uno*, 409–11.

19. *El lado oscuro del corazón*, 1:42:24.
20. *El lado oscuro del corazón*, 13:30.
21. Barry K. Grant, "Tradition and Individual Talent: Poetry in the Genre Film," in *Narrative Strategies: Original Essays in Film and Prose Fiction*, ed. Syndy M. Conger and Janice R. Welsch (Macomb: Western Illinois University, 1980), 93.
22. Grant, "Tradition and Individual Talent," 99.
23. Laura Harty, "La poesía y el cine: *El lado oscuro del corazón*," *Voz y letra* 32, no. 1 (2011): 99–113; Geoffrey Kantaris, "Deseos de literatura: Autores sucedáneos en dos películas de Eliseo Subiela—*Últimas imágenes* y *El lado oscuro del corazón*," *Revista Iberoamericana* 68, no. 199 (2002): 269–81.
24. Rountree and Membrez, "Poet of Argentine Cinema," 96.
25. *El lado oscuro del corazón*, 1:49:45.
26. *El lado oscuro del corazón*, 1:50:15.

Index

About the Editor and Contributors

Marlisa Santos is associate professor and director of the division of humanities in the Farquhar College of Arts and Sciences at Nova Southeastern University in Fort Lauderdale, Florida. Her research focuses on classic film studies and film noir, and she is the author of *The Dark Mirror: Psychiatry and Film Noir* (2010). She has also presented and published numerous papers on film at national conferences and in edited anthologies, including essays on Martin Scorsese, Edgar Ulmer, and Joseph H. Lewis.

* * *

Susan Redington Bobby is associate professor of English at Wesley College in Dover, Delaware. Her research focuses on adolescent literature, fairy tales, and gender studies. She is the author of *Beyond "His Dark Materials": Innocence and Experience in the Fiction of Philip Pullman* (2012) and the editor of *Fairy Tales Reimagined: Essays on New Retellings* (2009). She has presented papers and chaired panels at several national conferences and has published critical reviews for journals in her field.

Roberto Cavallini is currently a lecturer in film and media studies in the Faculty of Communication at Yaşar University (Izmir, Turkey). He is a graduate in art history and aesthetics from Cà Foscari University (Venice, Italy) and he holds a PhD in visual cultures from Goldsmiths, University of London. His research interests lie at the intersection between visual cultures and contemporary philosophy, film theory and documentary cinema, creative practices and digital media production. He has presented papers internationally, including essays on European cinema (Antonioni, Chabrol), video-art

197

(Fabrizio Plessi, Lida Abdul), and site-specific practices and documentary theatre (Rimini Protokoll).

Hugh Davis is associate professor of English at Piedmont College in Demorest, Georgia. He is the author of *The Making of James Agee* (2008) and the editor of *The Works of James Agee, Volume 3: Let Us Now Praise Famous Men* (2013).

Nichole DeWall is assistant professor of English at McKendree University, where she teaches medieval and early modern literature, as well as drama and composition courses. Her research focuses on teaching Shakespeare and representations of disease in Shakespeare's plays. She recently published "'Sweet Recreation Barred': The Case for Playgoing in Plague-Time" in *Representing the Plague in Early Modern England* (2010); she also has a forthcoming publication titled "Into the Archives: Using EEBO in the Early Modern Literature Classroom" in a collection on technology in the classroom. She frequently participates in the Shakespeare Association of America's seminars and workshops.

Liz Faber holds an MA in English from West Virginia University, and she is currently a PhD candidate in mass communication and media arts at Southern Illinois University, Carbondale. Her research interests include cinema sound/voice studies, psychoanalytic feminist film theory, and new media studies. She is also the author of "*Kitchen Sink*, or the Postmodern Prometheus: Alison Maclean's Reimagining of Mary Shelley's *Frankenstein* via the Cinematic Horror Genre."

Suzanne Ferriss is professor of English at Nova Southeastern University. Her publications have centered on the intersections of women's literature, fashion, and cultural studies. She coedited two volumes on the cultural study of fashion—*On Fashion* (1994) and *Footnotes: On Shoes* (2001)—and coauthored *A Handbook of Literary Feminisms* (2002). She has written articles about Jane Austen, Mary Shelley, and the Brontë sisters, as well as popular films based on literary texts by Austen, Virginia Woolf, and Helen Fielding. Most recently, she coedited two companion volumes on "chick culture" with Mallory Young: *Chick Lit: The New Woman's Fiction* (2006) and *Chick Flicks: Contemporary Women at the Movies* (2008). Her work on cultural studies has also led her into the emerging area of motorcycle studies. With Steven Alford, she is the author of the book *Motorcycle* and edits the *International Journal of Motorcycle Studies*.

Carolyn Kelley is adjunct lecturer for the Center of Women's Studies and Gender Research at the University of Florida in Gainesville. Her research focuses on Hollywood cinema and gender roles in media. She is the author of "Rejected Women in Film Noir" (dissertation; University of Florida, 2011) and the article "Aubrey Beardsley and H.D.'s 'Astrid': The Ghost and Mrs. Pugh of Decadent Aestheticism and Modernity" (2008). She has presented numerous papers at national conferences on art, film, and literature, including the artwork of Aubrey Beardsley, Jane Campion's *Holy Smoke*, and the American Beat poets.

Carrie Messenger is assistant professor of English at Shepherd University in Shepherdstown, West Virginia. She holds an MFA from the Iowa Writers' Workshop and a PhD from the University of Illinois at Chicago. Her research in film studies examines the narrative strategies of fiction versus film. Her writing has appeared in literary magazines including *Crab Orchard Review*, *Ecotone*, *Fiction International*, *Redivider*, and *Witness*.

Walter Metz is chair of the Department of Cinema and Photography at Southern Illinois University, Carbondale. He is the author of three books: *Engaging Film Criticism: Film History and Contemporary American Cinema* (2004), *Bewitched* (2007), and *Gilligan's Island* (2012). He is also the author of over forty journal articles and book chapters about the ekphrastic relationships between film, television, novels, poetry, and theater. He is at work on a new book about Dr. Seuss and Pixar Animation Studios.

Ellen Moll is lecturer in English and comparative literature at the University of Maryland. Her research and teaching interests include contemporary literature, film, and visual culture, with an emphasis on gender studies, feminist and critical race theory, science and culture, and digital humanities. Recent presentations at national conferences have discussed the films of Lynn Hershman, the plays of Caryl Churchill, and the poetry of Sherman Alexie.

Jennifer O'Meara is a PhD candidate in film studies at Trinity College, Dublin. Her research, funded by an Ussher Award, focuses on verbal style in art cinema, particularly how dialogue is integrated with both sound and image tracks. She has presented papers at international conferences on genre, film sound, and the representation of language on-screen. She has forthcoming publications in edited collections on independent cinema and genre in contemporary film.

Juan G. Ramos is assistant professor of Spanish at the College of the Holy Cross in Worcester, Massachusetts, where he teaches courses on Latin American poetry, as well as literature and language courses at all levels. He is working on a book manuscript around the concept of decolonial aesthetics, particularly in relation to the development of antipoetry, third cinema, and the "new song" movement during the 1960s and early 1970s in Latin America. He has also presented papers at national and international conferences on literature and adaptation to film, as well as aesthetic and postcolonial approaches to poetry and film.

Qi Wang is assistant professor of film in the School of Literature, Media, and Communication at Georgia Tech. She has published on independent Chinese cinema, documentary, and Japanese anime in a number of venues including *positions: east asia cultures critique*, *Journal of Chinese Cinemas*, *Asian Cinema*, *International Journal of Comic Art*, and Blackwell's recent *Companion to Chinese Cinema*. She is currently completing a book manuscript on contemporary independent Chinese cinema. Her research interests include issues of subjectivity and spatiality in cinema and media, Chinese cinema, documentary, Cold War Asian cinema, and dance film. She has also curated or cocurated a number of Chinese film events, including the 2008 REEL CHINA Documentary Biennial (New York and Shanghai), the 2011 Independent Chinese Cinema (High Museum, Atlanta), and the 2013 Independent Chinese Film Series (involving four universities in the Greater Atlanta area).